DELAYED JUSTICE

Jack Branson and Mary Branson

DELAYED JUSTICE

Inside Stories from America's Best
COLD CASE INVESTIGATORS

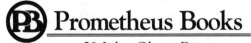 **Prometheus Books**

59 John Glenn Drive
Amherst, New York 14228–2119

Published 2011 by Prometheus Books

Cover image © Media Bakery.
Jacket design by Nicole Sommer-Lecht.

Inquiries should be addressed to
Prometheus Books
59 John Glenn Drive
Amherst, New York 14228–2119
VOICE: 716–691–0133
FAX: 716–691–0137
WWW.PROMETHEUSBOOKS.COM

15 14 13 12 11   5 4 3 2 1

Library of Congress Cataloging-in-Publication Data

Branson, Jack.
     Delayed justice : inside stories from America's best cold case investigators / by Jack Branson and Mary Branson.
          p. cm.
     Includes index.
     ISBN 978–1–61614–392–3 (cloth : alk. paper)
     ISBN 978–1–61614–393–0 (e-book)
     1. Cold cases (Criminal investigation)—United States. 2. Homicide investigation—United States. 3. Criminal investigation—United States. I. Branson, Mary Kinney. II. Title.

HV8079.H6B73 2011
363.250973—dc22
                                                                              2011004988

Printed in the United States of America on acid-free paper

In the midst of researching
the ugliness of humanity,

it's a respite to consider
Catherine Friedel Kinney
—a lady most beautiful and rare.

She brought out the best in every life she touched.
If all mothers were like her, the pages of this book
might well be empty.

Contents

Acknowledgments

Conducting an investigation is like putting together a jigsaw puzzle. Before the case can be closed with finality, you need every piece of the puzzle in place. Some elements of an investigation constitute the framework—the all-important edges of the puzzle. Who was the victim? Even when Jane Doe's killer is identified, the case cannot be closed with satisfaction until Jane's identity is known. Who was the perpetrator? No case can be solved without that piece of the puzzle.

With these primary pieces in place, a case may reluctantly be filed away, but it will never be closed for a dedicated investigator and for family and friends of the victim until all the puzzle pieces are identified and in place. Some pieces are hard to locate but are no less important to those involved. Why did the perpetrator commit the crime? Why did he or she choose the victim? As the framework of the case falls into place, missing pieces become more noticeable. Every piece of an investigative puzzle is valuable, and when it's missing, it's missed.

It's the same when writing a book. An author can create the framework for a book, but its richness comes from the pieces generously contributed by others. Some of these pieces have strong, vibrant colors, and some have deeper hues that make up the background. But a book is made strong by each contribution and enriched by their variety.

We created a framework for this book, but we are not presumptuous enough to think that we put together the puzzle. We're grateful to acknowledge the resources and the people who filled in the framework with their support, encouragement, expertise, insights, and experiences:

Our family—Penny, Adam, Taylor, Elliott, and Kayla—you make everything worthwhile, including writing. We love you.

Our friends and editors Bob and Ruth Hall—you find all the things we miss, and you do it diplomatically. We admire you.

Our agent, Claire Gerus—you have a knack for finding just the right publisher for each book. We appreciate you.

Editor in Chief Steven Mitchell, Prometheus Books—this book was originally your brainchild. We hope it meets your expectations.

Print Resources. Though we did not quote directly from print resources, we read as much as we could about the cases described to us by investigators, including reading from the (North) *Carolina News Channel* online version; the *LaGrange* (Georgia) *Daily News*; the *Virginia Pilot*; the *Red Orbit* (North Carolina) *News*; CharMeck.org (city of Charlotte, North Carolina, and Mecklenburg County government news); charlotte observer.com; WKBW-TV online news; the *Atlanta Journal-Constitution*; the *Madisonville* (Kentucky) *Messenger*; WGRZ.com (Buffalo, New York); latimes.com (Los Angeles, California); the *Gaston Gazette* (Gastonia, North Carolina); the *Washington Post*; Fox Radio online news (Redding, California); and the *Anchorage* (Alaska) *Daily News*. If you'd like to read an in-depth study of the Timothy Spencer rape/murder trial, we recommend Paul Mones's *Stalking Justice* (Pocket Books, 1995). For details of the Moore's Ford Bridge murders, see Laura Wexler's *Fire in a Canebrake* (Scribner, 2003). And for more information on murderer Russell Winstead, we suggest our own *Murder in Mayberry* (Berkley, 2009).

The victims of the violent crimes described in these pages. It is our hope that by telling your stories, you will be no longer victims but victors. If your stories can help readers understand the mind-sets and behaviors of perpetrators and learn strategies for bringing killers and rapists to justice, your already-valuable lives will be even more valuable. You are represented in the final chapter by Jessica, a victim who survived and tells her story. Jessica is one of the most courageous women we've ever met, and she speaks with candor about what it was like to be a victim, to wait ten years for justice, and to meet a cold case detective who cared about her as though she were his own sister. She relived her painful experiences in order to help cold case investigators understand the immeasurable gift they give families when they solve cases long forgotten by most.

The families of the victims whose stories we've told. We are the family of a violent-crime victim, and we know the pain of watching television reenactments and reading hundreds of newspaper articles describing the brutality of the crime. But we wrote about the murder in our own family because we believed it would help others going through similar experiences. We hope that you will see the retelling of events that are deeply personal to you as a way of helping investigators solve more cold cases.

The families of the perpetrators. You are the forgotten secondary victims, and you must suffer more than most of us can imagine. You face blame and public embarrassment while trying to reconcile the person you love with the crime that person committed. We know that environment can play a big part in shaping criminals, but we also acknowledge that some of the vilest perpetrators came from loving homes. We regret what you've experienced, and we understand your torn loyalty.

The investigators, prosecutors, and others who generously shared their expertise and insights. Throughout the interviewing and writing processes, you amazed us with your generosity in sharing what it took years to learn and what you're paid to share as you lead seminars and workshops. We sensed that, without exception, your primary goal is to get the bad guys. Here, in alphabetical order, are our cold case heroes extraordinaire.

Detective Troy Armstrong began his career as a street cop in Charlotte, North Carolina, in 1991. In 1999, he was temporarily detailed to a regional homicide cold case task force to assist in the investigation of the possible serial murders of more than thirty high-risk females. During this assignment, he discovered a keen interest and ability in handling older cases. When the task force disbanded in 2001, he joined Charlotte's Sexual Assault Unit.

In 2006, he became the first and only member of the Sexual Assault Cold Case Unit, which he now works with the assistance of what he describes as "a crack group of retired detectives." Troy has helped solve more than a hundred sexual-assault cold cases, resulting in the conviction of more than twenty suspects with combined sentences of more than 850 years.

Troy is in high demand as a speaker and instructor, and he generously shared his extensive experience and insights to enrich this book.

When asked the reasons for his success, Troy says, "Over the years literally hundreds of people have been involved in our cold case successes. The victims, their families, and I are forever grateful to everyone who played a part in the investigations. I especially appreciate some who have gone above and beyond in their dedication and pursuit of 'delayed justice': the CMPD (Charlotte-Mecklenburg Police Department) Crime Lab; Major Rick Williams; Sergeants Darrell Price, Marsha Dearing, and Dick Riedel (ret); Detective (ret) Linda Holmes, CMPD Lab Director (ret) Jane Burton; volunteer Halli Gomez; Assistant District Attorney Samantha Pendergrass; and most important, the victims and their families, whose courage never ceases to amaze me."

Investigator Clay Bryant has a law degree, and he's also a certified paramedic. But since childhood, when he rode with his dad, small-town police chief Buddy Bryant, all Clay had wanted was to be a law enforcement officer.

Clay served as an officer with the Georgia State Patrol before being appointed chief of police in Hogansville, Georgia. From 2002 to 2006, he served as an investigator for the Coweta County Judicial Circuit District Attorney's Office. During this time, he solved four intricate high-profile cold cases. Due to his diligence and expertise, five defendants are now serving life sentences for crimes once thought unsolvable.

Bryant was dubbed "Cold Case Clay" by an *Atlanta Journal-Constitution* reporter. His cases have been featured on *48 Hours*, Investigation Discovery Channel, A&E, and *Cold Case Files*.

Judge Dennis Delano Sr. grew up in Buffalo, New York, and has spent most of his life there. He married his wife, Cheryl, while in his late teens and immediately set about to accomplish his childhood dream of being a public servant. He began as a volunteer firefighter, then a full-time firefighter and paramedic, and eventually a uniformed peace officer. In 1985 he became a Buffalo Police Department patrol officer, later moving to the detective division's Auto Theft/Arson Unit, then to the Major Crimes Unit, and then to the Homicide Unit.

While working in homicide, Den taught himself about cold case investigations. When the department formed its first cold case unit in May 2006, Den's superiors recommended him for the unit's three-person team. A few months after the unit was formed, Den was reassigned to a multiagency task force formed to catch a serial killer/rapist who had been preying on young women in the western New York area for thirty years. The unit launched an intense two-month investigation that resulted in the suspect's capture and the freeing of an innocent man who had already served twenty-two years in prison. Den then returned to the cold case squad, where the team was able to identify another killer and free an innocent mother who had served thirteen years for her daughter's murder.

During his nearly thirty years of service to western New York, Den was awarded numerous citations for outstanding service. Now grandparents, Den and Cheryl still live in the area Den has loved and served for most of his life. He currently holds the position of judge for the City of Cheektowaga, New York.

Prosecutor Alan Goodwin graduated from the University of Alabama School of Law in 1998. Since that time, he has served as an assistant district attorney for the Alaska Department of Law and as a judge advocate in the US Air Force Reserve. Goodwin has primarily prosecuted violent crimes and crimes against children in Anchorage, Alaska, and has prosecuted Air Force Courts-Martial in California, Alaska, Japan, and Germany.

Alan credits detective Glen Klinkhart with solving the cold case he shared in this book, and he lauds his team for making the prosecution possible: case paralegal Marilyn Sansom and legal assistant Laura Bianchi. "This case was much more about the detectives, the analysts, and the evidence than it was about me," insists Alan.

Capt. (ret) Cindy Isenhour worked patrol, crime prevention, and vice and narcotics, but she spent most of her career working in criminal investigations, where she recently retired as captain and commander of the Criminal Investigation Division of the Gastonia (North Carolina) Police Department. She served as a detective, polygraph examiner, and supervisor in Criminal Investigations. She is a graduate of the FBI National Academy 199 Session.

Cindy was the first woman in her department to reach the rank of captain and the first woman to serve as commander of the hostage negotiations team. She was the first woman law enforcement administrator to serve as president of the North Carolina's FBI National Academy Association.

Cindy's husband, Jeff, recently retired as assistant chief of the Gaston County Police Department. Cindy's two sons and a daughter-in-law are all police officers.

NCIS Special Agent in Charge Joe D. Kennedy has served as a special agent for the Naval Criminal Investigative Service (NCIS) since 1986, where he now serves as director for the Joint Counterintelligence Unit (JCIU), Kabul, Afghanistan. Joe was instrumental in setting up the NCIS Cold Case Squad at NCIS headquarters in Washington, DC, where he and his team have investigated more than three hundred murders worldwide. Joe has gained national attention for his innovative approach to solving cold cases. He has provided training on cold case methodology and protocol all over the world, including in Asia, in Europe, in South America, and in the Caribbean.

Some of Joe's many strategic assignments include serving at Quantico, Virginia; Washington, DC; Puerto Rico; and Okinawa, Japan (where he served as a counterintelligence officer). He has been deployed to Afghanistan as deputy director for the Joint Counterintelligence Unit, and to Iraq as a supervisory special agent.

Joe is in demand as a cold case investigations trainer, and he spent years accumulating the wealth of information he contributed to this book. Many of the investigative steps and strategies in this book are adapted from Joe's presentations, with our comments and explanations added.

FBI Special Agent (ret) Art Krinsky is CEO of Arthur L. Krinsky & Associates, Inc., providing private investigations, specialized law enforcement training, and consulting services to business and law enforcement. He serves the National Center for Missing & Exploited Children (NCMEC) as a Team Adam Consultant in active cases of child abduction and sexual exploitation, and he is also an NCMEC Project ALERT volunteer working on cold cases.

During his more than thirty years as an FBI special agent, Art investigated numerous violations and violent crimes, and he was an FBI master police instructor, a legal advisor, an undercover agent, a critical incident debriefer, and a member of the Metro Atlanta Fugitive Task Force. After retirement from the FBI, Art was appointed by the Department of Homeland Security as senior instructor for the Federal Law Enforcement Training Center, with assignments in the Legal, Practical Applications, and Counterterrorism Divisions. He is a Georgia POST-certified law enforcement officer, a Georgia licensed private investigator and classroom firearms instructor, and a member of the Georgia and Ohio Bar Associations.

FBI Special Agent (ret) Steve Mardigian is president, CEO, and violent crime consultant with the Academy Group, the largest privately owned forensic behavioral science firm in the world. The Academy Group includes a cold case analysis program, enriched by its members' previous experience with the Behavioral Science Unit at the FBI Academy.

Steve served in the FBI for thirty-one years as a supervisory special agent, a regional field office program manager, a violent crime assessor, and as administrator of the FBI's National Center for the Analysis of Violent Crime (NCAVC). During his time in the Behavioral Analysis Unit at Quantico, Virginia, his work included helping law enforcement officers investigate cold cases. He now uses the expertise he gained in his years with the FBI to continue to assist law enforcement. He's a specialist in crime-scene and communicated-threat analyses.

Kentucky Commonwealth's Attorney David Massamore is our personal hero. He prosecuted the four-year-old murder case that brought justice for our family, and we witnessed the powerful way he reconstructed the crime for the jury and shared the investigators' findings with power and clarity. An outstanding litigator with a successful thirty-year career as a prosecutor, David has helped close a number of cold cases and has brought peace to countless families like ours.

David received his undergraduate degree in history, political science, and military science from Murray State University, Murray, Kentucky, and was then commissioned as a second lieutenant in the US Army. After his time in the military, David received his law degree from Cumberland School of Law, Samford University, Birmingham, Alabama. He has served as assistant county attorney and assistant Commonwealth's Attorney. He was elected Kentucky Commonwealth's Attorney in 1994 and has been reelected unopposed since that time.

David is quick to acknowledge that everything he's credited with accomplishing is the result of teamwork and that his team is exceptional: First Assistant Commonwealth's Attorney Kathryn Senter, Second Assistant Commonwealth's Attorney Kimberly Senter, administrative assistant Lisa Harris, victim advocate Charlie Weatherford, and secretary Amy Cline.

Detective David Phillips, Charlotte-Mecklenburg Police Department Cold Case Squad, credits his entire team with its phenomenal success solving cases: Charlotte-Mecklenburg Sergeant Melissa Mangum and Detective Steve Furr; FBI special agent liaison Ernie Mathis; and volunteers Dr. Vivian Lord (professor, University of North Carolina at

Charlotte); Brendan Battle (retired FBI special agent); Raymond Bowley (retired FBI special agent); Daniel Caylor (retired FBI special agent); Peter Dingee (retired Greenburg Police Department officer); Harvey Katowitz (retired New York Police Department captain); John Lambert (retired engineer from Duke Energy); and James Zopp (retired FBI special agent). The powerful backgrounds of the entire team combine to get powerful results.

David is a twenty-five-year police veteran, working as a uniformed patrol officer and as an investigator in the Property Crimes Unit before being promoted to the Person Crimes Unit, where he investigated robberies, sexual assaults, and homicides. In 2003, David became a member of the Charlotte-Mecklenburg Police Department's newly formed Homicide Cold Case Squad. He assisted in the formation of the unit's highly successful cold case volunteer team and helped implement many of the policies and practices the unit has adopted. David provides information and assistance to local, state, and federal law enforcement agencies and cold case units. Among the many awards David's squad has received are the 2005 Cold Case Unit ChoicePoint International Chiefs of Police Award for Excellence in Criminal Investigations and the 2008 US Attorney Generals Volunteer and Community Service Award.

FBI Special Agent (ret) Jim Procopio served in the US Air Force, attaining the rank of captain and receiving the Air Medal for combat missions flown in Vietnam.

Jim joined the FBI in 1969 and served most of his twenty-nine-year career in the Atlanta office. He worked a wide variety of cases, including the Atlanta penitentiary murder cases, the Atlanta child murders case, and the Moore's Ford Bridge murders cold case.

After retiring from the FBI, Jim served as senior security officer for a cruise line. He is now employed as a contract investigator by the US State Department.

Sgt. (ret) David Rivers, Miami Metro-Dade County Police Department, holds a master's degree in criminal justice from Florida International University, where he graduated with honors. Dave began his law enforcement career as a uniformed patrolman, later working vice, intelligence, and narcotics. He served as an investigator in the Felony Warrants Bureau and as a homicide detective. He was promoted to sergeant in 1981 and assigned to supervise an operational squad in which he responded to more than one thousand fatalities. In 1988, he was named supervisor of the Metro-Dade Cold Case Squad, one of the first cold case squads in the United States. Dave credits Sgt. Jimmy Ratcliff, Metro-Dade's first cold case squad leader, with creating the strong foundation from which he and future leaders benefited, and he credits his team of ten years with the success his squad achieved: Detectives John LeClaire, Greg Smith, Jarrett Crawford, Ramish Nyberg, and Jay Vas.

Along with his responsibilities on the cold case squad, Dave supervised the Polygraph Unit from 1990 to 1996. He retired in 1998 and became president of Voice & Ink Enterprises, Inc., a company that specializes in forensic consulting and instruction. The majority of his work involves conducting law enforcement trainings both nationally and internationally, along with testifying as an expert witness. He has served as a consultant or led trainings in more than 120 US cities in forty-six states, the District of Columbia, and three foreign countries. He graciously shared from his wealth of training experience to enrich this book.

Cold case investigator (ret) Greg Smith wanted to be an attorney, and after college he considered his time as a uniformed police officer a stepping-stone to a legal career. But something clicked in 1974 when Greg became a police officer for the Miami Metro-Dade County Police Department. He realized he enjoyed being, as his former supervisor David Rivers describes, "a nuts and bolts, boots-on-the-ground kind of guy."

Greg decided to remain in law enforcement, and after serving three years in the uniformed division, he served four years in general investigations, twenty-two years in homicide, and two years on the SWAT team. He was a founding member of the Metro-Dade Cold Case Squad, one of the first in the nation.

Now retired, Greg spends time with his family, volunteers at his church, and works with handicapped youth and adults.

Investigator (ret) Dan Tholson worked for the Evansville (Wyoming) Police Department for three years before joining the Natrona County Sheriff's Office in 1984. He retired as an investigator with the sheriff's office in 2006. Dan spent eleven years investigating child abuse and neglect and crimes against individuals. He also worked with juvenile offenders in the Youth Diversion Program for eleven years.

Dan has a keen understanding of investigative work and particularly of cold case investigations. He understands what it's like to work under the media spotlight and then to be faithful to a case long after reporters and publicity-seekers have moved on to the next high-profile case.

US Customs Branch Chief (ret) Mike Wewers became a Milwaukee police officer in 1965, working undercover with the vice squad. He was nominated for Officer of the Year in 1970, but before he could accept the award, he left for Chicago to work with IRS inspection.

That same year, he transferred to US Customs and moved to Miami. He became branch chief for Air Support and then branch chief for Marine Operations. He was involved in building the first regional intelligence center and the joint marine aviation command center.

When he retired, Mike was serving with the Vice Presidential Drug Task Force for Florida. He now lives in Cumming, Georgia, where he serves as an ALERT volunteer for the National Center for Missing & Exploited Children.

To every piece of the puzzle, thank you. Together, we created a book.

Introduction

Forgotten, As a Dream

TIME, LIKE AN EVER-ROLLING STREAM
BEARS ALL ITS SONS AWAY;
THEY FLY, FORGOTTEN, AS A DREAM
DIES AT THE OPENING DAY.[1]

Time softens the sharp-edged memories of injustice. It dulls pain and offers vague excuses for wrongs that were never righted. Years after the most violent crime, few people remember and even fewer are outraged. The greater the distance between the crime and the individual, the more muted seems the cry for justice.

Except for the rare individuals whose sense of justice spans time. They cannot rest until the victims rest in peace.

These people resist the smoothing down of anything reprehensible, and they meticulously keep painful memories sharp. For them, justice delayed is not justice denied. In fact, delayed justice means sweet and final closure, the last chapter to a life novel, and the beginning of a new existence for those close to the victim. For these people, justice trumps time.

These people are not seeking revenge. (Revenge is personal; justice belongs to society.) They simply view justice delayed as insurance against future crimes. Francis Bacon said, "If we do not maintain justice, justice will not maintain us." They want to send a message to tomorrow's criminals: crime will not be tolerated, nor will it be forgotten.

Every case that has been set aside needs such an advocate, and it is for these advocates that we write. As iron sharpens iron, we realize that even skilled investigators can benefit from the collective brilliance of their peers. We believe that we can multiply the efforts of some of the nation's most prolific cold case investigators by sharing their insights with new investigators and those from smaller departments with limited resources. And we recognize that occasionally the tenacious individual who keeps a case alive has no investigative training at all. Sometimes that person is a family member, sometimes a citizen who's haunted by a local unsolved crime, sometimes a member of the media. To these individuals, we offer a match for reigniting a dormant investigation.

In recent years, a variety of dedicated investigators across the nation have taken on the challenge of speaking for now-silent victims. They reinvestigate, re-interview, and revive cases that others once had put to rest. They present to families and friends of violent-crime victims some measure of closure. And for future generations, they give the assurance that justice, however delayed, will still be justice.

Without justice, lives are changed forever. The impact of traumatic life events was powerfully described a half-century ago as a nation grieved the loss of John F. Kennedy.

When Mary McGrory of the *Washington Post* learned that JFK had been shot, she told future US senator Pat Moynihan, "We'll never laugh again."

"No, Mary," said Moynihan. "We'll laugh again, but we'll never be young again."[2]

Closing cold cases makes it possible for families to once again be young, to move forward with hope and a future.

If closing cold cases brings vast rewards and sends a powerful message to criminals, why aren't more cases solved? Some viable answers are money, time, training, and the complexity of the cases. Funds are more readily available for cases that still make headlines. The overload of fresh cases often pushes colder ones to the bottom of the stack. Investigators may have difficulty finding appropriate training on cold case investigations. And cold cases are rarely solved quickly.

We hold a deep respect for those who solve cold cases. Experience has taught us that cold cases are a unique entity. They lie dormant for months, years, even decades. But each one is like a sleeping volcano that could erupt at any time—just when grieving families have given up hope, just when perpetrators are confident that their secret crimes are obscured forever. We hope this book will be used to awaken cases that have been silenced too long.

Delayed Justice looks at why cases are filed away without resolution, why cold case detectives sometimes have better results than the detectives who investigated initially, how cold cases are investigated, and how a reader can conduct his or her own cold case investigation. Though Jack has more than thirty years of experience at all levels of law enforcement, we do not claim the expertise necessary to write a book on cold case investigations. We have gleaned that content from successful prosecutors and investigators from across the nation. We simply present this wealth of information to you in the hope that life chapters will be closed and criminals whose crimes were hidden will be removed from our streets and made to face the consequences of the actions they thought they had concealed.

In this book, we've used actual cold case investigations to support ideas and investigative steps, and, most of the time, a story is shared in its entirety to illustrate a particular point. Occasionally, when a story strongly supports more than one point, you'll find a partial story, followed by an ellipsis (...) indicating that the story is continued farther into the book. Then an ellipsis will begin the next or final portion of the story.

You'll find that, like good reporters, we've referred to suspects, investigators, and witnesses by their last names after their initial mention. But as we studied the cases and our compassion for the victims grew, we felt it more appropriate to refer to them by their first names. These very real people are the heart of this book. We hope that you will also grow to care about them and use what you learn from their tragic stories to bring happy endings to other cases.

—Jack and Mary Branson

NOTES

1. From the hymn "O God, Our Help in Ages Past." Words by Isaac Watts, 1719.

2. Godfrey Hodgson, *The Gentleman from New York: Daniel Patrick Moynihan—A Biography* (New York: Houghton Mifflin Co., 2000), p. 85.

Chapter 1

How Old Is Cold?

As long as a dog has his nose to the ground, there's a chance of picking up the trail.
—Kentucky Commonwealth's Attorney David Massamore

In the summer of 1979, the death of an inner-city Atlanta youth wasn't all that unusual. Kids in the projects often fended for themselves, coming home late, and occasionally not coming home at all. But that summer, the number of missing and murdered children increased, and local law enforcement eventually suspected a serial killer. As the murders escalated, so did the pressure to find the monster behind the crimes.

In spite of working under the media spotlight, pressure from par, and a city in panic, Atlanta police could not bring a quick close murders, and as murder piled upon murder, the earlier cases grew

A COLD CASE CAN BE PART OF A LIVING ENTITY.

It was a time when *CSI* wasn't a household word, *The Sil* goal, and hadn't catapulted psychological profiling to a commor

DNA was studied only in college biology. It was twenty years before the Automated Fingerprint Identification System—AFIS—would be established, and fingerprints were checked manually and only against known suspects.

The murders crossed county lines, and coordinating the investigation was complicated. The Atlanta area had never faced a serial murder case of this magnitude, and certainly not one in which the victims were children. Overarching all these challenges was the inexperience of Atlanta Police Department officers.

After Atlanta's first black mayor, Maynard Jackson, assumed office in January 1974, he began an aggressive affirmative action program to increase the number of racial minorities in the police department. With fear that they would eventually be pushed out of their positions, many experienced white officers quickly retired or transferred. The inexperienced recruits who filled their vacancies found themselves in the midst of one of the nation's biggest manhunts. Many had not worked a murder case, and they certainly had not worked a high-profile serial murder case. They lacked experience, time, and resources. In addition to investigating the murders, they had a city to protect. The meager time they could have devoted to solving the initial murders was soon invested in dealing with new murders, as a conservative body count rose to twenty-eight.

When the FBI entered the investigation in November 1980, agents were dismayed at the cold trails on the earliest murders. Case reports were sketchy. Evidence, including a full-size bicycle, had been lost. The early cases were cold while the serial killer was still actively stalking young victims. But federal agents knew that one way to stop future murders was to identify evidence and suspects from the earlier, now-cold cases.

A case does not receive a "cold" classification based on age. A cold case is simply an unsolved case that is no longer being investigated. A viable case is one that can benefit from a reinvestigation, and the early child murders cried out to be reinvestigated. So the FBI started working with local police, they investigated each child's murder that had occurred that day, piecing together a complicated puzzle that eventually led them to Wayne Williams, who was convicted of two of the murders in February 1982. . . .

A CASE CAN BECOME COLD IMMEDIATELY.

On the evening of July 10, 1988, a twenty-nine-year-old preschool fitness teacher, Julie Love, left the Atlanta home of her fiancé, Mark Kaplan, and was never again seen alive. Julie's car was found, out of gas, half a mile from Kaplan's house.

Today, a young woman in Julie's situation would lock her car doors, dig her cell phone from her purse, call her fiancé, and wait till he arrived with a gas can and an admonition to watch the gas gauge. But it was 1988. Julie had no cell phone and her only choices were to stay in the car till morning or walk to a gas station. She chose to walk.

For months, Kaplan's answering machine posed this question about his missing fiancé: "If you have any information on Julie Love, please leave your name and telephone number." His plea generated no legitimate leads.

Posters—180,000 of them—blanketed the city of Atlanta, showing a smiling young woman with short, curly dark hair. Under her photo were these words: "Have you seen Julie Love? She's barely 5 feet tall, and she wouldn't hurt a fly." But while sympathetic subway riders read the posters and hoped the case would be solved, no strong leads surfaced. Someone knew what had happened to Julie Love, but no one was talking. Thirteen months passed as a city mourned and witnesses remained silent. . . .

It's not unusual for a case to go cold as quickly as Julie's case. It's common for someone to be killed in a drive-by shooting, creating a crime scene with no fingerprint or DNA evidence. Officers canvass the area, but neighbors state that they heard and saw nothing. Media encourage witnesses to come forward, but besides the usual flurry of sketchy leads and prank calls, the public is silent. From the start, investigators simply have no evidence, no suspects, and no leads. The case immediately becomes a box in the evidence room, awaiting the changes and illuminations that sometimes occur over time. With other cases pressing to be solved, the only reasonable and prudent action is to immediately classify the case as inactive.

A CASE CAN REMAIN WARM INDEFINITELY.

Some cases remain weak but never die. Leads trickle in, whether accurate or faulty. Each time the case receives media exposure, witnesses call to say they've spotted the missing child or they recognize the blurred face on the surveillance video. Strong media exposure seems to bring out people who think they see Jimmy Hoffa or an aging Lindbergh baby. But occasionally a lead is legitimate, and to find the real ones, all leads must be followed. Among the tedious and useless tips, an investigator may find someone or something to move the case forward.

Warm cases, though sometimes frustrating and time-consuming for investigators, often have a greater chance of being solved. "It's sort of like a bloodhound," explains thirty-year veteran Kentucky prosecutor David Massamore. "As long as a dog has his nose to the ground, there's a chance of picking up the trail. If you pull him away for a day or two, there's less chance of picking up the scent."

So sometimes an investigator chooses not to close a case, occasionally at the expense of other cases. He or she may have become close to the victim's family and made a promise to bring them closure. Or the investigator may take failure to solve the case personally and simply refuse to give up. Such a case remains indefinitely open but inactive, in a state of suspended animation, resurfacing occasionally like a weak shadow of its former self, vying for an investigator's attention. It's a whisper in a crowded room of shouting current cases, most of which are driven by media coverage, political pressure, and grieving families. But to an investigator with a special interest, the whisper is enough to keep the case on his or her desk.

The age and temperature of a case do not necessarily determine the amount of attention it receives. But when an investigator has mounting cases with strong, current leads, a deciding factor for classifying a case as cold must be the absence of viable leads. When the leads run out, it's probably time to label the case cold.

AN ACTIVE CASE MAY APPEAR COLD TO OUTSIDERS.

Sensationalism sells, and "Case Goes Cold" makes a better headline than "Police Still Plugging Away." Few investigations create a straight line from crime scene to courtroom, and the thoroughness and perseverance that produce a prosecutable case often include crucial blocks of time that appear unprofitable to media and families. When leads that must be followed go nowhere or when investigators are unable to share their progress without compromising the investigation, a healthy case can take on negativity. Investigators are quiet. Media are looking for someone to quote. And frustrated family members are all too willing to grant interviews. It's difficult to work under a negative media spotlight, but dedicated investigators must sometimes learn to do so.

SOME CASES ARE NEVER ALLOWED TO DIE.

Most frequently, cases remain active longer than would reasonably be expected for one of two reasons. An individual or group keeps the case before the police and the public. Or the victim is high profile—wealthy, influential, well known.

   … While the early victims in the Atlanta child serial killings are an example of cases that went immediately cold, the overall investigation was kept alive by the victims' mothers. Though many politicians and investigators may have preferred that the case be swept under the proverbial rug, the mothers refused to let that happen. They were the ones who first realized they might be dealing with a serial killer. With the high crime rate in Atlanta's inner city, that realization may have taken the police much longer if not for the mothers' insistence that the police dig deeper.

   The serial killings began as just more violence in the projects. On

July 28, 1979, when two murdered children were found fifty yards apart in a wooded area not far from downtown Atlanta, the story was just a short blurb on page 18 of the *Atlanta Journal-Constitution*. But the murders continued, and their frequency increased. And soon the mounting cases couldn't be attributed to simply living in high-risk neighborhoods.

In spite of life's challenges and regardless of their financial circumstances, the majority of mothers in the Atlanta projects loved their children. And so, as more and more of their children went missing, the mothers cried out. And their cries were heard in Washington, and eventually around the world. Without the mothers pointing the police to the possibility of a serial child-killer, the murders might have continued longer than they did. And without the mothers' cries, the nation might not have allotted extreme resources for solving the murders....

* * *

"Most often," says Georgia cold case detective Clay Bryant, "the family is the linchpin that keeps a case alive." With new cases piling up, an investigator has to consider which cases are most likely to be solved, which ones are receiving the most media attention (which translates to pressure from supervisors), and where the most pressure is being applied. A parent's anguish is often the pressure that forces an already overworked investigator to pull out a file for a second or third look.

On March 5, 1974, seventeen-year-old Amy Billig left her Coconut Grove, Florida, home with plans to stop by her father's art gallery to get money for a night out with her friends. Construction workers near her house noticed Amy's high-stepping gait as she walked by wearing the typical teen clothing of the era: a denim miniskirt and cork platform sandals. She never arrived at her father's office, and she didn't meet her friends that evening.

Amy left behind a journal in which she wrote that she was considering going to South America with someone named Hank, but no one by that name was located among her friends or acquaintances, so police could not follow the lead.

Two motorcycle gangs—the Outlaws and the Pagans—were known

to be in the area at the time of Amy's disappearance, and Amy's camera was found on the Florida Turnpike, at an exit that would have been on the route the bikers took as they traveled north. Investigators developed the film, but most photos were overexposed, and the remaining ones gave no clues to Amy's whereabouts—except for one photo of a white van. The license plate wasn't visible, so without a specific link to a white van, Amy's photos provided no plausible leads.

For Amy's parents, Susan and Ned Billig, the nightmare of losing their daughter was intensified by a series of cruel hoaxes and false leads. Sixteen-year-old twin brothers, Charles and Larry Glasser, called Amy's family and said they had kidnapped her and wanted a $30,000 ransom. Police ruled out the Glasser brothers as kidnappers but charged them with extortion.

Shortly after Amy's disappearance, her mother, Susan, began receiving phone calls from a man who claimed that Amy was being held captive by a ring of sex traffickers. The unrelenting calls—sometimes as many as seven in a night—continued for twenty-one years, bringing agony and false hope to the grieving family. But the Billigs refused to change their phone number in case Amy tried to reach them.

The family received tips that Amy had been kidnapped by bikers, with some tipsters claiming that Amy was alive and some saying that she'd been killed. Over decades, tips linking Amy to the biker gangs continued to trickle in from across the country and even from the United Kingdom, usually with enough details to drive Amy's parents to investigate them. They often felt as if they were just a few days or a few miles from locating Amy. Even the faintest hope kept them moving forward. They closed their art gallery and sold many of their possessions to finance their search.

They refused to give up, working with the police when possible and by themselves when necessary. Ned died in 1993, and Susan continued searching for Amy.

In 1995, the FBI finally identified the anonymous caller who had taunted Susan for twenty-one years.

"It was devastating to discover that the caller was one of our own," says former US Customs Supervisory Special Agent Mike Wewers.

"Henry Johnson Blair worked for me. He was a uniformed Customs agent who received several awards. He was married with two children—not the type of person you'd imagine taunting a grieving family. We called him Hank—the name Amy used in her diary to describe the man she considered running away with to South America. Hank was required to relocate briefly to South America about the time of Amy's journal entry. And in 1974, Hank drove a white van of the same model as the one in Amy's photo."

Blair claimed he had never met Amy and that alcoholism and an obsessive-compulsive disorder drove him to harass her mother. He was never linked definitively to Amy's disappearance but was sentenced to prison for two years for harassment. Susan Billig filed a civil suit against him and eventually settled for $5 million.

Susan continued her search, refusing to give up and determined that no one would forget her missing daughter. About four thousand children are abducted annually by strangers, but Susan kept her daughter's case at the top of the stack. She participated in an A&E Network documentary in 1998, which showed how she worked with law enforcement to keep Amy's case alive as decades came and went. In 2001 she coauthored a book about Amy's disappearance (*Without a Trace: The Disappearance of Amy Billig—A Mother's Search for Justice*).

Susan died in 2005, at the age of eighty, still clinging to the hope of finding Amy. Without Susan as the catalyst, Amy's story quickly faded from public interest. When the fire under the investigation was extinguished, Amy's case finally grew cold.

* * *

Perhaps the most high-profile twenty-first-century case that remained open longer than normal was the Natalee Holloway case. When Natalee disappeared on a high school trip to Aruba, her mother, Beth, kept the case high profile. She appeared on countless talk shows, accepted numerous print media interviews, and made sure most of America knew her daughter's name. She wrote a book, *Loving Natalee: A Mother's Testament of Hope and Faith*, and cooperated with a television movie, *Natalee Holloway*. As long as the case consumed the mother, it consumed the nation. And it consumed her until the prime suspect in Natalee's murder, Joran van der Sloot, was arrested for killing a young Peruvian woman.

* * *

And while John and Patsy Ramsey might have wanted to keep their daughter's December 25, 1996, murder from becoming a media frenzy, the Boulder, Colorado, story made national headlines within hours. The investigation stayed alive because the murder of six-year-old beauty-queen JonBenét Ramsey was a naturally high-profile case. Jon-Benét was the youngest child of a wealthy, prominent family, and when bigger-than-life videos of her pageant participations found their way to the media, America made her case their case.

The more the case was profiled, including features in at least eight books by detectives, true-crime writers, and profilers, the closer the bloodhound stayed to the trail.

With the death of Patsy Ramsey ten years after JonBenét's death, public interest subsided. But perhaps because the case was high profile and leaving it unsolved reflected badly on local police, in 2009 the Boulder Police Department took back the case from the district attorney's office and reopened it.

Quickly cold or forever warm, a cold case is not a closed case. It's simply one in which the evidence pool has dried up. All logical leads have been checked. The bloodhound has followed the trail until it ended, and he has nowhere else to go.

Yet.

Chapter 2

Why Temperatures Drop

IT'S CONSTANTLY A TRIAGE.

—Detective Troy Armstrong, Charlotte (North Carolina)
Sexual Assault Cold Case Unit

Once a bloodhound picks up the wrong scent, he's useless in finding the correct trail. In the same way, it's easy for an investigator to size up a crime scene, form an opinion or accept a suggested one, then direct all of his or her efforts toward proving the wrong theory. A theory can be workable and sound as long as it's not contradicted by fact. But it is still just that: a theory. No matter how compelling, a theory is not truth until it's substantiated by irrefutable data. And without truth, cases can go cold.

CASES GO COLD WHEN INVESTIGATORS HAVE TOO MANY CASES.

"All the cases are big in a metro agency," says Troy Armstrong of the Charlotte (North Carolina) Sexual Assault Cold Case Unit. "In a large agency like Charlotte, cases come in constantly, so workload plays a big part in cases going cold. Cases go farther down in the pile.

If a case has a better chance of being solved, it's moved up. It's constantly a triage."

CASES GO COLD WHEN AN INVESTIGATOR STOPS FOLLOWING THE EVIDENCE AND STARTS FOLLOWING A THEORY.

When Fred Wilkerson vanished in November 1987, his family immediately suspected his ex-girlfriend, Connie Quedens. Earlier that year, Quedens had started divorce proceedings on her husband, Fred had deeded his share of a fourteen-acre Troup County, Georgia, property to her "for love and affection," she and Fred had built their dream house on the property she now owned, Fred had made Quedens the beneficiary of his $10,000 life-insurance policy, and they had moved in together. But soon after moving in with Fred, Quedens wanted out of the relationship and Fred out of the house. Fred retaliated by filing a suit to regain his property. Two days after filing the suit, Fred went missing.

Police interviewed Quedens but found no solid evidence to connect her to Fred's disappearance. With no strong probable cause, they couldn't search her property.

Investigators found Fred's car at the Atlanta airport a month after he disappeared, wiped clean of fingerprints and DNA, with two of Fred's uncashed paychecks in the glove compartment. Quedens suggested that Fred might have left Georgia to start a new life, and despite the suspicious findings in Fred's car, investigators focused on that theory, to the exclusion of other leads.

When the meager leads that supported the flight theory were exhausted, the case went cold. Seven years later, on May 24, 1994, then–Probate Judge Gwen Prescott issued an order establishing a presumption of death. Now Fred's property and life-insurance money officially belonged to Quedens.

Then in May 2003 a tree fell on Coweta County District Attorney Pete Skandalakis's pickup truck, and Connie Quedens's comfortable existence crumbled. Skandalakis took his pickup truck to a body shop in LaGrange, Georgia. While chatting with body shop owner Tim Wilkerson, Skandalakis mentioned his occupation. Wilkerson immediately asked a favor.

Wilkerson told Skandalakis that his father, Fred Wilkerson, had gone missing sixteen years earlier, but he and his family were convinced Fred had been murdered. They knew who had murdered Fred. They just couldn't prove it. He asked Skandalakis to reopen the case.

Skandalakis assigned the case to Clay Bryant, a detective who was quickly gaining a reputation for solving cold cases. Bryant methodically reinvestigated the case, re-interviewing family and neighbors.

After three months, Bryant located a witness who had never been interviewed. The woman said she had picked up Quedens at the airport on November 28, 1987, shortly before Fred's car was found there. While Bryant's case against Quedens was growing stronger, he still had no solid proof that Fred hadn't done exactly what Quedens claimed—willingly left to start a new life.

But Bryant, sometimes described by fellow investigators and media as a cold case "bloodhound," refused to give up. His tenacity eventually led him to a reliable source with a strong suggestion: look in the well. Quedens had a well on her property, and sometime after 1987, it had been filled with dirt.

This time, the court decided Bryant had probable cause to search Quedens's property, and the area that was once a well was quickly revealed as the dumping spot for Fred's body. On September 30, 2003, just four months after Fred's son had asked the county DA to reopen the case, Fred's body was removed from the bottom of the old well on Ware Cross Road, just 120 yards from the house Fred and Quedens had shared.

Investigator Clay Bryant.
Courtesy of Clay Bryant.

He'd been shot once, execution style, in the back of the head (with a .32 caliber Walther PPK pistol).

The next day, Quedens, by then sixty-one, was arrested for the murder. A small crowd of Fred's family, friends, and neighbors flanked the street, cheering and applauding, as the Troup County Sheriff's Department cruiser drove Quedens from her property to the county jail.

Nearly a year later, at Quedens's trial, prosecutors presented this scenario: The couple's relationship had soured, and Fred began feeling that he'd been duped into signing over his half-interest in the fourteen-acre property. He filed a lawsuit against Quedens, hoping to regain the land. Fred was living in the basement of the house he and Quedens had built, giving Quedens opportunity to shoot him in the back of the head and drag his body to the nearby well. The prosecution's case was built on a strong theory that was available at the time of Fred's disappearance, and one the family had believed for sixteen years. But without Fred's remains, it would have been just a theory. The gunshot wound to the back of Fred's skull turned theory to fact. Fred had not left Georgia to start a new life. He had been murdered.

Though the defense argued that doing so would prejudice the jury, the prosecution brought Fred's skeletal remains into the courtroom, powerfully illustrating how long Fred's family had waited for justice, fitting one more stone into the wall that will enclose Quedens for life....

CASES GO COLD WHEN EVIDENCE POOLS DRY UP.

You cannot interview witnesses you don't have, and you cannot examine evidence that you have not received. As much as an investigator wants to keep a case open, as much as a family wants to see resolution, a case sometimes becomes cold in spite of the most skilled efforts. A wise detective knows when to classify a case as cold without feeling defeat. The situation, though painful, is clear: You can work only with what you have.

A case doesn't become cold at a certain age. It becomes cold when no more outstanding, logical leads remain. Some investigators insist, "If a case isn't solved in the first forty-eight hours, it will most likely go cold," and certainly the first two days are crucial to gathering evidence while it's still secure and available and to interviewing witnesses while their memories are relatively sharp. And, of course, the forty-eight-hour window is critical in a child-abduction or kidnapping case—when there's a chance that the worst of the crime hasn't yet been committed.

However, intricate cases with numerous leads and voluminous evidence can certainly take longer than two days to solve. As long as evidence is unstudied and witnesses are still surfacing, a case is vibrant. When the evidence pool has been exhausted, it may be time to meticulously file away every piece of evidence and every written report, waiting for the sometimes-surprising changes that occur over time, bringing new life to cases that once seemed hopeless.

CASES GO COLD WHEN WITNESSES ASSUME SOMEONE ELSE IS SPEAKING UP.

The desire not to become involved with an investigation can be strong, particularly in some cultures, so if it looks as though a case will be solved without their contribution, some witnesses won't come forward without strong prodding.

"People who have relevant information often assume that the case has been solved and their information isn't needed," says Alaska prosecutor Alan Goodwin. Sometimes a second interview or additional media coverage will help a witness realize that his or her help is still vital to solving the case.

CASES GO COLD WHEN WITNESSES HOLD INFORMATION FOR LATER NEGOTIATIONS.

As a prosecutor, Goodwin has encountered repeat criminals who had information that they knew could benefit them in the future, so they held onto it until it was most beneficial.

"People with checkered criminal pasts sometimes hold onto information like poker chips until they are in trouble again," explains Goodwin, "hoping they can 'cash in' their chips when it's to their advantage." After the particularly brutal murder of a homeless woman in Anchorage, Alaska, a career criminal offered information about the killer, saying he had been with the killer the night he committed the murder. But when this witness learned that the charges against him were less than he had anticipated, "He changed his mind," says Goodwin. "He said he'd hold onto the information until he needed it. With his minor charges, he wouldn't get much in return for his information."

CASES GO COLD WHEN CRUCIAL EVIDENCE IS MISSING.

Even a fresh investigation can be like picking up a stack of puzzle pieces, putting them together carefully, and finding that so many pieces are missing that you can't determine what the puzzle is supposed to be.

Sometimes big puzzle pieces are missing. You may not even know who your victim is. Perhaps no one steps forward to identify the body. Or you're dealing with skeletal remains that have yet to be identified. You may even be struggling to prove that the death was truly a homicide as opposed to death due to natural causes. As you wait for these crucial puzzle pieces, the temperature plummets.

It was the search for a shiny black 1988 Honda CRX Si with a sunroof and the Montana license plate "LILMISS" that drove the murder investigation of Lisa Marie Kimmell for nearly fourteen years. Eighteen-year-old Lisa had purchased the car from her salary as an Aurora, Colorado, Arby's restaurant employee, and she'd used a nickname given to her by her grandparents for the personalized plate.

The license plate implied beauty queen, and she certainly could have been one. She was a pretty, wholesome, hardworking girl who planned a career in management with Arby's and had just moved to the Denver area to work at her first restaurant.

On March 25, 1988, Lisa worked the day shift at the Aurora Arby's and left work about 3:00 p.m. She stopped by her bank and withdrew

Murder victim Lisa Marie Kimmel.
Courtesy of Dan Tholson.

$100 from the ATM at 5:14 p.m. She went to her apartment to pack, talked by phone with her boyfriend in Wyoming, and then drove her Honda with the LILMISS license plate out of Denver at about 6:30 p.m., heading north on I-25 toward her parents' home in Billings, Montana. She planned to stop in Cody, Wyoming, to pick up her boyfriend.

The wide stretches of countryside tempted her to drive a little too fast, and about 8:40 p.m. she was pulled over fifty miles outside of Casper by Wyoming State Highway Patrolman Al Lesco and given a ticket for driving 88 in a 65 mph zone. She didn't have the money to post the $120 bond, so Lesco escorted her to Douglas, a town with a population of less than five thousand, where she attempted to make a withdrawal from an ATM. Her card would not work at the bank's ATM. Lesco had the option of booking Lisa and taking her to jail, but he decided to let her sign the "promise to appear" section of the ticket and allow her to continue her trip. Lisa signed the ticket, and Lesco gave her directions back to the freeway. It was 9:08 p.m.

Lisa's signature on the citation was the last documentation of her life. Sometime after signing the ticket, she disappeared. When she failed to arrive at her boyfriend's Cody home, he called Colorado and

Wyoming highway patrols to see if she'd been in an accident. Then he called Lisa's parents.

At 3:30 p.m. on March 27, Ron Kimmell reported his daughter missing to the Yellowstone County Sheriff's Office in Billings, and he and his wife, Sheila, launched a frantic campaign to find their oldest child. They distributed hundreds of fliers throughout Colorado, Wyoming, Utah, and Montana. Billings law enforcement issued a regional alert, describing the Honda with the distinctive license plate.

On the day Lisa was reported missing, forty people reported seeing her car, in twenty-five locations. The following day, March 28, fifty people reported seeing her car, in twenty-five locations. On March 29, fifty-three people reported seeing the LILMISS car in thirty-one locations. On March 30, thirty-four people reported seeing the car in twenty locations. On March 31, forty-three people reported seeing Lisa's car in eighteen locations. On April 1, fifty-four people reported seeing her car in thirty-four locations. Investigators followed every lead.

But on April 2, two fishermen found Lisa's body floating in the North Platte River, near the Old Government Bridge about twenty-five miles south of Casper and about eighty miles from where Lesco had stopped her for speeding. Traces of Lisa's blood were found on the

Old Government Bridge from which Lisa Marie Kimmel was thrown.
Courtesy of Dan Tholson.

bridge, leading investigators to assume that she had been tossed from the bridge.

Lisa was nude except for panties and socks, but she was still wearing a gold ring, two gold necklaces, two diamond stud earrings in her left ear, and a gold watch that had stopped at 9:40. Forensic specialists determined that the watch had probably stopped when it came in contact with the water.

An initial autopsy report showed that Lisa had been bound, beaten, raped, and sodomized, then hit over the head with a blunt object and stabbed six times in a distinctive "hand" pattern: five stab wounds in the center of her chest and one stab wound under her sternum. The autopsy revealed that Lisa was killed not long before she was placed in the water. That information, along with the extensive abuse to her body, led to the theory that she had been held hostage for a week.

Lisa's car was missing, and police believed that if they found the car, they'd find trace evidence that would lead to the killer.

"The car became the key for fourteen years," says investigator Dan Tholson. "The car was 'spotted' everywhere. In the first three weeks, police had 576 sightings in 129 locations. Then the crime aired on *Unsolved Mysteries*, and police received fifteen hundred calls. When the show was rerun, they received seven hundred more sightings.

"The trouble with sightings," continues Tholson, "is that the majority go nowhere, and they take up valuable time and resources. But every sighting has to be checked out. Police ended up following four thousand to five thousand sightings of the 'Lil Miss car.' At one point, we received a report that the car had been spotted on a military base, and the base shut down all traffic coming and going. The lead turned out to be faulty."

While the car became the focus of the immediate investigation, Dr. James Thorpen, a Casper pathologist

Investigator Dan Tholson.
Courtesy of Dan Tholson.

who was later elected coroner, had the foresight to look to the future. In 1988, DNA was just beginning to emerge as a viable investigative tool, but Dr. Thorpen collected massive DNA samples in the hope that someday this new technology would tell them who killed Lisa Marie Kimmell.

Dr. Thorpen tried to persuade the sheriff to hire a private lab to compare the DNA found on Lisa with the DNA found on another young woman in the area who was kidnapped, abused, and then run down by a car. The sheriff said that DNA findings were too faulty, and he refused to give permission for the expensive tests. But the rape kit and other DNA samples were meticulously protected over time.

Years passed, and even the sightings of Lisa's car diminished. "But the case was never put away," observes Tholson, who joined the Natrona County (Wyoming) Sheriff's Department in 1984. "We had the DNA, and we were waiting for technology to catch up. And we were waiting to find the car.

"Eventually, we stopped believing we were actually tracking the car," recalls Tholson. "We'd talk to people who could place the car in New York, Washington, and California—all in the same day. We learned that the license plate wasn't as distinctive as we originally thought. Hundreds of people had similar plates with things like 'LILSIS,' and even though we had to follow the leads, we were pretty sure they weren't going anywhere."

The Natrona County Sheriff's Department asked other agencies to look at the case, hoping to get new insights. "And some agencies joined the investigation uninvited," recalls Tholson. "Everyone wanted to be the one who solved the Lil Miss case.

"Rumors about the case were flying," continues Tholson. "No one trusted anyone else. No one thought the sheriff's department was doing its job. At one point, a would-be informant told an officer that he'd been present when Lisa's heart was cut out. We told the officer that the autopsy report did not indicate that her heart had been removed, but he followed the lead anyway.

"We received a report that someone who was rumored to be a devil worshipper had a party in their basement, and partygoers saw the Lil

Miss license plate on the basement wall. Investigators went to the home, and the confused homeowner showed them that his house had no basement.

"Some agencies thought the case was drug-related, that Lisa was a drug carrier. That was one of the most damaging theories. From everything that was turned up, Lisa was a good, hardworking girl. Dr. Thorpen found no drugs in Lisa's system. He did drug tests on Lisa's hair and determined that she'd had no drugs in her system for at least ninety days prior to her death.

"A lot of people in prison offered information in exchange for a lighter sentence, but none of their 'information' led anywhere."

Tholson commends Lisa's mother for keeping the case before the news media.

Though the media were sometimes tough on the Natrona County Sheriff's Department, where Tholson worked as an investigator, he states, "If I had a violent crime in my own family, I'd contact law enforcement constantly. At least once a week."

In spite of Sheila Kimmell's love for her daughter and the perseverance of scores of law enforcement officers, fourteen years passed with no suspect and no black Honda with a LILMISS license plate.

George H. W. Bush and Bill Clinton passed through the office of president, and George W. Bush took office.

America fought Desert Storm.

The World Trade Center towers fell.

Lisa's friends married, started careers, and had families.

Meanwhile, dedicated scientists continued to refine DNA research, and investigators looked for ways to share their DNA findings. The FBI's CODIS (Combined DNA Index System) became fully operational in 1998.

And in 1997, Wyoming passed a law requiring that DNA samples be taken from anyone convicted of a felony or in custody for a felony conviction and that these DNA samples be entered into the FBI's CODIS database.

Then on July 5, 2002, the Wyoming Crime Lab notified the sheriff's department that they'd gotten a CODIS hit on Lisa's killer.

Murderer Dale Wayne Eaton.
Courtesy of Dan Tholson.

The suspect was a fifty-seven-year-old welder named Dale Wayne Eaton, serving a three-year sentence in a federal prison in Colorado.

Eaton was a divorced father of two sons. He had physically abused his family, so his wife had left with the children. At the time of Lisa's murder, he lived alone in an old school bus, with no running water, in Moneta, Wyoming, about seventy miles northwest of Casper.

When Eaton was younger, he was in and out of institutions. At sixteen, he stabbed a Greeley, Colorado, woman who complained that the watermelons he was selling were sour. After that, he'd been arrested numerous times for charges ranging from assault and battery to auto theft to grand larceny, and he'd served several prison sentences.

In 1997, he forced a husband, wife, and child into his van at gunpoint and forced the woman to drive. But his victims fought back. The woman swerved the car, and her husband attacked Eaton, severely beating him. When police arrived, the family gave them their statements and a relative's phone number where they could be reached. Then they headed on to California to visit family.

When Eaton's trial came up, police said they could not locate the victims. Eaton was found guilty, but because the family did not testify against him, he received a light sentence at a community correctional facility. He simply walked away from the facility.

In July 1998, Eaton aroused the suspicion of a park ranger while staying at Grand Teton National Park. The ranger ran a check and found that he had escaped from a correctional facility. Eaton was arrested and placed in the Wyoming State Penitentiary, and a DNA sample was taken. When he was arrested, Eaton had a weapon. Because he was arrested on federal property, the government charged him with possession of a firearm by a convicted felon. After serving time in the Wyoming prison, he was released to federal authorities, prosecuted, and placed in maximum security at the Florence, Colorado, federal prison to serve a three-year sentence.

Wyoming State Crime Lab personnel were unable to process DNA themselves, and they lacked the funding to pay for another lab to process samples. The DNA sample taken from Eaton was not processed for four years. When it was, Natrona County Sheriff's Department's DNA samples were waiting for the match.

"There is still a backlog of unprocessed samples, uncollected samples, changing DNA protocols, and other issues across the country," says Tholson. "I believe that when all these issues are worked out and the unknown samples and the known samples are in the same database, there will be a lot more cases solved."

By the time the Natrona County Sheriff's Department received word of the match, Eaton had killed his cellmate because he had perceived that he had made a sexual advance toward him. Described by his family as deceptively strong and quick, Eaton struck his cellmate in the left side of his jaw, twisting his head and tearing his carotid artery. His cellmate bled out before anyone could save him.

Tholson and investigator Lynn Cohee went to the federal prison to

Eaton's property as it was in 2002 at the time of his arrest. *Courtesy of Dan Tholson.*

interview Eaton. He had just met with his attorney about killing his cellmate, but he was calm and relaxed.

"When we started talking about Lisa's murder," recalls Tholson, "Eaton's mouth immediately became so dry that he was making smacking sounds and was having trouble talking. We had to get him some water before we could talk with him. He became extremely agitated as we talked, but he never confessed."

On July 29, 2002, investigators carried out a search warrant on Eaton's property. The school bus had been replaced by a beat-up mobile home.

At the bottom of an old well on Eaton's property they found hubcaps and parts of a taillight from a Honda. The front yard contained a suspicious mound, as if the ground had been dug up. A ninety-year-old neighbor, who had not been questioned in the past, said she had watched through binoculars in 1988 when Eaton dug the huge hole with a backhoe. She asked him what he was doing, and he said he was digging a well. She told investigators that he dug only about fifty feet deep and you couldn't find water in that area without digging two hundred or three hundred feet.

It was enough for investigators to get a warrant to dig up the property. The next day, they brought in their own digging equipment. The first day, they found a few car parts and considered giving up. But on the second day, after digging in several places near Eaton's mobile home,

Investigator Dan Tholson checking for the VIN as Lisa Marie Kimmel's car is dug up.
Courtesy of Dan Tholson.

they found Lisa's Honda, confirmed by the vehicle identification number. And they found part of the LILMISS license plate buried near the car. But the wheels, seats, stereo, and gear-shift knob were missing from the car. A pipe had been fastened to the car, and a siphon hose was hanging from the gas tank.

"Eaton had treated Lisa's car a lot like Native Americans treated buffalo," observes Tholson. "He used every part. He later claimed that the pipe was inserted because he'd wanted to use the car for a septic tank—not uncommon in this part of the country. He'd siphoned out the gas. And he'd recycled as many car parts as he could.

"One of Eaton's sons told us he remembered helping his father melt down four Honda wheels to sell as scrap. He was only sixteen at the time, but he was one of those kids who knew every make and model of car. He had no doubt the wheels they sold belonged to a Honda.

"And he said he helped his father install a Honda stereo and Honda seats into a pickup truck in 2001.

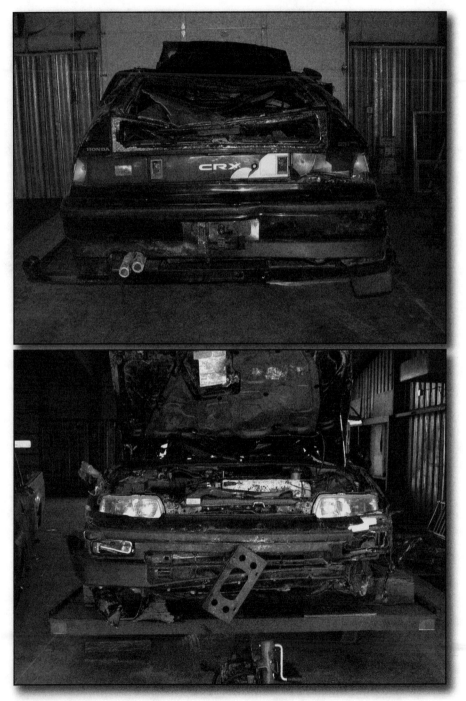

Lisa Marie Kimmel's car after being dug up. *Photos courtesy of Dan Tholson.*

"If he had buried the body with the car, he wouldn't have been caught," observes Tholson. Only one theory has surfaced about why Eaton made Lisa's body so easy to find. It goes against his diagnosis as a sociopath, but it fits the memories his sister has of Eaton as a child. His brother had muscular dystrophy, and Eaton pushed him to school every day in a wheelchair. Maybe somewhere, now deeply buried in his distorted psyche, was the tiniest bit of twisted compassion.

Eaton allowed his psychiatrist to testify at his trial, giving him permission to share information from their discussions. The psychiatrist shared this story:

Eaton was angry with his ex-wife when he spotted Lisa. He approached her with a rifle and told her she was trespassing on his land. He forced her into the school bus where he lived, bound her, and raped her repeatedly at gunpoint. She begged him to let her go, saying she wanted to be home in time for Easter. Her body was found on April 2. Easter 1988 was April 3.

Eaton's trial, including jury selection, took more than a month, but the jury deliberated for less than six hours before finding him guilty and sentencing him to death. He is currently the only Wyoming inmate on death row. Investigators suspect that Eaton was responsible for other murders in the area over a period of several years, but they have not yet been able to prove any connections.

In a wrongful-death suit, Lisa's family was awarded Eaton's property. On July 18, 2005—what would have been Lisa's thirty-sixth birthday—they burned the buildings to the ground. The car, which drove the investigation for so long and, along with the DNA, helped convict the killer, is still in storage.

CASES GO COLD WHEN LEADS ARE IGNORED.

In 1991, Sheila Jo Hargrove's body was found floating in Horseshoe Lake, not far from the small house she rented near Manitou, Kentucky. She had been stabbed multiple times. The county medical examiner went to Sheila's home to examine the crime scene. He followed the trail of blood through the house, out the front door, across the porch, down the stairs, and across the lawn. The blood trail stopped abruptly at the tailgate of a freshly washed pickup truck, with drops of water still in the truck bed.

Years later, the medical examiner stated that he'd thought at the time that the truck had been used to transport Sheila's body to the dump site, then washed of all evidence. He didn't express his theory to investigators, and eighteen years passed before the owner of the truck was convicted of killing Sheila....

CASES GO COLD WHEN NO ONE PURSUES THEM.

Every case needs an advocate, and sometimes an active case becomes dormant simply because no one can or will make it a priority. Cases pile up. Newer cases with fresher trails take precedence, even though older cases still have clues that have not been followed. A detective retires or changes assignments. Other detectives already have full workloads, so suddenly no one's working the retired detective's cases. If new developments arise, there's no one to receive them.

A cold case unit is a welcome resting place for such cases. Without such a unit, new evidence may simply be filed away. Cold cases aren't necessarily fifteen or twenty years old. They may simply be orphans in a monumental caseload.

But sometimes cold case detectives are hesitant to assume responsibility for a case until the original detective officially gives it up.

"One thing we were always concerned about was stepping on people's toes and taking a case away from someone who put their heart and soul in it but didn't have time to keep the investigation moving," says Greg Smith of the Miami Metro-Dade County Police Department. "To avoid crossing that line, we made a policy: The case was cold when the original investigator was no longer in the unit. He might have been promoted, moved to another unit, or left the department. Until then, the case was his unless he asked us to take it over.

"A couple of times," says Smith, "we took a case at a detective's request. Sometimes he'd say, 'You guys go ahead and run with it. I'm tied up with other cases.' That was the green light we needed."

CASES GO COLD WHEN THERE'S NOT ENOUGH TIME OR MONEY TO CONTINUE THE INVESTIGATION.

Money talks, and sometimes, to the chagrin of the investigator and the agony of the victim's family, it prioritizes. Just as most individuals find that their funds are limited and they must choose which charities to support, investigators also lack resources to invest in every worthy cause. A lack of time and money does not necessarily negate the worthiness of a case. It simply places it somewhere on an overloaded docket.

Cold cases are costly in budget and manpower, as Detective Greg Smith learned when he was assigned to the Metro-Dade (Florida) Police Department Cold Case Squad. Much of the population in South Florida is transient, so investigating cold cases places an unusual strain on resources. When detectives identify viable leads, they often discover that the perpetrators are no longer in the area. As a regular detective for the Metro-Dade Police Department, Smith traveled by plane for only one case. During his time with the department's cold case squad, he flew to thirty-six states and three countries to follow up on cold case leads. Squad members worked on so many cases at the same time that they often interviewed for multiple cases when they traveled. Even with careful travel planning, following out-of-state leads was costly.

CASES GO COLD WHEN BUDGETS ARE CUT.

Like South Florida, upstate New York has an unusually high crime rate. Over the years, as finances forced the city of Buffalo to reallocate manpower, fewer detectives were forced to work more cases.

"Buffalo's population has decreased over the years," observes former Buffalo Police Department cold case detective Dennis Delano, "so it appears on paper like we could do with fewer police personnel. In the past thirty or so years, police personnel have been reduced from fifteen hundred to six hundred.

"It's true that a lot of people left the area, but crime continued to rise. I guess more good guys left than bad guys. Now new cases come in faster than detectives can solve the existing ones, and the stack of cold cases gets higher."

CASES GO COLD WHEN PUBLICITY DIES.

"Time, money, and publicity drive cases," says Detective Troy Armstrong. "A crime can be the hot topic on Monday, and by Wednesday a more brutal or high-profile crime occurs and the media forgets the first case." The adages that are passed from generation to generation hold true: The squeaky door gets the oil. The crying baby gets picked up. The high-profile case gets the most attention.

That's not a reflection on the investigator or a devaluing of a less-prominent victim. It's sometimes the only way an investigator can survive.

CASES GO COLD WHEN NO ONE'S OFFICIALLY IN CHARGE.

In the early evening of June 15, 1993, the USS *Yorktown* docked in Saint Thomas, in the Virgin Islands. Its crew headed for shore, ready for some well-deserved R&R. And petty thieves were waiting for them.

Local criminals regularly kept track of ships coming into port, and they often followed sailors and attempted to rob them. While most of the sailors chose to begin their liberty with a celebration, three men headed for the nearest pay phone to call their families. Just after sunset, thirty-one-year-old US Navy lieutenant Dana Bartlett, Third Class Damage Controlman Michael Nendze, and US Coast Guard lieutenant Patrick Gardella walked five hundred yards to the end of the pier to use the phone. Dana planned to call his wife.

The phone was located next to a tennis court, so Dana and Gardella sat in the nearby bleachers while Nendze called his wife.

The two men noticed a black Suzuki Samurai with tinted windows drive by slowly. Dana became suspicious and told Gardella they should leave the area. The two men headed toward the phone booth to get Nendze, but three teenagers ran up to them from behind the tennis court. One carried a baseball bat with nails driven through it, turning it into a mace. The other two carried handguns. One of the assailants stuck a gun in Gardella's face and demanded, "Give me your money."

Gardella gave him the quarter he had for his phone call, his military identification, and his keys. The two other men approached Nendze and demanded his money, too. Then the one carrying the makeshift mace hit Nendze. As Nendze raised his hands to protect himself from the blow, another assailant shot him at point-blank range with a .22 pistol. The assailants then demanded money from Dana. As Dana reached for his billfold, the one with the mace began attacking all three men, beating them to the ground.

While Dana was on his knees, one of the assailants attempted to shoot him, but the pistol misfired. Dana rolled over and curled up into a fetal position to protect himself, and the assailant fired again. Again the gun misfired, but the assailant shot a third time, striking Dana in the face. The assailants fled into the night, leaving the victims' money.

Gardella told Nendze to stay with Dana while he got help. Weak from his own beating, Gardella struggled back to the *Yorktown* for help. When police and an ambulance arrived, Dana was barely conscious. He was placed in an ambulance and rushed to a nearby hospital. A Virgin Islands police officer rode with him in the ambulance. Dana told the officer exactly what had happened and gave a description of the assailants.

A few hours later, Dana lapsed into a coma and was flown to the Veterans Administration Hospital in Puerto Rico. He died nine days later without regaining consciousness. Nendze and Gardella survived, but both suffered some permanent injuries.

Initially, the case was worked by an overabundance of investigators as three agencies disjointedly studied evidence and followed leads: the FBI, NCIS, and the Virgin Islands Police. Each agency quickly identified a list of suspects, but without a strong sense of coordination among the investigations, all three agencies let the case go cold within weeks.

"Too many hands in the pot" is the way Special Agent Joe Kennedy evaluated the case two years later when he was appointed by NCIS Director Roy Nedrow to lead a reinvestigation of Dana's murder, along with five other NCIS investigators. This time, Kennedy was careful to establish a bond between the NCIS task force members and the Virgin Islands law enforcement officers. He enlisted the help of six local officers, bringing the investigation group total to twelve.

The combined group worked together so closely that they were soon known as the Virgin Islands Task Force. Local members knew the area, and some had investigated the case two years earlier. Within thirty days, the Virgin Islands Task Force made three arrests and obtained two confessions (the third suspect eventually pleaded guilty). All three suspects had been listed in the original report.

Eventually, all three assailants were sentenced. Two of the assailants received two consecutive twenty-five-year sentences. Because the third was a juvenile at the time he committed the crime, his sentencing is not public record. At the sentencing, Dana's wife, Gail, said, "My heart aches to think how frightened Dana must have been that night. I realize how lucky they [the assailants] are to beg for their futures. Dana didn't have that chance."

CASES GO COLD BECAUSE WITNESSES ARE AFRAID.

In 1987, Corinna Mullens's beaten and mutilated body was found inside the trunk of her car outside her Central City, Kentucky, apartment. The twenty-year-old single mother had been raped, sodomized, mutilated, and beaten to death. No physical evidence was found. Corinna's boyfriend was indicted, tried, and acquitted, primarily because a Central City police officer provided an alibi. With no further suspects, the case went cold.

It wasn't until 2006 that a witness came forward. The thirty-five-year-old woman had been just sixteen when she saw four men rape, mutilate, and murder Corinna. One of the men was Corinna's boyfriend, and one was the police officer who had provided his alibi.

The young girl was terrified to tell what she'd seen, and she had remained quiet until guilt became stronger than fear.

The woman's description of the crime matched the autopsy findings, and three of the four men were convicted of rape, sodomy, and murder. The police officer was also convicted of destroying evidence. But because the US Constitution protects against double jeopardy, Corinna's boyfriend could not be retried for murder. He was, however, found guilty of perjury, complicity to rape, and sodomy.

* * *

Fear is a common case-stopper, and sometimes it squelches an investigation permanently. Even if one person is brave enough to come forward, without the backing of other witnesses, who perhaps have been silenced by threats or assumptions of threats, one brave soul may not be enough to bring a case to closure.

On a January afternoon in 1992, a man called the Atlanta FBI office to say that he'd witnessed a murder forty-six years earlier. Special Agent Jim Procopio was assigned the case, and he flew to Panama City, Florida, to interview the witness. He met with a white man in his mid-fifties a few days later.

The overdue witness was Clinton Adams. He was quiet and subdued, and he showed very little emotion as he told Procopio that in 1946, as a ten-year-old boy, he was playing in a pine thicket in Morgan County, about forty miles east of Atlanta, when he heard several cars drive by, then stop on the Moore's Ford Bridge that crossed the Appalachee River connecting Walton and Oconee counties. He

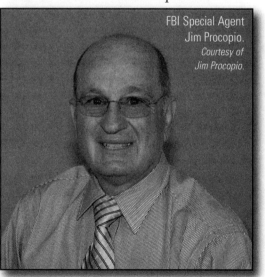

FBI Special Agent Jim Procopio. *Courtesy of Jim Procopio.*

saw at least a dozen unmasked white men drag two black couples from the cars and massacre them. The terrified Adams watched helplessly, not daring to move until the last killer drove away, leaving the unrecognizable, mangled bodies of the black couples. Long after the woods were silent, young Adams could still hear the frantic, animal-like sounds of the dying people, and then the laughter and casual talk of the white men as they loaded their weapons into their cars and headed home to wives and children and quiet evening meals.

Adams told his mother what he'd witnessed, but she said very little. A few days later, law enforcement personnel canvassed nearby neighborhoods as part of their official investigation. The sheriff came to Adams's house and asked his mother if she knew anything about the murders. Adams blurted out, "I saw what happened."

The sheriff told him, "Never tell what you saw. Those men could kill you, just like they killed the others." Adams had witnessed what the men were capable of. He had no doubt they could do just that.

Adams told Procopio that he'd been running from the Ku Klux Klan all of his adult life and that his fear was reinforced by the Walton County Sheriff. When a stranger rang his doorbell, even a Bible salesman, he assumed the Klan had found him, and he moved. He'd moved as many as four times in a year. Over the years, Adams said that the Klan let him know they were watching him. He kept his secret for forty-six years, in spite of constant nightmares. But instead of the memories easing as he got older, they grew worse.

Then Adams lost a leg in an industrial accident, and his rehabilitation included regular visits to a psychiatrist to help him adjust to losing his leg. The psychiatrist sensed that something was troubling Adams, and he was eventually able to get him to talk about what he'd witnessed forty-six years earlier. The psychiatrist urged Adams to contact the FBI.

Procopio believed Adams. Why would someone wait more than forty years to concoct such a dramatic story? And Adams didn't seem like the type to be seeking attention. "In fact," recalls Procopio, "it was just the opposite. I sensed that he wanted to fade into anonymity as soon as he left the interview." Procopio thought Adams seemed relieved to have finally told his story.

Procopio checked FBI records. The thinness of the Moore's Ford Bridge murders file troubled Procopio. "It seemed strange," he recalls, "that a case that was listed as a major case consisted of a paper-thin file. Each year, only a few cases nationwide are classified as major cases. The gruesome murder of four individuals, almost without a doubt racially motivated, definitely qualified as a major case, and the investigation would have been extensive." But there he stood, in front of the records file, holding a case file that was more the size of a citation for jay-walking. A lot was missing.

"If you have no starting point," observes Procopio, "you have no ending point. We had to go back, reinvestigate, and find a starting point. But everyone I interviewed and everywhere I checked, I was met with silence."

Adams admitted that he recognized some of the men, and he named several. All of the men he named were dead. It was clear that, even with decades separating him from the killers, he had no intention of revealing the identities of any guilty men who were still alive.

Adams wasn't the only one who knew what happened. Nearly everyone in Walton County knew, at least secondhand. They knew the names of a dozen or more men who had opened fire on sharecroppers Roger and Dorothy Malcom and George and Mae Murray Dorsey, shooting them with hundreds of rounds from shotguns, rifles, pistols, and a machine gun. Some people thought the murders were justified, so they saw no reason to point a finger at the killers. The rest saw the killings as savage, brutal, senseless murders, but like Clinton Adams, they were afraid to speak up. Whatever their reasons, the conspiracy of silence left the Moore's Ford Bridge murders, the last documented mass lynching in the United States, a cold case. (Lynching is broadly defined as being put to death by a mob without legal authority.) And the horror of the lynching is multiplied because those who know what happened have remained silent for more than six decades.

The story started eleven days before the murder, on a sweltering Sunday in July 1946: Roger and Dorothy Malcom went to church like nearly every other couple in the South, black or white. But after church, Roger began drinking, and he and Dorothy started arguing. Neither situation was unusual. But this time the black sharecroppers carried their argument onto the landowner's property, near his house. The landowner, Barnette "Barney" Hester, did his best to stop the couple from fighting. It wasn't the first time he'd had to tell an intoxicated Roger to quiet down and go home.

But this time, Roger had a pocketknife, and he threatened to cut Dorothy. Hester attempted to stop him, and Roger sank the knife deep into the left side of Hester's chest, right below his heart. As Hester crumpled to the ground, Roger darted away, but not before issuing Hester a drunken warning that, from now on, he was to address him as *Mr.* Malcom. Hester's family rushed him to the hospital, nearly ten miles away in Monroe, a town of five thousand residents and thirty-six churches.

While Hester was being transported to the hospital, his white neighbors went looking for Roger.

They found him hiding in a cornfield and tied his hands and feet, then called the Walton County Sheriff's Department. Two officers arrived, changed the ropes to handcuffs, and took Roger to Monroe. While doctors fought to save Hester's life at Walton County Hospital, Roger languished in the jail on the other side of town.

Hester survived, and Roger Malcom was bailed out of jail eleven days later, on July 25, 1946. Dorothy's parents had been begging white landowner Loy Harrison to bail Roger out of jail and let him work off the debt. He refused for days, then suddenly changed his mind. He took Dorothy with him to Monroe, and he took another black couple, George and Mae Murray Dorsey. Harrison signed a $600 bond to free Roger from jail. He left the county jail about 5:30 p.m., with the two black couples riding with him as he headed back toward his farm.

Harrison chose a winding dirt road, the longest route home. He claimed that when he reached the Moore's Ford Bridge, a car blocked his way and forced him to stop. Between twenty and twenty-five men, none of whom Harrison said he recognized, took the Malcoms and Dorseys by gunpoint into the woods, tied them to trees, and shot them. He claimed he had no part in the lynching, but Harrison was one of the men that Clinton Adams named as a shooter.

Despite Monroe County's desire to handle the situation on its own, soon FBI and Georgia Bureau of Investigation agents blanketed the county, interviewing hundreds of people. More than a hundred citizens were brought before the grand jury. While Monroe County afforded unusual privileges for blacks of that era—a "colored" library, a "colored" municipal swimming pool—the government was run by whites, and outside law enforcement agencies received limited cooperation. In the end, no one broke the county's code of silence, and no major evidence surfaced that could point investigators to the killers.

Fear silenced both blacks and whites who might have wanted to speak, and one by one, they have gone to their graves without revealing what happened on July 25, 1946, on a deserted Georgia road.

But each July in Walton County, Georgia, a memorial march challenges news media and local residents not to forget the last racially motivated mass murder in the South. It's not the immediate families who keep the case alive; it's the African-American community. At the time of the horrific murders, they were helpless to speak out. Now they're determined to be the voice for the victims whose mangled bodies were laid to rest nearly seven decades ago. The case remains open, at least in part, because a group of people refuses to let the community forget.

Will any of the men who brutally killed the Malcoms and the Dorseys be brought to justice before they die of natural causes? Hope fades with each passing year.

CASES GO COLD WHEN THERE'S A COVER-UP.

Four people killed in a matter of seconds. Surely some in Walton County still know what happened, but no one's talking.

"When reopening a cold case," says Procopio, "sometimes investigators hear the same story from nearly everyone they interview: 'We all knew who did it.' When rumors linger in a community, there's always the possibility of a cover-up."

It's a case that still haunts Procopio because he knows the answer is out there. People know what happened, but they're not talking. And with each year that passes, the chance of anyone coming forward diminishes.

* * *

When cold case detective Clay Bryant was fifteen, he accompanied his dad—Hogansville, Georgia, Chief of Police Buddy Bryant—on a call for assistance from the Troup County Sheriff's Department. A woman's body had been spotted at the bottom of a well, just outside of town. Bryant watched as police used a cable to pull the woman's body from the well, and he heard the murmurings in the crowd that had quickly

Well where Gwendolyn Moore's body was found.
Courtesy of Clay Bryant.

gathered: "Well, he finally did it." "No doubt about it. Marshall killed her." "I'm surprised she survived this long, the way he beat her."

The image of Gwendolyn Moore's body spinning on the cable haunted young Bryant for years. His father talked about the case until his death, regretting that the body was found just outside his jurisdiction, which kept him from participating in the investigation. But he always told his son that he had no doubt Marshall Moore killed the mother of his four sons. Gwendolyn had been trapped in an abusive marriage for half of her thirty years, and nearly everyone in the community knew Moore terrorized his pretty, petite wife.

Gwendolyn's husband was the town's suspect, too. He had a reputation for violence. His sons remembered being awakened many nights by the sounds of their father beating their mother, then crying themselves back to sleep.

The night before Gwendolyn's body was found, her husband beat her savagely. Neighbors on one side witnessed the beating from their front porch. Neighbors on the other side allowed her to take refuge in the crawl space under their house, as she often did.

"But Gwendolyn's truck-driver husband knew some influential

House Gwendolyn Moore hid under after many of her beatings (Moore house in background).
Courtesy of Clay Bryant.

people in the town," recalls Bryant. "He was rumored to be transporting illegal cargo and to be paying the police to look the other way.

"For whatever reason," says Bryant, "somebody didn't want to solve this case."

Bryant's father never forgot the injustice of the young woman's death. Bryant went to law school and eventually became a criminal investigator for the LaGrange County District Attorney. Then in 2002—on his father's birthday—he received a call from a local sheriff's deputy, asking him for help on the case. Perhaps, with the passing of time, someone would be willing to lift the veil from the cover-up that had left Marshall Moore a free man for more than thirty years....

CASES GO COLD WHEN A WITNESS
POINTS INVESTIGATORS IN THE WRONG DIRECTION.

A case can be the most active, viable case one day, and a few days later, the investigator finds that someone has provided false information. The investigator builds a case on a witness's testimony and later finds that things didn't happen just as the witness said. While investigators are following the wrong suspect or tracking down leads that go nowhere, the case goes cold. This is especially common in sexual assault cases.

CASES GO COLD WHEN INITIAL LEADS
AREN'T FOLLOWED THOROUGHLY.

It's not uncommon for cold case detectives to read over a case and see obvious leads that should have been followed and witnesses who were never interviewed. But the most productive way to approach a case is by concentrating on the evidence that's available.

Finding leads, interviews, and evidence that haven't been fully developed simply provide a cold case detective with a strong direction for the new investigation, and sometimes leads not followed can be beneficial. When Detective Troy Armstrong discovered an unprocessed rape kit among the evidence in a 1987 case, he considered it a bonus.

"In 1987, processing a rape kit only provided a possible suspect's blood type," Armstrong explains. "If the kit had been processed, we could have lost the DNA that we eventually used to convict the rapist."

If a case went cold because leads weren't followed, a present-day detective's best strategy is to say, "That's just one more strong lead I have now."

CASES GO COLD BECAUSE WITNESSES PROTECT THE GUILTY PARTIES.

…When preschool teacher Julie Love was abducted from the dark Atlanta street where her red Mustang convertible had run out of gas, the two men did not take her immediately to a deserted woods and kill her.

The abductors, Emmanuel Hammond and his cousin Maurice Porter, transported Julie around in their car for more than four hours. Hammond's girlfriend, Janice Weldon, was with the men when they abducted Julie. The three were driving around on the evening of July 11, 1988, in Hammond's maroon Oldsmobile Cutlass sedan. They spotted Julie walking by the side of Howell Mill Road. Hammond told Porter to stop the car. He called to Julie and offered her a ride.

Julie declined and pointed to a nearby house, assuring Hammond that she lived there. She walked up the driveway. As they drove away, Hammond saw Julie turn around and walk again toward the street. Hammond told Porter to turn around and drive by in the opposite direction with his bright lights on.

As they drove past Julie, the bright lights made it impossible for her to recognize the Cutlass and she had no idea she was being stalked. Hammond, Porter, and Weldon drove a little farther and saw Julie's abandoned car. Hammond assumed Julie either had car trouble or had run out of gas, so he told Porter to drive back to the area where they'd seen her. When they reached Julie, Hammond jumped from the car, pointed a sawed-off shotgun at her, and forced her into the backseat of the car.

They drove to Grove Park Elementary School, which Hammond had attended, and searched Julie's purse. They forced her to provide the PIN for her bank card, and Weldon and Porter drove to a local bank and attempted to withdraw cash. When the access code didn't work and the machine kept the card, they returned to the elementary school. An angry Hammond struck Julie repeatedly with the barrel of the shotgun, and Porter raped her.

Julie begged them not to hurt her and said she had more cards at home. They drove to her apartment complex, but when they saw a security guard at the entrance of the complex, they turned around. At this point, Weldon told the men to drop her off at her apartment. Instead, Hammond and Porter stopped by to see Hammond's mother in Cobb County, and they took Julie inside her house. Hammond's mother was standing in the kitchen, reading a newspaper, and she said nothing about the terrified young woman. Hammond led Porter and Julie back to his bedroom and went to the kitchen, where he talked to his mother for about five minutes.

Hammond and Porter then drove Julie back to the school and attempted to strangle her with a wire coat hanger. The petite woman fought hard and eventually struggled free. Hammond told Porter to drive to Grove Park and stop by the side of the road. He dragged Julie into the woods and shot her, later telling Weldon that Julie put her hands in front of her face and he "blew the side of her face off."

Even with this knowledge, Weldon remained silent for thirteen months, even pawning Julie's earrings for $140....

CASES GO COLD WHEN THE HEART OF THE INVESTIGATION IS GONE.

When a dedicated family member dies or a relentless detective retires or is transferred, the temperature drops quickly on the case they'd been keeping warm.

...In 1991, Kentucky State trooper Stan Jones was called to the

Manitou, Kentucky, home of thirty-year-old Sheila Jo Hargrove. Family had reported her missing, and when Jones saw the trail of blood from Sheila's front porch to her driveway, he wasn't surprised later that day when a local fisherman discovered her body floating in nearby Horseshoe Lake. She had been stabbed multiple times in the chest, back, and head.

The prime suspect was Sheila's married boyfriend, Bradley Dale Day, but Day's wife provided an alibi.

Investigators were able to lift several palm prints from the door through which the body had been dragged. None were clear enough for a match, with the methods and resources available at that time. But Jones carefully stored the evidence. For the next eight years, he followed every lead, re-interviewed witnesses, and otherwise kept the case alive.

When Jones retired in 1999, the bloodhound was pulled from the trail, and the case's temperature dropped for nearly a decade. But the evidence remained, meticulously catalogued and stored, waiting for the technology that would allow it to speak for the victim....

CASES GO COLD WHEN INVESTIGATORS RUN OUT OF LOGICAL LEADS.

In 1975, Sam Guy was a high-spirited Atlanta police detective moon-lighting as a security guard at the Howard Johnson motel near the Atlanta-Fulton County Stadium. On January 7, two men entered the motel lobby and demanded cash. Gunfire erupted, and when the thieves rushed out with $275, Sam Guy lay dying on the lobby floor, shot once in the shoulder and once in the leg. The bullet that entered his leg severed his femoral artery.

Guy's son, David, was also an Atlanta police officer. When he heard the dispatcher say that an officer had been shot at the Howard Johnson motel, he knew the victim was his father. By the time he picked up his mother and rushed to the hospital, his father was dead.

Investigating the death of their fellow officer became a priority for the department. Using the resources available at the time, investigators meticulously combed the crime scene, sending any possible evidence to the lab. They painstakingly compared fingerprints to known criminals'. They interviewed and re-interviewed. They cooperated with media in keeping the story alive. One by one, suspects were eliminated, and they were left with no evidence to bring before a grand jury.

One woman knew the truth about Sam Guy's murder, but she kept her secret for seven years. And without solid leads, Atlanta police could not find the men who killed one of their best-loved officers....

CASES GO COLD BECAUSE CURRENT TECHNOLOGY CAN'T TELL THE WHOLE STORY.

In 1986, an attractive newlywed, Sherri Rae Rasmussen, was found bitten, beaten, and shot to death in her condominium in the Los Angeles suburb of Van Nuys. At the time, the blood and saliva at the crime scene held little meaning to investigators, but they carefully collected it anyway.

Days after Sherri's murder, two men robbed another woman in the area at gunpoint, and police assumed that Sherri had surprised these same two men as they burglarized her home. Crime was at an all-time high in LA, and police had inadequate time to search for the killer. They accepted the theory that the two cases were linked. The robbers were never found, and both cases were filed away.

After twenty-three years, when LA's crime rate had dropped dramatically and investigators had a little more time, they took a fresh look at some cold cases, including Sherri's. They now had the capability and the time to test saliva and blood found at the crime scene and suspected to have belonged to the killer. Blood tests showed that the killer was a woman, something police had not considered when they focused on the two armed robbers.

The officers reread police reports, looking for women associated with the victim. When they found a mention of Stephanie Lazarus, they froze. Twenty-five years ago, Stephanie had been a young LAPD cop. Now she was a forty-nine-year-old detective who worked high-profile cases and had earned public commendations. She was married to another LAPD detective, and they had a young daughter.

The investigators realized that keeping the case quiet was crucial since Lazarus and her husband were privy to information passed through the department. They trailed their fellow cop until she discarded a plastic fork at a fast-food restaurant. They grabbed the fork and tested the DNA, comparing it with the blood and saliva found at the cold case crime scene.

When the DNA samples matched, the officers told Detective Lazarus that there was a break in an old case and she was needed in the interrogation room. Following standard procedure, Lazarus removed her weapon as she entered the room, expecting to interrogate a suspect. Instead, she faced her peers for the crime she had committed twenty-five years earlier.

Lazarus was arrested the same day, June 5, 2009, for what police now call a crime of passion instead of a burglary. Sherri's husband was Lazarus's former boyfriend. Soon after breaking up with Lazarus, he married Sherri. And soon after the wedding, Lazarus released her rage.

CASES GO COLD BECAUSE INVESTIGATORS HAVE TO MOVE ON TO OTHER PRESSING CASES.

In 1986, when Sherri Rae Rasmussen was killed, LAPD officers were overworked, and they had little time to follow leads. Today, LA's crime rate is at a historic low. In addition to making LA safer for its residents, the new low crime rate allows officers time to reinvestigate cold cases.

Sherri's murder had not gone unsolved because officers lacked concern. As soon as they were able, they pulled the files for her case....

* * *

It's not unusual for departments to go into minor or major case overload. An extreme surge in crime was the impetus for the first official cold case squad in the United States.

In the 1960s, the Miami Metro-Dade County, Florida, area was relatively quiet. A local homicide made the front page of the *Miami Herald*. By the 1980s, the number of murders was so large that the paper simply published a daily total of homicides. By 1984, Miami Metro-Dade County had a backlog of sixteen hundred unsolved cases, not counting the enormous increase in cases that were successfully prosecuted as the department worked at full speed.

"When cocaine hit the country, crime increased nationwide," observes Miami Metro-Dade County Police Department Sergeant David Rivers (now retired). "Our worst year in Dade County was 1981. We had more than six hundred murders, and a larger percentage of crimes were committed against unknowns. That makes tracing suspects harder, and cases go cold faster. In the 1970s, we had a closure rate of ninety percent. Now, the closure rate is a little more than sixty percent."

During this time of extreme case overload, Rivers says that, at best, investigators had two or three days to work a case before another case took priority, causing what the department labeled the "back-burner effect." Even viable cases with strong leads had to be placed on the back burner. All detectives could do was write a case summary and attach it to the front of the report. Then they reluctantly filed away the case. Soon so many cases were on the back burner that the outlook for solving them with the existing staff and resources became dismal.

Any sudden increase in crime can cause a back-burner effect, regardless of the size of the department. If ten detectives can't handle a surge from ten to a hundred cases, two detectives will struggle when their caseload increases from one to ten.

In most departments, cases must be prioritized. A high-priority case can move an existing case farther down in the pile. Joe Kennedy, the first leader of the Naval Criminal Investigative Service Cold Case Squad, divides cases into three categories: freezer, icebox, and microwave. Those that can be solved quickly—microwaved—are addressed first, but all cases are considered.

CASES GO COLD WHEN AN INNOCENT PERSON CONFESSES.

When someone confesses, for all legal purposes, the case is solved. Investigators have no reason to look further into the crime unless new evidence surfaces or the crime repeats itself.

On January 14, 1984, Carolyn Hamm, thirty-two, a white Arlington, Virginia, woman who worked for a Washington, DC, law firm, was raped and murdered in the apartment where she lived alone. Detective Joe Horgas of the Arlington Police Department assisted in the investigation, and the crime scene was etched in his memory for years.

The assailant had entered Carolyn's residence through a back window. He'd moved through the house, opening drawers and scattering the contents of Carolyn's purse, apparently looking for valuables. But in spite of the disarray of the house, investigators saw no signs of a struggle.

Carolyn's nude body was found facedown in her basement. Her wrists had been tied behind her back, using venetian-blind cords and a rope. Another rope had been fashioned into a noose and was tied round her neck. The long end of the rope was draped over a ceiling pipe and

Scene of Carolyn Hamm murder. *Courtesy of Steve Mardigian.*

then tied to the bumper of her car. She had died of ligature strangulation. She had no bruising or trauma to her body, but medical examiners determined that she had been raped.

David Vasquez was questioned about Carolyn Hamm's murder. Detectives confronted him with evidence that, though circumstantial, pointed to him as a likely suspect: he lived in the area, and witnesses had seen him near the crime scene. With the limited technology of the time, experts could only show that hairs found on Carolyn's body were "similar" to those of Vasquez, but those findings included him in the list of possible suspects.

Vasquez maintained his innocence, but his attorney persuaded the mentally challenged man to avoid the death penalty by taking an Alford Plea: He asserted his innocence but acknowledged that the prosecution had sufficient evidence to convince a jury of guilt beyond a reasonable doubt. Vasquez was imprisoned, and the case was officially closed.

CASES GO COLD WHEN DETECTIVES DON'T CONNECT THE DOTS.

But on December 1, 1987, Susan Tucker, another young white Arlington woman, was raped and murdered in a similar manner. Like Carolyn Hamm, Susan was also in her thirties. She was married, but her husband was out of the country at the time of the murder. They lived just four blocks from where Carolyn had been murdered four years earlier. Again, the assailant had entered the victim's house through a back window. Susan's belongings had been searched and the contents of her purse scattered. A collection of commemorative coins was strewn across the room, but no coins were missing. And again, there was no sign of a struggle.

Susan's nude body was lying facedown on her bed. Unlike Carolyn, Susan had been savagely beaten. Her face was completely blackened, and her eyes were swollen shut.

But like Carolyn, she had been raped and strangled, and the elaborately staged murder scene was eerily similar to Carolyn's. Susan's hands were tied behind her back. A nylon rope was tied tight around her neck.

Detective Horgas was assigned to lead the investigation, and as he examined the crime scene, he remembered Carolyn's murder and sensed he was dealing with a serial rapist and murderer. And Vasquez was already in prison. He could not have committed the second murder.

The week after Susan's murder, Horgas received a copy of a memorandum sent from the Richmond Police Department to regional law enforcement agencies. The memo had been sent two months earlier, but it had just reached Horgas's desk. Richmond police were investigating two homicides: On September 18, 1987, a thirty-five-year-old white Richmond woman was found raped and murdered in her apartment. Her hands had been bound behind her back. The assailant had entered the apartment through a rear window. There were no signs of a struggle. Then, on October 3, 1987, a thirty-two-year-old white Richmond woman was found raped and strangled in her bedroom. The assailant had entered the house from a second-story rear window. There were no signs of a struggle. The Richmond police asked regional law enforcement officers to contact them if they'd had similar cases.

In mid-December, Horgas contacted the Richmond police. He told them about the two Arlington murders, and though the detective he talked to didn't see a strong connection, he invited Horgas to join the next meeting of the task force Richmond had organized to find their killer.

During his initial phone call with Richmond police, Horgas asked the other detective whether they'd had any other unusual cases lately. The detective said a black man had broken into the residence of a thirty-two-year-old single white woman about 3:00 a.m. on November 1. The woman's first-floor apartment was only a couple of miles from the scene of one of the homicides. The woman woke up to find the man on top of her. He was in his late twenties, approximately six feet tall. He was wearing a ski mask, brown cotton work gloves, and dark pants. He wielded a carving knife with an eight-inch blade, and he threatened to kill her if she resisted. He carried a knapsack that contained a bottle of whiskey and some rope. He bound the victim with the rope, then spent three hours raping her and forcing her to perform oral sex. He spent a lot of time at her residence and eventually forced her to shower. Then he forced her to drink half the bottle of whiskey. The assailant remained silent throughout the assault.

About 6:00 a.m., the rapist took more rope from his knapsack and tied the victim's ankles. She sobbed throughout the attack, but it wasn't until her upstairs neighbors arrived home that anyone heard her. As the rapist bound her ankles, her neighbors heard her sobs and came downstairs to check on her. When the rapist heard the neighbors at the door, he escaped through his point of entry—a kitchen window.

Horgas asked whether the rape could be connected with the Richmond homicides, and the detective said no. The Richmond detective pointed out that the rapist hadn't killed his victim. He was a black man, and the FBI had already told the Richmond police that their suspect was a white man. The victim was petite and weighed less than a hundred pounds—much smaller than the murder victims. The rape had occurred on a Sunday morning, and the murders had occurred on Friday and Saturday nights. And the rapist had not put a noose around the woman's neck.

Horgas traveled the one hundred miles to Richmond to attend a murder task force meeting. The task force said they were dealing with two murders in Richmond, as well as a murder in nearby Chesterfield, which they did not believe was related. Horgas shared the details of Carolyn's and Susan's murders, including crime-scene photos, then listened as the Richmond detectives discussed their cases:

On September 18, 1987, Debbie Davis, thirty-five, was found lying facedown on her bed in her home. She'd been raped and murdered. The attacker had entered Debbie's residence through a window above the kitchen sink. The house, as well as Debbie's purse, had been searched, but there was no indication that the victim had struggled with her attacker. Debbie was nude except for a pair of blue jean cutoffs.

Debbie had died of ligature strangulation. A blue wool knee sock was wrapped around her neck and knotted in the back. A vacuum cleaner extension tube had been stuck under the sock and twisted like a tourniquet. It was so tight that investigators couldn't remove it manually. Her right wrist was tied with a black shoestring, and the other end of the shoestring was wrapped around her left wrist.

Then, on October 3, 1987, Susan Hellams, a thirty-two-year-old

Scene of Debbie Davis murder.
Courtesy of Steve Mardigian.

neurosurgery resident, was found raped and murdered in her bedroom. She lived just half a mile from Debbie. The assailant had entered the residence from a second-story window.

Susan's body was found lying on its side, on the floor of a closet. Her hands were bound with an extension cord. A red leather belt was tied and knotted around her neck. A second belt was knotted around her left ankle and then looped around her right ankle. The killer had held her down with his foot while he strangled her. Susan's right calf was smudged with a black footprint.

A third murder, which the Richmond police assumed was unrelated, involved Diane Cho, a fifteen-year-old high school freshman who lived with her Korean-American family in Chesterfield, just over the county line. Diane's parents and twelve-year-old brother were home when she was murdered, but they had heard nothing. They lived in a three-bedroom first-floor apartment. The last sounds they heard coming from their daughter's room were the sounds of a typewriter as she finished a term paper about 11:30 p.m. on November 22, 1987. Diane's parents woke the next morning at 6:00 a.m. Their daughter's room was quiet, so they didn't wake her, assuming she'd stayed up late the night before working on her term paper. The couple owned a small grocery, and they slipped quietly out of the house to go to work. At noon, they called their home, and Diane's brother answered. He said his sister was still sleeping. He said he didn't want to wake her because she would get mad at him. Diane's parents returned home around 3:00 p.m. By now concerned about their daughter, they opened her bedroom door. Diane was under a blanket, nude. A white rope was knotted into a noose around her neck, and her wrists had been tied with a darker rope. Her mouth was sealed with duct tape. An infinity mark—a horizontal figure eight—was painted on her thigh with nail polish.

Semen samples indicated that the two murders in Richmond had been committed by the same man, so Richmond police realized they were dealing with a serial killer. They had already contacted the FBI Behavioral Analysis Unit (BAU). Though the BAU stresses that profiling is an investigative tool and certainly not an exact science, they offered a profile for the Richmond killer: a white male in his thirties who lived in the Richmond area. Richmond police accepted the profile as a paradigm that they seemed unwilling to adjust as new evidence surfaced.

The Richmond police mentioned in their task force meeting that, right before the two rapes and murders, a black man in his twenties had raped several women in the area, using a similar method to that of the killer. But the detectives asserted that the crimes were unrelated because the FBI profile had said the killer was a white man in his thirties. They said they also doubted that Diane's murder was related because the killer would have had to change his victim preference and rape and murder a much younger girl of a different race.

Horgas asked about a link with his cases. At the time, he had no semen analysis to offer, but the Richmond detectives said they didn't believe the murders were connected anyway. They asked why a rapist would travel a hundred miles to commit a rape. They said they were convinced their rapist/killer was from the Richmond area.

Horgas told the detectives that they had had a series of rapes in Arlington just before Carolyn was killed in January 1984. The rapes occurred during the summer of 1983 and early winter 1984. Then, around the time of Carolyn's murder, a woman in her thirties was raped and cut viciously with a knife just a few blocks from Carolyn's home. The rapist in all the cases was a masked black man. The Richmond police said the rapes were just a coincidence. They reiterated that they were looking for a white man.

But the Richmond police knew about a new technology that Horgas had not heard of. A lab in New York could get more information from blood and semen samples than just blood type. Richmond police had already sent the semen samples from their two murders to the lab to test for DNA. The Richmond lab could tell only that the killer in both cases had the same blood type. The New York lab might be able to connect the samples as accurately as it would connect two fingerprints. Horgas knew he had to find out more about DNA.

Horgas left the meeting convinced that the Richmond and Arlington murders were connected. The Richmond detectives left with the opposite opinion.

Horgas checked further into the Arlington rapes. Within six months, nine Arlington women and one woman in nearby Alexandria had reported being raped and sodomized by a young masked black man wielding a knife. He stole only cash from their purses. Horgas hoped the hair and semen samples in the rape kits could be tested to prove a connection among all the crimes. Only three of the nine rape kits could be located. Other critical evidence, such as the victim's clothing, had also been destroyed or misplaced. Because space was limited, the department's policy was to discard evidence in cases that showed little hope of being solved. One rape kit had sat on a shelf in the evidence room for four years and had not been processed. Though the situation was frustrating, the samples were still available for later DNA processing.

In Susan Tucker's murder, hairs found on her body were identified as belonging to an African American. Semen reports showed the blood characteristics in the Arlington murders and the Richmond murders were the same. The simpler blood analyses narrowed the suspects to 13 percent of the population. If race were taken into account, the percentage dropped even lower.

Horgas interviewed one of the surviving Arlington rape victims. She told him that, as she approached her car in the parking lot of a supermarket around 1:00 a.m. in June 1983, a thin black man in his twenties grabbed her and held a knife to her face. He had a white T-shirt pulled over his head, with eye holes cut out. His hands were covered.

He told her to drive to a wooded area, where he forced her to perform oral sex before he raped her. He forced her to lie on the ground, naked. He said he was going to the car but that he'd be back. He did not return, and eventually the woman got up, dressed, and drove for help.

Everything seemed to point to a black rapist whose crimes eventually had escalated to murder. The links were strong, but not strong enough. Horgas contacted the New York DNA lab and asked for their help on the Arlington cases. He flew to New York right after Christmas to meet with the lab, Lifecodes. Lifecodes had been in business for five years, doing pioneer work in cancer, paternity, and prenatal testing. The technicians had recently added forensic DNA testing to the services they offered. Lifecodes analyzed the DNA samples and found that all the Arlington rapes and murders had been committed by the same man.

Armed with strong evidence that he was dealing with a serial rapist and murderer, Horgas contacted the FBI himself. He talked with Supervisory Special Agent Steve Mardigian of the BAU, and according to Mardigian, Horgas was organized and prepared. "He showed us facts about the Northern Virginia series of rape cases," remembers Mardigian. "He presented his evidence, and we saw the connection."

Mardigian and his team agreed to help. Others from the BAU had worked previously with the Richmond police. This time, Mardigian worked with the Arlington Police Department.

Horgas shared facts about the serial rape cases that occurred in the Arlington, Virginia, area just prior to Carolyn Hamm's murder, and he provided Mardigian with specific details surrounding the murder investigation of Carolyn Hamm. Mardigian began piecing together a possible scenario. The Northern Virginia serial rapist showed proficiency as a burglar. FBI rape studies showed that serial rapists do not normally stop committing rapes. Since Horgas said there had been no similar rapes and murders reported in the Arlington area after Carolyn Hamm's death in 1984 or in Richmond before Deborah Davis's murder in 1987, Mardigian speculated that during this period the rapist/murderer may have been arrested and served time for charges stemming from his other profession: burglary. In Virginia, a burglar might serve three or four years before being released, and parolees could be released anywhere in the state.

FBI profiler Steve Mardigian at time of investigation. *Courtesy of Steve Mardigian.*

Mardigian knew that sex offenders often begin their assaults near where they live or work. This comfort zone may later be expanded to larger areas as a perpetrator becomes more successful in his criminal activities. Mardigian recommended that Horgas look for suspects who had lived or worked in the area where the first rape occurred and who had been convicted, possibly for burglary, and then released in the Richmond area in 1987.

DNA evidence was still new in the late 1980s. CODIS wasn't established until 1994, and it wasn't until 1998 that all fifty states had passed laws requiring local police departments to collect DNA samples. Horgas needed a suspect before he could match DNA. And he needed the suspect's DNA.

One day, while checking the criminal history of a parolee on his computer, Horgas remembered a burglary investigation he'd participated in ten years earlier. A woman reported that a teenage boy had broken into her house. No arrest was made, but Horgas remembered that the suspect had been accused of causing other problems, including setting a fire. One of the Arlington rape victims had been shoved into the trunk of her car and her assailant had set fire to the backseat of the car. It was a long shot, but Horgas decided it was worth checking.

Eventually, Horgas traced down the suspect from ten years ago: Timothy Spencer. He traced Spencer's current location: Richmond. And as he checked Spencer's criminal history, the Arlington-Richmond connection fell into place. Spencer had a long criminal history as a burglar. The first burglary had occurred in Fairfax County near Arlington. He was arrested five years later for another burglary and served two years in prison. After he was released, he was arrested three more times. Spencer had been arrested in December 1982 for burglary and sent to prison. He was released in May 1983, a month before the first rape. As Horgas checked the rest of Spencer's criminal history, he realized that when Spencer was in prison, the rapes stopped. When he was released, they started again. And when the rapes occurred in Richmond, Spencer was living in a halfway house as part of his reintegration into the community. Horgas checked the records at the halfway house. Spencer had been signed out on the dates of the murders.

When Horgas, working with the FBI, had enough evidence to arrest Spencer, he did so as Spencer returned to the halfway house after work. Before Spencer was taken to jail, Horgas asked him if he would submit a blood sample. Knowing he'd left no blood at the crime scenes and unfamiliar with DNA evidence, Spencer willingly submitted his blood. It matched the DNA taken from the semen samples in the rape kits.

Eventually, through the careful and cooperative work of the FBI, the Arlington Police Department, and the Richmond Police Department, Spencer was convicted—through DNA evidence—of eleven rapes, thirty burglaries, and five homicides. He was the first person to receive the death penalty based on DNA evidence and one of the last to face the electric chair in Virginia.

Law enforcement found satisfaction in stopping a vicious killer, but they received equal satisfaction when they were able to free an innocent man. Mardigian and his team did a comprehensive analysis of the Carolyn Hamm murder case and submitted a report through the Commonwealth Attorney's Office to Virginia's governor. David Vasquez received a pardon.

"A cold case detective can have a win-win-win situation," observes Jessica, a rape victim. "Cold case detectives can help victims and families have closure. They can prevent new crimes that would be committed by these same perpetrators. And they can get innocent people out of prison by finding the truth."

CASES GO COLD WHEN INVESTIGATORS
ARE TOO CLOSE TO IDENTIFY VIABLE SUSPECTS.

In small towns where everyone knows his neighbor, it's sometimes difficult to see a friend as a suspect. When easygoing, affable Russell Winstead began surfacing as a murder suspect, the Madisonville (Kentucky) Police Department had trouble imagining him as a cold-blooded killer. Winstead and his kids had ridden four-wheelers with the police captain and his family. He was part of the K-9 officer's wedding party. But as evidence mounted, these officers realized that their stable, respectable mining-engineer friend had attended church one cold January night in 2003, dropped his children off at their mother's house, and driven to his wealthy aunt's house. There he bludgeoned his aunt and stabbed her ninety-seven times, showered a few feet from the body, and went home to his wife and children.

* * *

Murderer Russell Winstead hears jury's verdict.
Courtesy of the Madisonville Messenger,
Lowell Mendyk *photographer.*

…Even investigators in large cities can have difficulty viewing someone they know as a suspect, especially if that person is one of their own. At the time of Sherri Rasmussen's murder, her parents told the original investigators that LAPD cop Stephanie Lazarus had come to their daughter's condo in uniform and threatened her. The investigators had the lead, but without the undeniable DNA evidence, they apparently could not see their fellow officer as a suspect.

CASES GO COLD WHEN INVESTIGATORS LACK RESOURCES.

… The earliest Atlanta child-murder cases went cold quickly because city investigators lacked the personnel to do extensive interviews, the time and training to write thorough reports, and skill in collecting and maintaining evidence. The cases were revived when the FBI became involved because they brought with them these valuable resources.

Though the FBI had no jurisdiction in local murder cases, Atlanta and the nation wanted all possible resources directed at stopping the killings. So more than a year after the first murder, on November 6, 1980, the FBI opened ATKID (ATlanta KIDnappings), Major Case 30, with Atlanta's Special Agent in Charge John Glover heading the FBI's portion of the investigation. The Bureau's only official link to the murders was the possibility that one or more of the still-missing children were being held in violation of the Federal Kidnapping Law, so the FBI entered the investigation on that premise.

The FBI supplied what the city of Atlanta could not: virtually unlimited manpower, experience in writing thorough reports, and top-notch investigative training. And whatever the local field office lacked was immediately supplied by a support network that included a direct line to the White House.

A group of Atlanta field agents was assigned to the case, and their sole responsibility was to investigate the murders. But even though they could work full time on the case, they soon found that they needed additional help. As the number of missing and murdered children increased, Glover submitted requests for more cars, more investigators, and more money. The FBI complied. Additional agents were TDY'd (brought in on temporary duty) from other field offices. Money was transferred. No reasonable request for resources was denied.

Like the Atlanta Police Department, the FBI Atlanta Field Office was made up of relatively new investigators. Many were first-office agents.

But unlike the APD, these rookie agents did not work alone. They were supported by the most bountiful investigative resources of the nation. They called on Quantico's BAU, and its profilers flew to Atlanta. When they wanted information about race-related crimes, child murders, or serial killings, they simply sent a memo to headquarters.

As they reinvestigated the early murders, they created a strong paper trail. Special Agent Jim Procopio managed the administrative side of ATKID, including hundreds of pages of memorandums and 302s (FBI investigative reports). These detailed reports provided quick access to what had been done and why, allowing new agents and those on temporary assignments to jump onto the investigative train that would run at top speed for the next several months. And eventually those mounds of written reports would make it possible for prosecutors to convict the killer.

The case went cold because investigators lacked resources. It heated up when resources were added to the investigation.

As a cold case investigator reexamines a case, it's easy to think, "Why wasn't this lead followed?" or "How could anyone have missed such obvious evidence?" Cases go cold for a lot of legitimate reasons that have nothing to do with an inept investigation, and an investigator can waste significant time and energy analyzing what went wrong and placing blame. It's better to place the emphasis on solving the case instead of unconsciously investigating the original investigator.

You can spend your time obsessing about what should have been done and why it wasn't, or you can pursue the case. A good investigator makes the productive choice.

"Get over the why-didn't-they-do-this syndrome," says David Rivers. "The fact is, they didn't. You have to pick up the good stuff and forget what wasn't done or what was done poorly. Learn to live with it."

Chapter 3

Turning Up the Heat

SOMETIMES YOU FIND A NEEDLE IN A HAYSTACK AND YOU FIND THE
EVIDENCE THAT SETS THE HAYSTACK ON FIRE.
—Cold case detective Clay Bryant

"The resurrection of cold cases is just as diverse as the people who committed the crimes and as varied as the victims," observes Clay Bryant. "Just about anything can generate interest in an old case, but interest has to be there. More and more often, a cold case is solved when the state compares DNA with CODIS, through standard practice. But for all other cases, there has to be interest in the case itself. A family member, police officer, somebody has to care about the specific case. They have to be concerned about why the case hasn't moved and what will move it forward. It takes legwork.

"And after the legwork comes science and technology. Advances like mitochondrial DNA can seal a verdict because sometimes the major part of the defense trial will be 'you have the wrong guy.'"

Many law enforcement agencies have formed cold case units, and the news media report widely on their success. Television programs and movies have created a strong interest in cold cases, but they often make solving cold cases appear easy. In reality, few easy investigations reach the desk of a cold case detective. If they had been easy, someone would already have solved them. But renewed interest in a case, for whatever reason, is an opportunity to satisfy justice.

Formal cold case squads are relatively new. According to NCIS Special Agent Joe Kennedy, cold cases began being actively investigated after World War II, with an astounding 90 percent success rate. By the 1960s, the success rate had taken a sharp decline, most likely because America's society became more mobile and tracing suspects became more complicated.

The term "cold case" started to surface in the 1970s at the Los Angeles County Sheriff's Department and the Atlanta Police Department. By the 1980s, a few cold case squads had been formed. Kennedy credits the Miami Metro-Dade County Police Department and the North Carolina State Bureau of Investigation as two of the first. By the 1990s, cold case units were popping up across the United States and in many other countries. The news media caught on, and television programs began portraying real and fictional cold case stories. By the turn of the millennium, state and federal agencies were actively resourcing cold case squads, and the phenomenon of the 1970s and 1980s became standard fare for law enforcement of all levels and for the military.

When a cold case unit in one area loses funding, another surfaces somewhere else. Cold case investigations have come to be expected. Where once a family who had not received justice lost hope with the passing of time, a similar family today would expect the case to be passed on to a cold case investigator or cold case squad. With cold case investigators, there is always hope.

And it's good that cold case units have sprung up because it's easier and easier for a case to go cold. In addition to society's ever-increasing mobility, Kennedy offers other insights into why cases are more likely to go cold today than they were a generation or two ago:

- More crimes are now committed randomly by strangers, making identifying the perpetrator more difficult.
- Our country has experienced an overall increase in its murder rate, causing more cold cases by sheer volume, as well as making

it difficult for law enforcement officers to spend ample time on a case before moving to the next one. The increased rate of violent crime creates what retired cold case detective David Rivers calls the back-burner effect—moving cases to the "back burner," where they're still warm but probably not anyone's focus.

- Gang- and drug-related violence has created a relatively new category of vengeance killings: the drive-by shootings. These acts of violence are less likely to result in DNA evidence, fingerprints, or even eyewitnesses, making it more likely that the cases will go cold.
- Bystanders are now less likely to be Good Samaritans. People no longer want to become involved, and those living in high-crime areas are sometimes too terrified of retaliation to speak up.

Kennedy says that three components are crucial for solving cold cases: time, technology, and tenacity. Often, the new focus is on technology, but even technology is only as good as the tenacious individuals who faithfully take DNA samples and those who patiently enter them into databases. And more often than many people realize, crime scenes produce no usable fingerprints or DNA.

"The general public doesn't understand that a case can be solved without DNA," says former FBI profiler Steve Mardigian. "As technology moves us forward, it can have an adverse effect if the general public assumes that, without direct physical evidence like DNA, a case cannot be proven beyond a reasonable doubt. Most jurors have to be reminded that reasonable doubt is not beyond all possible doubt. Reasonable doubt is simply proof that can satisfy a juror's judgment and conscience that the crime was committed by the person charged. Sometimes that evidence is circumstantial."

The more the public hears of advances such as touch DNA—a method of analyzing skin cells left behind when the assailant simply touches the victim or an object at the crime scene—the more juries will expect, even demand, DNA evidence. This jury expectation, often called the *CSI* effect, may soon make once-strong cases appear weak simply because no DNA or fingerprints are available. The *CSI* effect may harm cold cases more than others, since witnesses and crime scenes may no longer be available.

"When you open a cold case file, you can often figure out whodunit. The problem, just like years ago, is proving it," says New York judge and former detective Dennis Delano. "Juries are reluctant to put people away after so many years without undeniable evidence."

But cold cases have their advantages. "When you're working a new homicide, you're putting the case together as you go along," says Delano. "You don't always know what's going on with other detectives on other shifts. With cold cases, you have the advantage of having the beginning and end, all spread out together. When you have the whole case in front of you, it reads like a novel. A large percentage of time, the perpetrator's name is in the file. Your objective is to find out which name did it."

When you find that name, that lead, that revelation of truth, you have a viable case. But first, a cold case file has to make it to an investigator's desk, and that can happen in countless ways.

CASES ARE REVIVED WHEN COMMUNITIES ARE CONCERNED.

FBI Special Agent (ret) Art Krinsky points to a few of the ways community interest can be revived:

- If a family member takes a re-newed interest, particularly in a close-knit community, interest can escalate quickly.
- Or sometimes a reporter, sifting through archives as part of a different story, reads about a case and can find no article that states that the perpetrator was identified. Concern, mixed with curiosity, creates more digging,

FBI Special Agent Art Krinsky.
Courtesy of Art Krinsky.

and eventually the reporter writes a story about the unsolved crime.

- When a similar crime occurs, even years later, a community may become concerned that the perpetrator is still active. The desire to solve the cold case is driven by a desire for present-day protection.

CASES ARE REVIVED WHEN NATIONAL DATABASES IDENTIFY SERIAL OFFENDERS.

Krinsky points out that databases such as ViCap (the FBI's Violent Criminal Apprehension Program) allow investigators to find similarities in cases that previously seemed unrelated. When investigators faithfully submit data for national databases, they often find that their suspect has committed other crimes over the years, and sometimes they find the suspect already serving time in a prison far from where he or she committed the old crime.

CASES ARE REVIVED BY ROUTINE REVIEWS BY COLD CASE SQUADS.

Some departments use volunteers—often retired law enforcement officers—to periodically screen cold cases. A routine check of an old file may show no viable leads one year. The next year, because of some new technology or a development in a different case, another routine check of the same file may produce a hot case that can be solved quickly.

Funding qualified personnel to screen and prioritize cold cases is difficult for most departments, and some departments have found that skilled volunteers can do just as good a job in the initial screening process as paid investigators. Detective David Phillips credits the Charlotte-Mecklenburg Cold Case Squad's use of carefully selected volunteers as a key to the team's success. "All our volunteers have some connection with law enforcement," says Phillips. "We have retired FBI agents, a retired NYPD captain, a retired police officer, an engineer, and a criminal justice college professor.

Charlotte-Mecklenburg cold case unit.
Courtesy of David Philips.

"We realize that we're dealing with sensitive information, so we screen every team member. We do a background check and drug testing. We determine their motive for wanting to be part of the cold case unit. We strongly prefer that volunteers have prior law enforcement and investigative experience. We require that volunteers receive a recommendation from our command staff and go through an interview process.

"We consider how the potential volunteer would handle confidentiality, if they would work well with the team, whether they could be objective in their evaluations, and whether they could make a time commitment to the team."

Using volunteers to staff a review team has saved Charlotte-Mecklenburg untold hours of paid time. A detective simply reads the final summary and begins the investigation within hours of picking up a case. "Our volunteers use a standard format that's easily read," says Phillips. "Their work frees up the detective to work the actual cases."

CASES ARE REVIVED WHEN FAMILY MEMBERS REFUSE TO GIVE UP.

...While going through another aunt's photo albums after her death, Leslie Ianuzzi learned of her aunt, Gwendolyn Moore, who had been murdered thirty years earlier. After she saw Gwendolyn's photo and asked her mother who the pretty young woman was, the story of Gwendolyn's death haunted her until she contacted the district attorney's office and asked officials to reopen the case....

...Amy Billig's mother kept her daughter's investigation open thirty-one years, until she herself died at the age of eighty.

"The sad reality," observes Dan Tholson, retired from the Natrona County (Wyoming) Sheriff's Department, "is that if the family doesn't keep a case alive, it can die."

Dennis Delano agrees that families sometimes hold the key to reviving a case. "They call the department and get referred to the cold case unit. They may talk about a case that's twenty years old, and they're talking about it like it was yesterday. Knowing that case was on the forefront of their minds all those years is what kept me working on a case," says Delano. "Sometimes I picked up a case just because the family kept calling and calling, keeping the pressure on."

CASES ARE REVIVED WHEN VICTIMS KEEP THE HEAT UP.

In 1987, a woman and her three-year-old daughter left a mall in Charlotte, North Carolina, in the middle of the day. As they reached their car, a man forced them into the car and told the woman to drive. When they reached a secluded area, he sexually assaulted the woman in front of her daughter, repeatedly threatening to kill her and her daughter. In spite of the woman's description of the suspect, the case went cold.

When Charlotte formed a sexual assault cold case unit in 2006, the *Charlotte Observer* ran a story about the new unit. By that time, the 1987 rape victim was living in Florida, but she saw the article online and called Detective Troy Armstrong, asking him to reopen her case.

In his initial conversation with the victim, Armstrong told her he would do what he could, but he advised her not to get her hopes up. The chances were slim that physical evidence remained from the crime.

Armstrong had difficulty finding the actual case file, but when he did, he discovered that there was a rape kit that had never been processed. It was the best scenario. If the kit had been processed in 1987, all they could have gotten was the blood type of the suspect. Now the pristine kit was available for processing with more advanced techniques. Armstrong had the kit processed, and the rapist was identified as an already-registered sex offender. By the time the case went to trial, three of his victims from across the country converged on Charlotte, and the fate of the rapist seemed inevitable. But before the trial ended, the suspect committed suicide. Still, the victim who pressed for the case to be reopened stopped him from harming more women.

CASES ARE REVIVED BY CHANCE.

While recuperating from surgery on his shoulder, Troy Armstrong was put on desk duty and was unable to open any of the twenty-five-plus new sexual assault cases that poured in monthly. A history buff, Armstrong decided to look at the older cases he and the other detectives rarely had time to consider.

He pulled out dusty files from the 1980s and 1990s, reading the narratives on cases that few remembered other than the victims. Most of the investigators who initially worked the cases had been transferred or had retired. As he searched the files, he mentally separated the cases with strong leads or possible DNA. He began seeing patterns and similarities in some of the cases, and he marked them as possible serial rapes. He requested DNA tests from the crime lab.

Armstrong's shoulder healed, and he began working new cases again. But now he had folders from some of the older cases. He had DNA matches and viable leads. And he had a thirst for working cold cases that eventually led to working full time in that arena.

Fred Wilkerson's case was revived when a tree fell on the prosecutor's truck and he took it to a body shop owned by Fred's son.

In Charlotte, a homicide detective named Linda attended a craft class where she became friends with another participant. As the two women discussed occupations, Linda noticed that the other woman became extremely interested when she learned that Linda was a detective. The woman asked for Linda's help. She told Linda that, fifteen years earlier, while she was doing landscape work at her church, a man had dragged her into the woods and beat her, raped her, and left her for dead. The case was never solved, and she asked Linda if she could look at her case.

Linda found the file, which contained evidence that had new meaning in light of today's technology. Within a few days, the evidence was sent to the lab. The nuclear DNA evidence did not have sufficient sample for a full DNA profile. It was, however, sufficient for a Y-STR (Y chromosome-Short Tandem Repeat) database. The Y-STR profile has been used for direct comparison and has excluded two suspects who were developed early in the investigation. The case remains open and is still being actively investigated.

CASES ARE REVIVED WHEN NEW INVESTIGATORS ARE INTRODUCED.

When Troy Armstrong joined the Charlotte, North Carolina, cold case unit in 2006 he received a two-year-old e-mail, forwarded to him by another investigator.

On May 14, 1998, a young college student named Jessica was awakened at about 11:30 p.m. by the sound of someone trying to enter her apartment. Her roommate was out of town, and she was immediately on alert. A man forced his way into the apartment and brutally raped Jessica for several hours before slipping out into the night. Jessica didn't see her rapist's face, and he left no fingerprints. In 1998 that left very little to go on.

It was a time before DNA was standard procedure for criminal cases. A time before CODIS. An era when a case that went cold stood

Detective Troy Armstrong.
Courtesy of Troy Armstrong.

very little chance of revival. After that night, Jessica slept fitfully, looking suspiciously at every stranger, and yearning for justice. Each year, on the anniversary of the rape, she called or e-mailed the police department. Though the original detectives who investigated Jessica's case were no longer with the sexual assault unit, she continued to contact anyone who would listen.

Eventually, one of her e-mails reached Armstrong. At first he was unable to advance the case, but because of Jessica's e-mail, he couldn't forget that the crime had happened. He suspected Jessica's rape was part of a series of college rapes that had occurred at about the same time, and he was eventually able to positively link Jessica's case, through DNA evidence, to a second case involving the 1998 rape of another college student.

The man who raped Jessica was finally apprehended, and she and the other victim were able to testify against him in court. He was found guilty on all charges.

CASES ARE REVIVED WHEN THE RIGHT QUESTIONS ARE ASKED AT THE RIGHT TIME.

...Cold case investigators are sometimes surprised to find eyewitnesses who were not interviewed when the crime occurred, who simply weren't asked the right questions, or who were once unwilling to speak but are now cooperative.

Kentucky Commonwealth's Attorney David Massamore remembers the Sheila Hargrove murder case: "The defendant got his wife to give him an alibi, and no one followed up to verify it. When she was approached years later, at first she stuck to her original story. But during a later interview, when presented with evidence that Day could not have been home at the time she'd originally said, she finally admitted that she'd lied."...

CASES ARE REVIVED WHEN COLD CASE UNITS ARE FORMED.

Sometimes a city council is alarmed by the backlog of cases and reassigns one or more investigators to work full time to reduce the backlog of unsolved cases. Sometimes media shine the spotlight on the high number of cold cases in an area. Sometimes a lone detective notices the stacks of evidence and file drawers of old records and thinks, "These people need justice."

Federal grants are sometimes available to start cold case units. Alert departments and investigators watch for such opportunities, then write grants, make contacts, and do proposals.

However a cold case squad is formed, its members have a full slate of business on their first day in the office. A cold case squad breathes promise into dusty evidence files and brings the hope of closure to families who might have long since given up. While many investigators struggle to balance cold case investigations with a regular workload, the formation of a unit specifically designated to investigate cold crimes is probably the most positive step that can be taken toward solving unsolved crimes.

CASES ARE REVIVED BY POSITIVE PUBLICITY ON OTHER CASES.

It's what retired cold case investigator Greg Smith calls being a victim of your own success.

"When we solve a case, it generates publicity, and publicity generates phone calls," says Smith. When victims' families read about a successful cold case investigation, they feel encouraged, possibly for the first time in decades. If a detective or cold case squad can solve someone else's case, maybe they can solve theirs. Soon detectives are flooded with more requests. So many requests can be overwhelming, but they remind investigators of how many people are carrying the daily burden of unsolved violent crimes.

CASES ARE REVIVED BY A CLOSER LOOK AT VICTIMOLOGY.

Today's investigators often focus more intensely than their predecessors on victimology. Sometimes collecting information about the victim—victimology—is necessary before identifying suspects, and a thorough study of the victim—friends, work habits, degree of risk in the normal daily schedule—can be time-consuming. But the victim's story is a vital puzzle piece, and it's worth waiting for. For instance, if a murdered suburban housewife was moonlighting as an exotic dancer, that information may not be available immediately, but discovering it points investigators to an entirely new group of potential suspects. If a victim routinely stopped for coffee each morning at 6:00 and arrived at work by 7:00, and one morning he stopped for coffee but failed to show up for work, you can pinpoint his time of disappearance with a fair degree of accuracy.

. . . In recent years, investigators have focused as much on the victim as the perpetrator, and many times understanding the victim will lead to the killer. Such was the case when the Kentucky State Police reopened the Sheila Hargrove murder investigation. A combination of improved fingerprint analysis techniques and victimology eventually brought the case to a successful conclusion.

When David Massamore came into his position as Kentucky Commonwealth's Attorney in 1994, Hopkins County had six hundred open cases. One of those cases was labeled "Sheila Hargrove." Though her name began as a file designation, Sheila soon became real to Massamore. The crime was too brutal and too senseless to dismiss, and the case became personal. In September 2005, the Kentucky State Police became interested in the case as well.

Though both the Kentucky State Police and Massamore wanted to solve Sheila's murder, other cases continued to fill the docket, and much work had to be completed on personal time. That's not unusual. For a dedicated investigator to find time for a case that everyone else has forgotten, often he must carve out time from his off-duty hours.

The more Massamore thought about Sheila's case, the more senseless her murder seemed. In 1991, Sheila was a single mom in her mid-thirties who loved her three small boys and worked hard to support them. She worked at the Shoney's restaurant in Madisonville and had just moved into a small rental home in a nearby rural area. Like many rural homes in Kentucky at that time, Sheila's home had a cistern, so she arranged for city water to be delivered. Sheila spent her days working or enjoying time with her family and friends. It was difficult for Massamore to imagine Sheila doing anything to invoke the degree of rage that was carried out on her body.

As with all inactive Kentucky cases, an investigator was always assigned to Sheila's case, and regular reports were required, even if the report was simply "no new evidence." "In Western Kentucky," explains Massamore, "no case goes into a box and is forgotten."

Massamore was sure the case could be solved if only someone could spend some concentrated time studying reports and piecing together the story of Sheila's final hours.

A Kentucky State Police detective did just that, putting in most of his hours on his own time. He set up an office in his home, spreading out newspaper articles and police reports. After working a full shift with the KSP, he spent time with his family and then retreated to his office where, nearly every night, he tried to piece together the puzzle of Sheila's murder, sometimes working late into the night.

Because of meticulous police work at the time of the murder, investigators had an accurate picture of the crime, and the frame of the puzzle was nearly complete when they reopened the case:

Area businessman Bradley Dale Day delivered water to Sheila. On the morning of June 4, 1991, Day called a friend of Sheila's several times, saying he was having trouble reaching her by phone. Then he called Sheila's mother at about 7:30 a.m., asking if Sheila was with her.

Day called Sheila's mother again a little before 8:00 a.m. He said he was at Sheila's house, that there was a lot of blood, and Sheila wasn't there.

Sheila's mother called the emergency room and asked if anyone had been admitted the night before who had lost a lot of blood. Hospital officials said no, so she knew she had to get to her daughter's house quickly. She rushed the mile and a half to Sheila's house.

When she entered the living room, the most noticeable part of the crime scene was bloody drag marks. They stretched from a pool of dried blood to the front door. Sheila's mother opened the door and saw that the drag marks continued across the porch, down the stairs, and across the lawn. Then they ended abruptly, right at the base of Day's freshly washed truck.

As Sheila's mother reacted to the horror, Day finally called 911.

When the police arrived, they found Day sitting calmly on the front porch. Though Day was married, he described Sheila to police as his girlfriend. He said she was supposed to go with him that morning to haul water.

Sheila's mother told investigators a different story: Sheila had planned to go swimming with a friend that day. Three swimsuits were draped over Sheila's couch, as if she'd been in the process of deciding which one to wear, corroborating the mother's story.

Day told police that when he knocked at Sheila's door that morning, no one answered. He tried the door, but it was locked. He found her car keys and house keys in her car, so he entered the house through the back door. Music was playing on a radio in the kitchen, but Sheila wasn't in the house.

Police checked the doors and found no sign of forced entry. They took photos of the entire house, capturing clues that meant nothing to them at the time but would later fill in the gaps of Sheila's story. They found a couple of partial palm prints on the otherwise clean front door, but in 1991 palm prints were difficult to identify. Police took the prints anyway, and carefully stored them.

While police were outside looking for Sheila, they received a call that a fisherman had found Sheila's body in Horseshoe Lake. She was clothed only in panties, and she had been stabbed fourteen or more times in the chest, back, and face—then dumped in the former coal mine strip pits that were now a lake.

Day told police he was in love with Sheila and planned to marry her. When asked where he was at the time the murder would have occurred, he said he was home with his wife. He'd gotten home at 9:00 p.m., and he and his wife had argued about Sheila. Day said he called Sheila about 11:30 p.m. so she could reassure his wife that their relationship was not serious.

Police made an appointment to talk to Mrs. Day. Her story paralleled Day's, perhaps too perfectly. But with his wife as an alibi and no evidence to tie him to the murder, Day was not questioned further. Though police suspected Day, they shifted their investigation to Sheila's ex-husband.

Sheila's ex-husband sold cocaine, and one night undercover narcotics officers went to the couple's house while Sheila's husband was away. Sheila sold them the drugs, and she was arrested. Sheila pled guilty and received probation. Her ex went to prison. He had been released several months prior to the murder. Though Sheila wanted nothing further to do with him, they remained on good terms and even used the same attorney for the drug charges.

This was the information Massamore found in Sheila's file when he became Commonwealth's Attorney. The detective at the time was Herman Hall. Hall and Massamore looked over the case summaries and studied the physical evidence. They both felt that either Bradley Dale Day or his wife had committed the murder.

Unfortunately, Hall was transferred soon after Massamore arrived. As standard operating procedure, Massamore continued to receive periodic updates about Sheila's case, but it wasn't until the Kentucky State Police assigned an officer to work on the case that Massamore found someone who shared his concern for finding Sheila's killer. Massamore had renewed confidence that Sheila's family would finally have justice.

One of the first things the Kentucky State Police detective did was develop a relationship with Sheila's family. "When you get to know the family," observes Massamore, "you feel like you know the victim, even if that victim is deceased."

But building a relationship with Sheila's family was a little difficult at first. Sheila's mother had lived for fourteen years without justice for her daughter. She was impatient with police efforts. Establishing a relationship took time, but the detective kept coming back.

On a later visit, the detective told Sheila's mother that he promised to do his best to solve Sheila's murder case and that he would try harder than anyone ever had. With so many variables on any case, specifically one that had been cold for more than a decade, that's all an investigator can—or should—promise.

Massamore talked with Sheila's children. He told them that their mother deserved peace and the family deserved peace. "Now," reflects Massamore long after the conviction, "I can go to sleep at night knowing that one family no longer has to wonder."

The investigators read the police reports and pored over crime-scene photos. It was obvious from the massive amount of blood and the blood spatter patterns that the killing had occurred in Sheila's house and the body was dragged outside and driven to the Horseshoe Lake dumping spot.

Many years later, the crime-scene photos told Sheila's story. They showed a wet washcloth on the bathroom floor. Powder-blue shorts, a powder-blue T-shirt, and a pink visor tossed into the laundry basket. Three swimsuits on the couch. Sheila's nightgown and the telephone lying on the floor.

In the kitchen, a photograph frame, with no photo, lay beside Sheila's keys. Her purse lay on the kitchen counter. A nearby ashtray contained a single cigarette butt. It looked as though Sheila had gotten home from work, taken a bath, and opened her house to a visitor. Since there were no signs of forced entry, the investigators believed that Sheila's visitor was someone she knew.

Day was an immediate suspect, and so was his wife. But Massamore used logic to rule out Mrs. Day.

"There was an area in Sheila's kitchen where you could see who was outside," remembers Massamore. "You could see who was knocking at the door. We asked ourselves, 'Would Sheila have opened the door in the middle of the night to her boyfriend's wife—possibly enraged—or to a stranger? It was more likely that she'd opened her door to a friend. Or a boyfriend."

When they felt confident that they understood the crime and the crime scene, they studied the victim. The Kentucky State Police interviewed Sheila's mother. She told them that Sheila was killed on a Monday. The week before her murder, Sheila's ex-husband had picked up the children for summer vacation, and Sheila was alone, something unusual for a mother of three.

That Saturday evening, Sheila's mother stopped by and offered to help her clean the house she'd recently rented. She thought cleaning the house would take Sheila's mind off missing her children. They scrubbed every room, and Sheila's mother said that she remembered cleaning the front storm door, which was half screen and half glass, with Windex. She said that Sheila rarely used the front door. Since palm prints were found on the front door, it was highly probable that they would have been made by someone leaving through the front door the day of Sheila's murder. Chances were good that the palm prints belonged to the killer.

The next evening, Sheila's mother got home from work at 9:30. Sheila drove up at the same time, and they walked into the mother's house together. Sheila was looking for a cool dessert to take the edge off the ninety-degree weather. She told her mother that she'd just talked to her brother David on the phone and asked if he had any ice cream. When she learned that David had none, she said she was going to drive to a nearby store to pick some up. David suggested that Sheila go to their mother's house instead. He said their mother had fresh strawberries and would make Sheila some strawberry shortcake. Her mother prepared the strawberry shortcake and she recalled that Sheila had seemed distracted and a little irritable as she ate her dessert.

The Kentucky State Police detective remembered that the well-known forensic scientist Dr. Henry Lee had solved a case by digestion rate. He checked the autopsy report. Sheila's stomach had contained undigested strawberries. He tracked down Henry Lee and asked his advice. Lee said that strawberries digest in one-and-a-half to two hours. After that time, they can't be identified visually. Sheila called her brother at about 9:00. She ate strawberries at her mother's house at 9:30 and her mother was confident that her daughter left her house around 10:00, wearing a powder-blue T-shirt, powder-blue shorts, and a pink visor.

Massamore built a timeline of Sheila's activities and narrowed the time of the murder, based on what he knew about the victim's final hours.

Since Sheila's family said she always used the kitchen door instead of the front door, the investigators surmised that Sheila had entered the house through the kitchen door around 10:15 p.m., most likely bolting the door at that time of night. She put out her cigarette, removed her sweat-drenched clothing, and washed her face. Then she heard a knock at the door. She looked out and saw someone she trusted enough to welcome inside.

Massamore tried to understand how Sheila reasoned that night, and what she did. He asked for input from women in his office.

- What's a single female coming home alone going to do?
- Would she leave the doors open?
- Would she open the door in the middle of the night to her possibly irate boyfriend's wife or to a stranger?
- What would she do if she came out of the bedroom to find an unwanted intruder? What is the likelihood she would have screamed loud enough for neighbors to hear?

The KSP canvassed the neighborhood, asking neighbors if they'd seen or heard anything. Those who had lived in the area at the time of the murder still remembered that Sunday night in 1991. Normally, those memories would have been wiped clean, but learning about the gruesome murder the next day had etched the events into neighbors' memories. No one had heard sounds coming from the Hargrove house or from the quiet neighborhood, except for Sheila's own brother.

Sheila's brother, David Levill, lived just three hundred yards from Sheila, on Roscoe Veazey Road. He'd watched the 10:00 p.m. news, hoping the weather report would promise a little relief from the ninety-degree heat the community had faced recently. But he fell asleep before the weather report, sleeping fitfully in the hot, muggy night. He was awakened by noise outside. Going to the window, he saw Bradley Dale Day's water truck coming from the direction of Sheila's house, driving fast. Levill had a security light, which lit up the road, and he saw Day's truck clearly. He looked at the clock: 10:57 p.m. Levill told the police his story in 1991.

The investigators added Levill's information to the timeline. Now they had Day's truck leaving the crime scene right before 11:00. His wife had said he came home at 9:00 p.m. and never left.

"We think she covered for him just because he was her husband," says Massamore.

If Sheila ate strawberries at 9:30, they would have been digested by 11:30. She would have already been murdered when Day drove past her brother's house at 10:57.

The KSP detective re-interviewed Day's wife. The couple were now divorced, but at first she stuck to her story. The detective told her about the strawberries and the eyewitness, warning her that she risked going to prison if she was caught lying. After a moment, she responded, "You're right. He told me to lie."

Getting to know Sheila Hargrove through family and friends was the investigators' first step in closing the young mother's murder case. All of the information about Sheila's habits and her actions on the night of the murder was available in 1991. It's possible that the case could have been solved quickly through victimology. In Sheila's case, the victimology information waited eighteen years for someone to place it into the puzzle, alongside the advanced technologies that would bring it into better focus.

Massamore shared Sheila's story with the jury, and he helped them realize how horribly she died. "He not only stabbed her," he explained, "but then he dumped her in the strip pits like she was a piece of garbage."

Day maintained his innocence, and since the prosecution had no DNA evidence and no eyewitnesses, Massamore was unsure whether the jury would convict Day of murder. Rather than risk a not-guilty verdict, he chose to give the jurors a lesser option to be sure Day didn't walk. They found him guilty of first-degree manslaughter.

The prosecution's strongest arguments were the palm prints, the timeline, and the inconsistencies in Day's testimonies. During the penalty phase of Day's trial, Massamore asked the jury what a life was worth. He said that Sheila's children and family were finally coming to a point of closure in her death. He asked the jury to give Day the maximum sentence, which was twenty years in prison. He said that Day had walked free for eighteen years, then he added, "Sheila will never walk again." The jury recommended the maximum twenty-year sentence.

CASES ARE REVIVED WHEN SOMEONE BRINGS A NEW PERSPECTIVE.

Cold case detective Clay Bryant observes, "When you look at a case with a fresh perspective, opinions and self-evaluations change. You can sometimes find peripheral people who can bring secondary evidence. Sometimes you find a needle in a haystack and you find the evidence that sets the haystack on fire."

When the Kentucky State Police looked at Sheila's murder scene and dump site with a fresh eye, it was easy to see things that a longtime resident of Western Kentucky might have overlooked. No road directly connected the murder scene and the dump site. A driver had to go through a series of connecting roads, and you would have to know the area well to do so. The lake was not visible at night from the road. For someone to drive the route at night and dump the body into the lake, he or she would have to be familiar with the area.

"Killers don't hang around the murder scene too long," observes Massamore. "Every second you're at ground zero is a chance to be exposed. This person took time to move the body. We believed that the killer needed to separate the body from the scene because the crime scene implicated them. It had to be somebody who knew Sheila, knew her patterns, and knew the path to the dump scene.

"This was a woman who was always at home with her children at night," says Massamore. "The killer had to be familiar with her circumstances and know that on this particular night she was alone. And Sheila had just moved into the house about a week or so earlier. Few people knew where she lived."

A fresh approach led to new theories. Once earlier detectives learned that Sheila's ex-husband was a drug dealer and she'd testified against him, they decided that he'd had Sheila killed for informing on him. A fresh investigation proved that Sheila and her ex-husband hadn't seen each other in two years and they'd had a friendly divorce. The children were Sheila's by a previous marriage, and she and her drug-dealing ex-husband had no reason to communicate after the divorce.

Even after his wife said he'd forced her to lie, Day stuck to his story. The investigators went over the crime-scene photos, the witness statements, and the police reports, looking at everything with a fresh eye. They looked for discrepancies in witness timelines and used other logic from the case to measure the accuracy of individuals' statements. Sheila's brother said Day drove past his house at 10:57 p.m. Day and his wife claimed he was home by 9:00 and never left. Who was correct? The partly digested strawberries provided the answer.

Massamore read Day's statement about how he got into the house the morning after the murder. "I realized that 'the key was the key,'" he recalls. "I used that theme in my closing arguments. Day said that when Sheila didn't answer the door, he'd found a set of keys in her car and let himself in. But an investigator who went with the photographer when he took the crime-scene photos remembered hearing a detective tell the photographer to give the family the key as soon as he finished because it was the only key they had. We checked with Sheila's family and confirmed that she had only one house key. She would have needed the key to let herself into her house, and she couldn't have put the key in the car after she was murdered."

"What makes cold cases doable is that facts never change," says Massamore. "The only thing that changes is their significance. Sometimes you don't know the significance until years later. The facts are always there."

CASES ARE REVIVED WITH THE HELP OF NEW NATIONAL RESOURCES.

New DNA and fingerprint identification techniques surface constantly, and a small technological advance may bring a cold case back to active status.

Investigators found that the police had taken partial palm prints from the inside portion of Sheila's freshly cleaned front door. The top of the door was screen, and the bottom was glass. At the time of the murder, partial prints were not easily identifiable. The partials were later identified as belonging to Bradley Dale Day, but since partial print identification hadn't been proven 100 percent reliable, nothing was done. Eighteen years later, the prints were sent to AFIS, and they were all confirmed as belonging to Day. The prints were left palm prints on the inside of the door, where he would have pushed if he'd been dragging a body. Experts established that Sheila had been dragged with someone's right hand.

"Solving Sheila's case involved accurate evidence collection eighteen years earlier," says Massamore, "and modern technology to analyze it."

CASES ARE REVIVED THROUGH HINDSIGHT.

When someone calls a department about a cold case, a detective is usually assigned to find the case file and give it at least a brief examination. Sometimes while examining the file, the detective remembers a similar case that occurred after the one now under examination.

"As you study an old case, sometimes similarities to other cases jump out. There's a big advantage to hindsight," says Troy Armstrong.

CASES ARE REVIVED WHEN THERE'S PUBLIC PRESSURE.

When the public begins asking, "Why wasn't this case solved?" law enforcement supervisors and city officials feel pressure to counteract with good news about the case's resolution. The pressure can come from a number of sources, including discouraged family members, but if the case is in the public eye, pressure has a trickle-up effect. When supervisors or officials begin feeling pressure to solve a case, investigators may discover that they finally have personnel and other resources allotted to a case they've wanted to solve for a long time.

CASES ARE REVIVED WHEN LOCAL MEDIA RUN A NEW STORY.

People have short memories, and most often, public interest is more of a here-and-now factor. But occasionally, a case is brought before the public in a compelling way and the pressure is on.

When a reporter notices a story in the crime archives, searches for a resolution, and, finding none, writes a story about the case, a public outcry for justice is often the result.

If family or investigators want to open a case, asking a reporter to write a story is often a quick and effective way to generate public interest.

Dan Tholson considers media as allies and suggests, "Work with the media. Sometimes putting things back on TV or in the newspaper works."

CASES ARE REVIVED WHEN AN OFFENDER COMMITS A NEW CRIME.

When today's offender enters prison, his DNA and fingerprints go on file. If a determined investigator has entered data from an older crime committed by the same perpetrator, he'll get a hit. The system fails only through human neglect. Until data is entered into databases, it's unavailable to those searching for matches. Because prisons are over-worked and understaffed, with no one monitoring how quickly inmate DNA is entered into databases, sometimes hits take longer than they should.

CASES ARE REVIVED WHEN SOMEONE WANTS A DEAL.

When criminals languish in jail, they often look for ways to lessen their sentences, going back over what they know that could translate into reduced jail time. Jailhouse snitches can offer good evidence, but they seldom make reliable, convincing witnesses. When an investigator establishes that information funneled through the jail is accurate, the job is then to make the information credible.

"In 1987," says David Rivers, "the Florida State Legislature changed the sentencing rules so life became real life—no possibility of parole. The only hope lifers had was offering substantial support to the police. We started getting jailhouse calls. There's a grapevine out there. Inmates wanted to reduce life sentences by giving information on unre-lated cases.

"Jailhouse information is often good. Criminals hang out with other criminals. They hear things no one else hears. Some departments have stacks of cases waiting to be reviewed, cases that started with a phone call from jail. Countless cases are closed by inmates. But you, as a detec-tive, have to make that person credible. "

Boat racer Don Arnow was killed in 1987, and a driving force in solving the crime was a defrocked lawyer who had defended drug dealers. He was convicted of money laundering and racketeering. "When we found out he had information," says Greg Smith, "we spent six months nurturing him to make him a credible witness. The lawyer learned that Don's murder was a contract killing arranged from the jail. We checked visitor logs to prove the credibility of the witness. We're obligated to make sure jail witnesses are telling the truth.

"Our job was to make the lawyer's information credible. We used his information to obtain a search warrant. After we found the incriminating records, *then* we subpoenaed the attorney. We were able to convict both the shooter and the one who did the contract."

CASES ARE REVIVED WHEN ANOTHER CRIME IS COMMITTED.

Mill Creek is a small town in Pennsylvania. Violent crime, especially when directed toward a child, is rare. So when a young girl disappeared in 1986, the investigator immediately remembered a similar case that had occurred twenty years earlier. In 1966, nine-year-old Christine Watson was playing near a creek with her younger brother when an adult male invited her to go walking along the creek bank. Christine agreed to go, but her brother refused and ran home to tell his parents. Christine was found farther down the creek bank, lying on her back. Her throat was slashed so brutally that she was almost decapitated.

Christine's brother provided a description of the man who lured his sister away. Witnesses described a car they saw leaving the scene. A suspect surfaced and was interrogated. But with no concrete evidence linking him to the crime, the case was eventually filed away.

The current investigator pulled the old file and saw numerous parallels. Though the two cases ended up being unrelated, in the course of the second investigation, the old case was solved. Simply reopening the case and looking at it under a new light were enough to bring resolution....

Though the two Pennsylvania cases were not related, sometimes a new case links an earlier one to the work of a serial killer, such as in the case of the Arlington-Richmond rape/murders.

CASES ARE REVIVED WHEN CRIMINALS BRAG.

In the criminal culture, crimes are often extolled, and many criminals enjoy bragging about their crimes, though even criminals have standards, however low.

It's more difficult to find a bragging rapist than a bragging murderer. "Murder is a badge of honor in some circles," states Troy Armstrong, "but even in the criminal world there's a stigma to rape. Rapists are targeted in prison."

But finding a perpetrator's confidant can be a vital link to solving a case. "In the vast majority of cases closed by cold case investigators, the suspect, for any number of reasons, told at least one person about his or her involvement in the murder," observes Joe Kennedy.

David Rivers agrees, stating that in nearly all of the 187 cold cases closed by his Miami, Florida, squad during his ten years as supervisor, the offender told someone about the crime. Rivers acknowledges that locating these witnesses is sometimes tedious, but their testimonies can solidify an arrest and conviction.

CASES ARE REVIVED WHEN INVESTIGATORS BROADEN THE LIST OF SUSPECTS.

It's not uncommon for an investigator to focus exclusively on one suspect, and when the evidence doesn't point toward that suspect, to file the case away. New investigators without preconceived theories often see different things and interpret information in an entirely different way. And with new perspectives come new suspects. Sometimes a cold case investigator is simply a new pair of eyes looking at the same information.

CASES ARE REVIVED WHEN REWARDS ARE OFFERED.

Investigators are often divided on the effectiveness of rewards, based on their personal success in offering them. Some investigators believe that those who come forward at the announcement of a reward would have done so anyway. Others can point to cases they believe were solved when the family or community established a reward.

The case of Russell Winstead represents what is probably an accu-

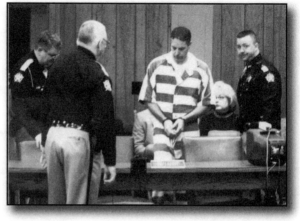

Murderer Russell Winstead at
arraignment March 2006.
Courtesy of the
Madisonville Messenger,
Jim Pearson photographer.

rate cross section of the value of offering a reward. After bludgeoning his eighty-five-year-old aunt and stabbing her ninety-seven times, the thirty-seven-year-old Kentucky engineer and father of three fled to Costa Rica, a choice he made based apparently on the abundance of casinos to feed his gambling habit and the country's strict extradition laws: not even a cold-blooded killer could be extradited until the country receiving the suspect agreed not to pursue the death penalty or life imprisonment without the chance of parole.

Winstead lived well in Costa Rica, with no visible means of support, for more than a year, supported by money from his murdered aunt's estate, before he became the FBI's Fugitive of the Month, with a $10,000 reward attached to the designation. Soon after, *America's Most Wanted* profiled Winstead.

Three people called the *AMW* tip line, stating that they had seen Winstead often in San José's Horseshoe Casino. He was picked up by Costa Rican authorities, and US Marshals brought him back to Kentucky to face trial.

At that point, the FBI contacted the three informants, offering them the reward. One turned it down, stating that he had just wanted to see a killer apprehended. The second donated his portion to charity, and the third accepted his share of the reward.

In December 1997, Michael LeJeune and his girlfriend, Rekha Arnand, both twenty, hosted a drug party at their Roswell, Georgia, apartment. LeJeune and one of the guests, thirty-nine-year-old Ronnie Davis, began arguing over a $250 cocaine debt. Perhaps to show the other party guests that he meant business when collecting debts, LeJeune left the room and came back with a handgun. He shot Ronnie once in the back of the head. The stunned guests left the party, but no one went to the police.

The grisly cover-up that followed made front-page news. LeJeune went to a local hardware store and purchased a chainsaw. He decapitated Ronnie and dismembered his body. He stuffed the body parts into the trunk of his car, keeping Ronnie's head in the apartment. He and his girlfriend drove to nearby Forsyth County, where they tossed the body parts in a cemetery, doused them with gasoline, and set them on fire. The body was identified by the fingerprints on one hand, which was not consumed in the fire, and by a Harley-Davidson tattoo on Ronnie's left arm.

With Ronnie identified, LeJeune and Arnand were even more concerned that they would be traced to the murder. They put Ronnie's head in the trunk of LeJeune's car and drove to LeJeune's parents' lake house on nearby Lake Lanier. They placed Ronnie's head in a vise on a workbench and tried to remove the bullet so it couldn't be traced to LeJeune's handgun. When they were unsuccessful, they sealed the head in concrete and dropped it into the middle of the lake.

Despite heavy media coverage, no one who witnessed the murder spoke up. With no physical evidence, no motive, and no eyewitnesses, it seemed doubtful that Ronnie's killers would ever face justice.

Then, in January 1998, Ronnie's family offered a $10,000 reward for information leading to their son's killer. Ten thousand dollars buys a lot of cocaine, and soon a party guest called the tip line. LeJeune and Arnand were arrested and their apartment and car examined for the plentiful blood evidence that linked the couple to Ronnie's death. Arnand languished in the Fulton County Jail for five years before entering a plea bargain to testify against LeJeune in exchange for a lesser charge punishable by time served.

Greg Smith also had eventual success in offering a reward. "We had a 1967 unsolved murder of a police officer," recalls Smith. "He was killed in the line of duty, and the case was never solved. We put together a reward, working with the Police Benevolent Association. We asked the media to make people aware of it. At first, it generated nothing, but media kept up interest and eventually someone responded to the reward. We were able to solve the case because we offered a reward.

"We've used rewards quite a bit," continues Smith. "We offered a $50,000 reward for information on the triple murder of Genevieve Abraham and her friends Bea and Sam Joseph during a 1983 home invasion. Genevieve's husband, Anthony, kept the media involved. Each year on the anniversary of his wife's murder, he did a media tribute, and he reminded people of the reward. Ten years later, someone called to ask if the reward was still being offered. He was the cousin of one of the men involved in the home invasion." ...

CASES ARE REVIVED AS LAWS CHANGE.

A case must be investigated and tried under the laws that existed at the time of the crime. However, state laws vary and this may not apply to the statute of limitations. If an eleven-year-old rape case was filed away when the ten-year statute of limitations ran out and a state increases the statute of limitations to twenty years, the case is once more viable. The wisest step when considering opening a case where the statute of limitations may have run out is to meet with the prosecutor as early as possible. In today's cases, says Rivers, "You've got a lot of new toys, but you're still working off statutes that were in effect when the crime happened."

CASES ARE REVIVED WHEN SOMEONE NEW TAKES AN INTEREST.

A young adult may hear about a family crime from a generation ago and bring a fresh enthusiasm to solving the case.

... That's what happened in the case of Gwendolyn Moore, the thirty-year-old mother of four whom many believed was beaten to death by her husband. More than thirty years later, Gwendolyn's aunt died, and her sister and her niece, Leslie Ianuzzi, were sorting through her belongings when they came upon a photo of Gwendolyn.

Ianuzzi had never heard anyone mention Gwendolyn, and as she heard the story of her gruesome murder, she became outraged. She called the prosecutor's office and asked officials to take another look at her aunt's case. This time, the office included a new investigator, Clay Bryant, who as a fifteen-year-old boy had been present when Gwendolyn's body was pulled from a well. Bryant had a passion for solving the case, but it was Ianuzzi who initiated its resurrection....

CASES ARE REVIVED WHEN WITNESSES FINALLY DECIDE TO TALK.

...Moore's Ford Bridge, 1946. A ten-year-old white boy tried to tell the sheriff that he'd witnessed the execution of two young black couples. The sheriff told him not to tell anyone what he'd seen or the same thing might happen to him. The frightened boy kept his secret for forty-six years before calling the FBI's Atlanta field office.

...When people come forward after years of silence, guilt is sometimes the catalyst. For ten years, a young man suffered guilt because he knew who killed Miami socialite Genevieve Abraham and her close friends Bea and Sam Joseph. All three were shot to death in the Josephs' Coral Gables, Florida, apartment on December 4, 1984.

"Genevieve's husband, Anthony Abraham, was a Miami car dealer, but we heard that he was also an honorary Consul General for Lebanon," explains David Rivers, who reinvestigated the case. "He had rich friends in high places. Two of his employees were Watergate burglars. So much was going on that we didn't know if we were dealing with a random burglary and murder or something more sinister. We did everything from investigating gypsies to checking with Langley to be sure we weren't in over our heads in an international situation.

"No leads panned out. But in 1992, just before Hurricane Andrew, we received a call on our Crime Stoppers hotline. The tipster was

Ralph Rodriguez of Miami. He identified his cousin, Luis Rodriguez, as one of the killers.

"Ralph was so emotionally torn up over the murders that he almost died of a perforated ulcer. He'd promised God that, if he survived, he'd make everything right. As soon as he recovered, he gave us the case.

"We took Ralph to Orlando, wired him up, and tried to get Luis to cop out. Though Luis didn't implicate himself, we arrested him after a lengthy investigation. He eventually confessed and then implicated Manuel Antonio 'Tony' Rodriguez [no relation] in the murder, agreeing to testify against him for leniency for his own involvement.

"Ralph's family disowned him for turning in his cousin, so we thought it was best to send him out of the state while we prepared for the trial. He came back without our knowledge and married his old girlfriend. They got into a dispute one night. Ralph fired a gunshot into the ground and was arrested. While Ralph was in jail, he broke his ankle, and it became infected. Diabetes complicated the infection, and he lost his sight. He was blind when he testified at the trial.

"Luis Rodriguez was given a life sentence for his part in the burglary and murders. Tony Rodriguez was convicted of instigating the murders and was given the death penalty."

"Sometimes a case requires a phone call," says Rivers. "The detective has to wait until someone else makes the call. And you never know who that caller will be."

CASES ARE REVIVED WHEN LOGIC IS APPLIED.

With all the new technology, it's easy to assume that technology can answer every question. But nothing beats the determination of a dedicated detective for reviving a case—a determination that Alaska prosecutor Alan Goodwin declares to be "good, old-fashioned hard work. And ample shoe leather."

Chapter 4

New Hope for Old Cases

YOU DON'T APPROACH A COLD CASE AS A STANDARD INVESTIGATION.
IT'S MORE OF A CHESS GAME. YOU CAN'T HAVE TOO MUCH PATIENCE.
—NCIS Special Agent Joe Kennedy

C hange brings hope to dormant cases. And when these cases are reopened, they're investigated in ways the original detectives could not have imagined.

During an era of unsurpassed technological advancements, no book or manual could remain up-to-date on investigative resources. "The Internet is the best investigative tool," says Judge Dennis Delano. "You can find information on how to investigate, what techniques are available, and new resources. That's the best way to find the absolute newest technology."

New technology, new databases, and new methods of analysis are developed constantly, and a case that was virtually unsolvable last week may be closed today with a simple data entry. Though the following resources can serve as a guide, pointing an investigator in the right direction, new resources are as available as the daily news, and a skilled investigator stays current on the tools that can help convict the bad guys.

ADVANCES IN FINGERPRINT IDENTIFICATION

Just a few decades ago, fingerprints were sent to a lab where someone used a magnifying glass to study them and then compare them with prints taken from a known suspect. Now, those same prints are shot into a system that gives a clear and quick answer, possibly matching them to an unknown suspect living thousands of miles away.

When investigators looked through the Sheila Hargrove murder file, they saw several steps they could take to start their reinvestigation, but one portion of the report leaped out at them. The original investigators had found several palm prints on the door the killer used to exit the house, dragging Sheila's body behind him. In 1991, palm prints were difficult to match, but in 2009 they were routinely used as convicting evidence.

When Sheila's mother said that she and Sheila had cleaned the front door with Windex two days before the murder and Sheila rarely used her front door, the investigators realized that the old evidence, carefully collected eighteen years before, could identify Sheila's killer. And it did....

Today fingerprint analysis is constantly improving, and an investigator should not discount any quality or portion of a print that can be lifted from a crime scene. And a cold case detective should reexamine old evidence to see if advanced techniques can harvest new print evidence.

"We had some weird letters and cards sent to the department sixteen or seventeen years ago," recalls cold case detective Troy Armstrong. "The papers were processed at the time with a chemical called ninhydrin, and some prints were documented. But with new technology, I requested that the envelopes be pulled to extract DNA from the stamps. When the lab pulled the envelopes out to work for DNA, they were surprised to find that more prints had shown themselves after sitting for nearly two decades."

The use of lasers for lifting and reading prints has enhanced fingerprint analysis in recent years. And one relatively new advancement in fingerprint analysis is cyanoacrylate fingerprint development, sometimes referred to as the "super-glue" technique. This technique makes it possible to lift prints from surfaces such as leather and cloth, which could previously yield no prints.

Where once fingerprints could be compared only with those of a known suspect, national fingerprint databases now allow an investigator to compare fingerprints with criminals, past and present, local and far away, free and imprisoned. With the combination of new fingerprint lifting and reading techniques and national databases in which to search for matching prints, a criminal can never be sure he or she has wiped a crime scene clean.

AMERICA'S LAW ENFORCEMENT RETIREMENT TEAM (ALERT)

America's Law Enforcement Retirement Team (ALERT) is a branch of the National Center for Missing & Exploited Children (NCMEC). It's a consulting service staffed by retired law enforcement officers and is available to all law enforcement agencies.

Project ALERT representatives specialize in missing-children cold cases. Their services include case review, organization and analysis, investigative strategy recommendations, assistance with case interviews, and technical meetings with law enforcement personnel to discuss additional resources.

ALTERNATE LIGHT SOURCE (ALS)

An alternate light source (ALS) uses a light such as a laser or incandescent bulb and filters that allow all but the selected wavelengths of light to be screened out. The result is an illuminating of the evidence.

An ALS can be used at the time evidence is collected, as well as when evidence is evaluated. Identifying evidence immediately with an ALS can help an investigator avoid destroying or contaminating physical evidence that might easily be moved or lost through indirect transfer.

An ALS can detect:

- Body fluids. Most body fluids, including semen, saliva, urine, and vaginal secretions, will fluoresce when exposed to an ALS. Blood does not fluoresce. Instead, it absorbs light and darkens.
- Bruising beneath the skin. This can be helpful when investigating an unexplained death.
- Forged or altered documents. An ALS will show when multiple types of ink or multiple pens were used to alter a document.
- Gunshot residue. An ALS can detect tiny particles of gunshot residue on skin, in hair, and on clothing.
- Hair and fibers. Using an ALS on smooth or carpeted surfaces will make fibers and hairs, as well as small particles such as paint fragments and glass, more easily visible.
- Latent fingerprints. Prints that might not be identified with standard methods of lifting can be illuminated using an intense blue-green laser light. The organic materials in the fingerprint will fluoresce yellow without the use of powders or dyes. Fingerprints can be detected with an ALS on skin, paper, rubber, and cloth.

ALS is now being considered for detection of drugs and for arson investigations. Like fingerprint and DNA analysis technology, ALS is making it more and more difficult for an offender to effectively cover his tracks.

AUTOMATED FINGERPRINT IDENTIFICATION SYSTEM (AFIS)

See IAFIS for a description of the national fingerprint database.

BEHAVIORAL ANALYSIS UNIT (BAU)

The FBI's Behavioral Analysis Unit is a component of the National Center for the Analysis of Violent Crime. The unit assists local, state, federal, and international law enforcement agencies with criminal investigative analyses. The BAU staff review crimes from both a behav-

ting iris data is nonintrusive and requires no physical contact.
idual is detected automatically as he or she approaches the
nera. Just a glance at the camera lens is sufficient for the
photograph the iris and digitally process it.

tting iris data is voluntary, so there are no privacy issues. And
pted data can be accessed only by a positive match, so the
on is secure.

cognition is excellent for identifying prisoners and prison vis-
though it cannot prevent child abductions, it's an effective
lentifying missing children and senior adults. More and more,
nition is replacing child fingerprinting efforts.

BDUCTION AND SERIAL MURDER
GATIVE RESOURCES CENTER (CASMIRC)

's Child Abduction and Serial Murder Investigative Resources
CASMIRC) is a component of the National Center for the
of Violent Crime. The center offers federal law enforcement
s, training, and expertise to all levels of law enforcement for
ductions, mysterious disappearances of children, child homi-
hd serial murders. CASMIRC provides on-site consultations
ess to its centralized database of child abduction and serial
cases that have been submitted by state and local authorities.
SMIRC works in coordination with the National Center for
and Exploited Children and the Office of Juvenile Justice and
ency Prevention to provide training in dealing with cases that
children.

HONE TRACKING

ividual can now be tracked in real time by cell phone signals
ng off towers. The cell phone does not have to be in use; it just
be turned on.

ioral and an investigative perspective.
behavior and how the offender intera
provide crime analysis, interview strate
search warrant assistance, prosecution :
testimonies. The BAU maintains a refer
forensic disciplines such as odontology, :
pathology.

The BAU also produces the *Child A*
enforcement agencies and a PDF file rep
A Threat Assessment Perspective, availabl
teachers, parents, and law enforcement.

BIOMETRICS

Biometrics are technologies that capture, s
identity by comparing characteristics in real
the same type of pattern. The most comm
fingerprint, iris, DNA, face, hand, palm, sign;

Software programs for these scans are a
agencies through privately owned companie
Much like they've done with traditional chi
local law enforcement personnel can now c
them for entry into national databases. The
or senior adult, then has information stored 1
tification must be made some time in the futu
by prison personnel for inmate intake, bookir
well as for tracking inmates' visitors.

The most accurate biometric solution is
even more accurate than fingerprints or fac
matches have been found in more than two m
Every human iris is unique, even between twi
vidual's left and right eyes. After the age of
throughout a person's life, and it positively id
possesses it.

Colle
The indiv
digital ca
camera to

Subm
the encry
informati

Iris re
itors, and
tool for i
iris recog

CHILD A
INVESTI

The FB
Center
Analysis
resource
child ab
cides, a
and acc
murder

CA
Missing
Delinq
involve

CELL P

An in
bounc
has to

Even more accurate cell phone tracking is possible via GPS or GSM using one of several software programs. It's necessary to install a computer chip in the phone or download software from the Internet to the cell phone for this type of tracking to work. Other systems can locate a cell phone and attach a tracking device without having access to the phone.

With a court order, it's permissible to use the spy software programs now available that allow you to gain access to cell phone information without the user knowing it. You can track the cell phone's location at any time, record and monitor incoming and outgoing text messages, listen in on calls, and record phone conversations.

COMBINED DNA INDEX SYSTEM (CODIS)

The Combined DNA Index System (CODIS) is a resource of the FBI. It is available to local, state, and federal crime labs in the United States and to a selected group of international law enforcement crime labs.

CODIS is a comprehensive index of DNA that is constantly updated as law enforcement personnel submit samples from convicted felons and samples extracted from crime scenes. CODIS is a powerful tool for identifying serial offenders. After DNA is inputted into CODIS, if a matching DNA sample is later submitted, the agency submitting the first DNA sample will be notified of the hit, as well as the agency submitting the most recent DNA.

DEOXYRIBONUCLEIC ACID (DNA)

Our bodies have 100 trillion cells. Inside every one of those cells is a microscopic strand of DNA that, if uncoiled and stretched out, would be six feet long. Yet it's so narrow that when it's coiled up, it fits into a cell that's also microscopic.

Every cell has its own strand of DNA, and that DNA is exactly like the DNA in every other cell in the same body. And it's different from every other person's DNA in the entire world. Identical twins have the same DNA, but it's expressed differently.

Even when six people look so much alike that a victim can't identify them in a lineup, DNA will unmistakably point a finger at the true offender.

Because of DNA, justice is no longer blind. A little nearsighted sometimes, but definitely not blind.

DNA has done more than identify criminals. It's taken the responsibility of identification off victims and witnesses. "If I had been forced to choose a mug shot," says Jessica, a rape victim, "I would have chosen the wrong person over and over. DNA took the burden of guilt off of me, the burden of choosing the wrong person based on memory.

"The rapist had a twin brother. Even if I had been able to identify him in a lineup, without DNA, the defense attorneys would have pushed back with 'It could have been his brother. How can you say for sure it was him?'

"Don't give up," stresses Jessica. "If you have DNA, there's somebody out there."

"In the 1990s when DNA started being used for criminal forensics, you needed a bloodstain about the size of a nickel for a good analysis," says Troy Armstrong. "Now we use samples that can't be seen with the naked eye. Touch DNA allows us to collect DNA from a victim's clothing or off a weapon. You can run DNA on fingerprints and extract DNA off cells of a print.

"We can now narrow the male portion of DNA and use a smaller portion to get results. DNA testing can determine race and ancestry, which can point an investigator in the right direction even without a DNA match.

"The O. J. Simpson trial was the first time most people heard of DNA, including the jury." It was difficult for a jury to convict on evidence that, at the time, seemed arguable, but prosecutors now have the advantage of nearly every juror understanding that DNA is molecular fingerprinting. Its testimony is as strong as a surveillance video of the crime. It's the gold standard of evidence, but surprisingly, even many present-day cases must still be presented without it. Cold case investigators must sometimes be creative in finding DNA evidence.

"Look outside the box for places to find DNA," advises Armstrong. "I recently worked a brutal rape cold case where no DNA was at first available. As I read the police report, I noticed that the victim stated that the suspect performed oral sex on her. When the hospital does a rape kit, they comb through pubic hair and do numerous swabs. We checked the rape kit and all the items were folded into sterile paper. Hospital personnel had put the comb, and everything gathered with the comb, into the paper. We got saliva from the comb used on the victim's pubic hair, and we had our DNA. You can't collect too much evidence."

Armstrong feels fortunate that the hospitals in the Charlotte, North Carolina, area are skilled at collecting forensic evidence. "They have a forensic nursing program," explains Armstrong. "They're trained to treat a victim first as a patient but they're also skilled in protecting evidence."

With the abundance of DNA sources, collecting evidence is now more complicated than in previous years. "When I was on the homicide task force, we worked a case of a waitress who went off with some men. She was found beaten to death and submerged in a tub at a motel," says Armstrong. "The crime-scene photos showed empty beer cans. Investigators had dusted the cans for fingerprints but they didn't collect and save the cans. And even if they had, when you dust for prints, you can destroy other evidence."

"A lot of evidence that was worked for DNA ten or more years ago was useless for a while," says Armstrong. "When CODIS increased the number of markers, a lot of cases weren't translated over. The cases sat for years because they weren't formatted the right way. When they reformatted and resubmitted them, they got matches."

"When opening a cold case," says retired cold case investigator Greg Smith, "pull out all the physical evidence and see what new tests can be run. Occasionally, you'll find that no evidence has been stored. But with refined fingerprint studies and DNA, your chances of success are good if evidence has been preserved properly.

"We received a tip not long ago that caused us to reopen a 1971 case. A sixteen-year-old girl and her sixteen-year-old date were attacked by several males when they left their Christmas prom. They gang-raped the girl and beat them both. Then they shot them. The girl lived, but the boy died. The case wasn't solved, but the investigators carefully stored the evidence.

"The evidence included the girl's prom dress. It had been perfectly preserved in a box—a lot of times you'll find evidence stored in plastic, but that damages the evidence. Little splotches on the dress had been cut out and tested in a 1971 lab, but the rest of the dress had been preserved. We found two DNA profiles and entered them in CODIS."

After a suspect's DNA is in the national database, investigators wait for a hit. "People who do things like this don't do it once. They're either dead, out there still stalking victims, or when they were put in prison no one took DNA samples," asserts Armstrong.

"What couldn't be done in 1971 was a simple lab test thirty years later," says Armstrong. "And the lab test was possible because of the conscientious preservation of evidence at a time when the ones preserving it had no idea of its future significance."

Storing evidence is a problem for most departments, but it's crucial for future investigators who may pick up the case a decade or more from now. "Your files have to be maintained correctly, in a secure area, in an area accessible only to detectives," admonishes Smith. He's seen the power of evidence carefully stored by investigators now retired or dead, and he's reaped the rewards of their conscientious work.

Cold case detectives owe a great deal to the faithful investigators of past generations. If they find DNA in evidence boxes, it's because someone, years ago, stored it for them.

ELECTRONIC ADVANCE PASSENGER INFORMATION SYSTEM (EAPIS)

The Electronic Advance Passenger Information System (eAPIS) is provided by the Department of Homeland Security and is available to commercial airline and vessel operators and law enforcement agencies that apply with the Customs and Border Protection section of the US Department of Homeland Security. The system determines whether suspects have traveled outside of the United States and can see if they traveled on specific flights.

ENHANCED HAIR AND FIBER DETECTION METHODS

… The Atlanta child murders case was the country's first high-profile case that presented fibers as a major prosecution tool. The first bodies were discarded in remote land areas, and forensic pathologists identified unusual carpet, drapes, and bedspread fibers, as well as human hairs, on the victims. When the press leaked this information, the killer, later identified as Wayne Williams, began tossing the bodies into nearby rivers.

Determined investigators changed their strategy and began keeping guard at night under bridges in the area, using rookie Atlanta cops and bringing FBI agents to Atlanta for temporary details as part of what the investigators dubbed the Troll Patrol. Each night, investigators camped out on and under many of the city's bridges, hoping to catch the killer dumping a body. It was the type of reactive investigation that no law enforcement officer wants, and it was a last resort. The only way they could catch the killer with this type of surveillance was if he had already killed another child.

The FBI approved a thirty-day bridge surveillance. On the last night of the month-long detail, some damp, cold, exhausted investigators hovering under the James Jackson Parkway Bridge, dazed with exhaustion, heard a sound that eventually put an end to the terror that had gripped the city. It was the sound of a splash, and one rookie APD officer stationed under the bridge, who had been a competitive swimmer in high school, said with confidence, "That was the sound of a body hitting the water."

The Atlanta Police Department and the FBI immediately stopped Wayne Williams as he turned around and circled back over the bridge, which crossed the Chattahoochee River. It was 2:52 a.m. on Friday, May 22, 1981—just three hours before the thirty-day bridge detail was scheduled to end. Two days later, the body of Nathaniel Cater, an Atlanta inner city youth, was found floating in the Chattahoochee River, just 1.2 miles from the James Jackson Parkway Bridge.

Because it was dark and no one had actually seen Williams toss Nathaniel's body into the water, prosecutors had a tough job building their case. They chose to try Williams for only two of the murders, the ones for which they felt they had the strongest evidence. The fibers became a major aspect of the trial, as prosecutors struggled to explain the unique fiber findings—something most jurors had never before considered solid-enough evidence to take away a man's freedom for life.

The fact that Williams had driven onto the bridge and stopped for a moment, then circled back in his original direction did not prove he had dropped a body into the water. The fiber evidence did not prove him guilty either. Fibers are not unique to a particular person. Unlike fingerprints or DNA, they cannot pinpoint an offender beyond a shadow of a doubt. Anyone who comes in contact with a carpet, bedspread, or jacket can pick up its fibers, so fiber evidence is strongest when used to corroborate other evidence. Together, two inconclusive aspects of the investigation—the bridge stop and the fibers—combined to create a strong case.

Lab technicians studied the fibers found on the Atlanta victims and painstakingly matched them with those from Wayne Williams's bedroom. Their findings had an effect similar to blood typing. Williams could be included, along with countless others, as a possible suspect in the murders.

Investigators further narrowed the list of suspects by identifying the carpet mill where the fibers were produced and determining the time frame in which the particular carpet was sold. They researched how much of the carpet was sold in the Atlanta area, and the odds that a suspect would have that carpet in his or her house. The results of their research greatly narrowed the possibility that any one person would be associated with all twenty-eight fibers found on the victims.

Wayne Williams's house, bedroom, and vehicles contained all twenty-eight types of fibers. Fiber analysts speculated that the fibers found on the victims were most likely transferred to the victims from contact with Williams's environment, thus connecting him to the murders.

But in the end, the fiber evidence was circumstantial. It proved Williams probably had association with the victims but not that he killed them. But coupled with the bridge incident, fibers became twenty-eight powerful pieces of the puzzle that, when assembled, produced a picture of guilt.

Fibers helped convict Wayne Williams and served as a landmark case for future cases built on fiber evidence. In the decades since, fibers have become an acceptable form of supporting evidence, and hair can now be undeniably linked through DNA.

FINANCIAL CRIMES ENFORCEMENT NETWORK (FINCEN)

The Financial Crimes Enforcement Network (FinCEN) consists of records from financial institutions that are required by the Bank Secrecy Act, such as Currency Transaction Reports (CTRs) and Forms 8300. The information is provided by the US Department of the Treasury to financial, law enforcement, and regulatory communities.

FinCEN information helps prevent and detect money laundering. Laws such as the Bank Secrecy Act require that banks and other financial institutions report and keep records of suspicious currency transactions. This recordkeeping creates a financial trail for investigators to follow as they track criminals and their assets.

Financial institutions are required to file a CTR with the Treasury Department when they have a cash transaction of $10,000 or more. A conscientious banker will also file the form for a transaction that appears planned to avoid the $10,000 criterion, such as two $5,000 transactions or a $9,700 transaction.

If a $10,000 cash transaction occurs with an entity other than a bank, that entity is required to file a Form 8300. Jewelry stores, casinos, car and boat dealerships, and real estate companies usually keep the form on hand to report large cash transactions.

FinCEN also provides intelligence and analytical support to law enforcement. FinCEN staff combine information reported under the Bank Secrecy Act with other government and public information. This information is then provided to law enforcement agencies in the form of intelligence reports. These reports help law enforcement agencies build investigations and plan new strategies to combat money laundering. An investigator who suspects that a case includes money laundering may acquire FinCEN intelligence by subpoena.

INTEGRATED AUTOMATED FINGERPRINT IDENTIFICATION SYSTEM (IAFIS)

The Integrated Automated Fingerprint Identification System (IAFIS) is provided by the FBI and is available to local, state, and federal law enforcement agencies.

IAFIS is the largest biometric database in the world. It contains the fingerprints and criminal histories for more than sixty-six million individuals in the criminal master file, including seventy-three thousand known or suspected terrorists. The database also contains more than twenty-five million civil fingerprints, including prints from those who have served in the military, those in law enforcement, those whose companies have had federal contracts, and those who have worked for the federal government.

IAFIS provides automated fingerprint search capabilities, latent search capability, electronic image storage, and electronic exchange of fingerprints and responses. IAFIS provides not only fingerprint information, but also corresponding criminal histories and supporting information such as mug shots, scar and tattoo photos, aliases, and physical characteristics such as height, weight, hair color, and eye color.

Before the 1999 launch of IAFIS, the FBI compared fingerprints manually, and it often took weeks or months to obtain a single ten-print report. Now IAFIS processes about 162,000 ten-print submissions per day, with an average response time of ten minutes for criminal fingerprint reports.

Submitting fingerprints and criminal history information to IAFIS is done on a voluntary basis by state, local, and federal law enforcement agencies, and IAFIS information is only as up-to-date as the agencies submitting it.

Many states have similar AFIS systems, which are now tied to the national IAFIS system.

INTEGRATED BALLISTIC IDENTIFICATION SYSTEM (IBIS)

Integrated Ballistic Identification System (IBIS) is the equipment necessary to carry out the National Integrated Ballistic Information Network (NIBIN) system. It's provided by the Bureau of Alcohol, Tobacco, Firearms and Explosives to all levels of law enforcement. This equipment allows firearms technicians to create digital images of the markings made by a firearm on bullets and cartridge casings and compare these images with other bullet and cartridge casing markings in an automated system. The automated system eliminates most choices, allowing a firearms examiner to make a much quicker confirmed match.

INTERNATIONAL CRIMINAL INVESTIGATIVE ANALYSIS FELLOWSHIP (ICIAF)

The International Criminal Investigative Analysis Fellowship (ICIAF) is an FBI-sponsored organization dedicated to the training, certification, and support of police psychological and geographic profilers.

Candidates for the ICIAF Criminal Investigative Analysis Understudy Program must be law enforcement officers with a minimum of three years' experience in interpersonal violent crime investigation. They must be sponsored by an ICIAF Fellow and by their own law enforcement agency.

ICIAF helps ensure that criminal analysts meet a minimum standard of competency before offering their opinions as criminal investigative analysts to the police or courts. Through the Understudy Program, they pass on the collective knowledge, skills, and experiences of the Fellows to new criminal profilers; train and accredit new criminal investigative analysts and geographic profilers; contribute to research into criminal behavior analysis; and provide training to law enforcement officers in criminal investigative analysis and geographic profiling topics.

IRBSEARCH

IRBsearch (www.irbsearch.com) is a privately owned company that provides online risk assessment information to private investigators, process servers, bail bondsmen, and others who document the legitimacy of their intended use of the system. The fee is based on usage, and the system allows individuals to search billions of records quickly and efficiently.

IRBsearch provides information not available to the general public, such as criminal histories and vehicle information. Private investigators, as well as law enforcement, will find the information helpful in tracking down subjects.

LAW ENFORCEMENT ONLINE (LEO)

Law Enforcement Online (LEO) is provided by the FBI to individuals employed by law enforcement agencies, the criminal justice system, or public safety agencies or departments if their positions require secure communication with other agencies. It's a method of transmitting sensitive but unclassified information throughout the world and a vehicle to exchange such information. LEO provides online education programs and hosts professional Special Interest Groups (SIGs) that are controlled-access areas for specialized organizations or disciplines. Each SIG contains a public area accessible to all LEO users and may also contain a restricted-access area for members approved by the SIG's moderator.

The FBI's Violent Criminal Apprehension Program (ViCAP) maintains a public SIG, which is open to any LEO member. The ViCAP SIG provides access to the ViCAP Web Crime Database (by authorized users), information on ViCAP services, ViCAP staff and assignment charts, and ViCAP alerts, newsletters, forms and reference material, and events calendar.

To obtain a LEO account, contact LEO at 304-625-5555, 1-888-334-4536, or leoprogramoffice@leo.gov.

LEXISNEXIS

LexisNexis is a privately owned electronic research database that compiles public information from a number of sources. Nexis.com makes available content from more than 20,000 global news sources, company and industry intelligence providers, biographical and reference sources, intellectual property records, public records, legislative and regulatory filings, and legal materials, with archives dating back to the 1970s for some sources.

LexisNexis can be used to obtain case law, newspaper stories, and public information on individuals and companies. The service is not free, and the cost is based on usage. Though LexisNexis makes research faster and easier, law enforcement officers in smaller departments may find it difficult to sell their superiors on the need to pay a substantial amount of money for information that is available free in other places, though the cost in human resources to gather the information should be taken into account.

NEXT GENERATION IDENTIFICATION (NGI)

The Next Generation Identification (NGI) program was initiated to reduce terrorist and criminal activities by improving and expanding biometric identification and criminal history information. Though initiated by the FBI, the NGI is a collaborative effort among local, state, federal, and international representatives.

Over a period of several years, NGI will replace current IAFIS technical capabilities, while introducing new functionality.

MEDIA ARCHIVES

Many cold case investigators rely heavily on newspaper archives, which often contain a plethora of stories about the crime and the early investigation. When police reports are sketchy or no longer available, archived newspapers can provide substantial information.

"A young man asked us to follow up on his grandfather's death," recalls Greg Smith. "He died in 1959 and his death was ruled a suicide. But the grandson told us that he believed his grandfather had been murdered.

"We agreed to follow up, but our police files on suicides are destroyed after ten years. I only had a name and the fact that he committed suicide. But I had a media contact who gave me access to the newspaper archives.

"The old articles showed that the grandfather was high-profile and involved in organized crime. I gained enough information about the grandfather to locate his file in the medical examiner's office. The medical examiner still had photographs and part of a police report. It was definitely a suicide."

But Smith learned that the grandson wanted more than closure. "It turned out that he was trying to open the case to get a movie deal," says Smith. Media archives foiled his plans.

NATIONAL CENTER FOR MISSING AND EXPLOITED CHILDREN (NCMEC)

The National Center for Missing and Exploited Children (NCMEC) has no arrest powers and does not take charge of cases. Instead, it assists law enforcement personnel in locating both newly missing children and those whose cases have gone cold.

NCMEC sponsors the Jimmy Ryce Law Enforcement Training Center, which provides national and regional training and technical-assistance programs for local law enforcement officers, prosecutors, and educators to enhance the investigative response to missing and exploited children. The center is named in memory of nine-year-old Jimmy Ryce, whose story is included in chapter 5.

NATIONAL CENTER FOR THE ANALYSIS OF VIOLENT CRIME (NCAVC)

Services of the National Center for the Analysis of Violent Crime (NCAVC) are provided by the FBI to local, state, federal, and foreign law enforcement agencies investigating unusual or repetitive violent crimes. NCAVC also offers assistance in nonviolent matters such as national security, corruption, and white-collar crime investigations.

NCAVC is staffed by experienced FBI special agents and other professionals. They provide advice and support in child abductions, mysterious disappearances of children, serial murders, single homicides, serial rapes, extortions, threats, kidnappings, product tampering, arsons and bombings, weapons of mass destruction, public corruption, and domestic and international terrorism.

NCAVC is organized into three components: Behavioral Analysis Unit (BAU), Child Abduction Serial Murder Investigative Resource Center (CASMIRC), and Violent Criminal Apprehension Program (ViCAP).

Requests for NCAVC services are typically facilitated through NCAVC coordinators assigned to each FBI field office.

NATIONAL CRIME INFORMATION CENTER (NCIC)

The National Crime Information Center (NCIC) is a computerized database in which criminal justice agencies input and access information about crimes and criminals, including criminal histories and information on stolen vehicles and other stolen items; wanted persons including international fugitives; missing persons; and gang members. The database is provided by the FBI to local, state, federal, and foreign criminal justice agencies and authorized courts. NCIC information assists authorized agencies in apprehending fugitives, locating missing persons, and locating and returning stolen property. The information is limited to the information that has been entered by law enforcement agencies. For example, if a law enforcement agency fails to enter the serial number and description of a stolen firearm, no record would exist if the weapon were used to commit a crime in another location. However, if information is entered into the system, it's available immediately when an officer makes a routine traffic stop.

Many states have their own version of NCIC, such as Florida's FCIC. For a while the state and federal systems weren't tied together, but now the systems communicate.

NATIONAL INTEGRATED BALLISTIC INFORMATION NETWORK (NIBIN)

The National Integrated Ballistic Information Network (NIBIN) is a program provided by the Bureau of Alcohol, Tobacco, Firearms and Explosives (ATF) to law enforcement agencies. Through the NIBIN program, ATF provides Integrated Ballistic Identification System (IBIS) equipment to local, state, and federal law enforcement agencies for imaging and comparing evidence from crimes where firearms were used.

NIBIN provides law enforcement agencies with an effective intelligence tool that many could not afford on their own. The system also makes it possible to share intelligence across jurisdictional boundaries, enabling all levels of law enforcement agencies to work together to stop violent criminals.

The equipment allows firearms technicians to take digital images of bullet and cartridge case markings made by a firearm. The system then automatically compares the images with those in the system, identifying similar results. Firearms examiners then check the results to confirm a match. The automatic screening minimizes the amount of nonmatching evidence that firearms examiners must inspect to confirm a match, enabling law enforcement agencies to discover links between crimes more quickly, including links that would have been lost without the technology.

INTERNATIONAL JUSTICE AND PUBLIC SAFETY INFORMATION SHARING NETWORK (NLETS)

Originally called the National Law Enforcement Telecommunications System, the system is now called the International Justice and Public Safety Information Sharing Network. However, many officers still refer to it as NLETS.

NLETS is a nonprofit corporation owned and operated by the states and funded by fees for service. Its services are available to all levels of law enforcement. NLETS is an international, computer-based message-switching system that links local, state, and federal law enforcement and justice agencies for the purpose of information exchange. It provides information services support for a growing number of justice-related applications.

NLETS users include law enforcement agencies in all US states and territories, all federal agencies with a justice component, selected international agencies, and strategic partners, all cooperatively exchanging data, including motor vehicle and driver's data, Canadian Hot File records, INS databases, and state criminal history records. Nearly ninety million messages are transacted each month through NLETS.

SAFE STREETS TASK FORCE

The Violent Gang Safe Streets Task Force is the vehicle through which all local, state, and federal law enforcement agencies join to address the violent crime plaguing their communities. The Safe Streets Violent Crime Initiative allows each FBI field office to address violent street gangs and drug-related violence through long-term task forces focusing on violent gangs, crimes of violence, and the apprehension of violent fugitives. The FBI's Safe Streets and Gang Unit works with 160 Violent Gang Safe Streets Task Forces in cities and regions across the country.

These task forces actively pursue violent gangs, with a goal of prosecuting gang members for racketeering, drug conspiracy, and firearms violations. The Safe Streets Task Force encourages cooperation among all levels of law enforcement to increase productivity and avoid duplication of efforts.

A key facet of a Safe Streets Task Force is the Enterprise Theory of Investigation (ETI). The ETI's goal is to identify and prosecute entire gangs, from street thugs and dealers to the top leaders in the gangs' structures. They use a combination of investigative techniques, from immediate, street-level enforcement to sophisticated techniques such as consensual monitoring, financial analysis, and Title III wire intercepts investigations to root out and prosecute the entire gang.

SOCIAL NETWORKING

From checking Facebook to purchasing access to LexisNexis, the Internet has opened an entirely new world for investigators. And they've found that everyone, including those wanted by the police, like to stay connected with old friends.

Sometimes, when investigators can't find suspects through traditional channels, they turn to Facebook and other social networking sites, and they're discovering that sometimes even if individuals have half a dozen aliases on the FBI fugitive list, they're still using the name their high school buddies will recognize on Facebook.

VIOLENT CRIMINAL APPREHENSION PROGRAM (VICAP)

The Violent Criminal Apprehension Program (ViCAP) is a national database of violent-crime information, primarily homicides, sexual assaults, missing persons, and unidentified human remains. The database is maintained by the FBI and is available to all law enforcement agencies.

Law enforcement agencies submit comprehensive information about their cases to ViCAP. The information maintained in the national database automatically compares the newly submitted case to all other cases in the database to identify similarities. Individual cases submitted to ViCAP are analyzed by crime analysts, and Crime Analysis Reports (CARs) are provided to the case investigators.

ViCAP captures detailed administrative, investigative, and behavioral data about violent crimes, such as agency information, victim information, offender/suspect information, offender timeline information, modus operandi, dates and exact geographic locations, crime-scene information, types of trauma inflicted on a victim, weapon information, sexual activity, vehicle information, evidence tracking, narrative summary, holdback information (which has access restrictions), and attachments such as photographs, crime-scene diagrams, and composites.

Criteria about cases stay in the FBI-ViCAP national database indefinitely and are compared against all other cases as they are entered into the system.

VICTIMOLOGY

Victimology is a branch of criminology that studies the background and habits of the victim, the relationship between a victim and an offender, and why the victim was targeted for a crime.

"Profiling can make a strong contribution to victimology," says retired FBI profiler Steve Mardigian. "We look at old cases by going right back to the beginning. We look at the dynamic interaction between the victim and the offender. We look at the behaviors of the offender and the victim. We ask what aspects of the victim's personality could have made him or her more likely to be a victim. Then we develop a profile about who the suspect could be.

"But profiling the suspect is only one aspect of how a profiler

FBI profiler Steve Mardigian now.
Courtesy of Steve Mardigian.

can contribute. We deal with the crime scene and crime reconstruction. We look for motivation—was it a stranger or someone the victim knew? From those things, we look at how the case could or should be investigated, and we make recommendations to investigators.

"We make suggestions on how to engage the media, and we offer resources for getting information to the public. If media information is dealt with appropriately, you can communicate with the public and with the offender.

"We make an indirect assessment, looking at a suspect's strengths and weaknesses. And once someone's been charged, a profiler can help with how to interview and how to deal with them in court."

... Victimology played a strong part in solving the July 1966 Christine Watson murder case. At the time of Christine's murder, twenty-three-year-old Eugene Edward Patterson was a suspect. He had a criminal record for indecent exposure, and he closely resembled Christine's brother's description of the man who approached the two children near their home in Mill Creek Township in Erie, Pennsylvania—the man Christine was walking away with the last time her brother saw her.

Twenty years after the murder, FBI profiler Steve Mardigian received the case. His initial analysis showed that nine-year-old Christine was a low-risk victim. She wasn't exposed, in her regular daily schedule, to unusual risks. Her parents weren't involved in illegal activities. She was a typical little girl from a typical family, so Mardigian and his team needed to discover if Christine was a random victim or if she had some connection with the offender.

"We got autopsy reports," recalls Mardigian, "and we recommended that the police investigators re-interview the original witnesses. A minister had inter-

Child killer Eugene Patterson arrest photo.
Courtesy of Steve Mardigian.

acted with Patterson at the time of the murder. He'd been the one to take Patterson to the police department for his original interview. When police didn't have enough to hold him, the minister said Patterson had told him he needed to go back and talk to the police some more. But he decided to talk to his mother first, and he never returned to the police. With no solid evidence to connect Patterson to the murder, the case went cold.

"When the police interviewed the minister twenty years later, they showed him a toy deputy badge that police had found under Christine's body. He said he'd seen a badge like it on Patterson's coffee table.

"With Patterson's history of indecent exposure, we felt that he'd probably started out exposing himself to Christine. She was four feet three inches tall and weighed fifty-three pounds, but he would have felt threatened by her if she'd said she was going to tell what he did. We believe he killed her to keep her from identifying him.

"We analyzed how Patterson would have reacted after committing the crime, and we felt that he would have been anxious and would have shut himself off from society immediately after the murder. If we could take him back to the crime, we might be able to re-create those emotions. Since we had the minister putting the evidence in the suspect's house, we suggested that police resurface the case in the media. We hoped to make Patterson anxious.

"At the time of the murder, he lived on a farm with his mother. She had since died, he'd married, and he was living on the same farm with his wife.

"We got word that he was feeling pressure from the new media exposure, and police found him driving erratically up and down the road. We felt it was a good time to interview him.

"We developed strategies for interviewing him. We suggested not bringing him to the police department, so police took him to a hotel room.

"The police interviewers attempted to take him back in time to the crime by showing him articles about the murder and photos of Christine. They suggested that maybe it was an accident. He said, 'I don't remember killing that little girl.'

"The police decided they had enough to bring him in to be

processed and later asked what he wanted them to tell his wife. He said, 'Tell her I'm sorry.'

"During Patterson's trial, we advised the prosecuting team to take him back in time to when the event happened. We suggested that they hand him things from the crime scene and, specifically, while he testified, to show him the badge.

"The prosecutor laid the badge on the witness stand in front of him, and Patterson stood up and pointed to the badge and said, 'I won't touch that. I'll never touch that.' That had a strong impact on the jury."

…FBI profiler John Douglas advised the prosecution team on how to question Wayne Williams in the Atlanta child murders trial. Williams had soft, almost feminine features, and he was usually calm and mild-mannered. Douglas knew it would be difficult for a jury to imagine him as a serial killer. But he predicted that, under extreme duress, Williams would become agitated, letting jurors see that he was indeed capable of murder.

When Williams took the stand, defense attorney Al Binder attempted to use Williams's gentle appearance to prove he was incapable of murder. At one point, he grabbed Williams's soft, feminine hands and asked, "Are these the hands of a serial killer?"

But the prosecution team countered Binder's efforts by following Douglas's suggestion. They continued Williams's cross-examination for hours. At Douglas's suggestion, prosecutor Jack Mallard also took Williams's hands as he asked him, "What was it like to kill? Were you afraid?" Williams said very quietly, "No."

Williams then lost control, showing the rage Douglas had hoped for, as he told the prosecutors, "I know you have a profiler and I'm not going to fit your profile."

Then on February 24, 1982, during an emotional outburst, Williams boosted the state's case against him. The previously reserved Williams hissed, "You want the real Wayne Williams? You got him right here." It was the perfect time for the state to rest its case. Two days later, after closing arguments, eight black and four white jurors deliberated just eleven and a half hours before finding Williams guilty of both murders that the prosecution had chosen to charge him with, the two they considered the strongest.

Y CHROMOSOME-SHORT TANDEM REPEAT (Y-STR)

The Y Chromosome-Short Tandem Repeat (Y-STR) database was created by the National Center for Forensic Science (NCFS), in conjunction with the Y-STR Consortium.

Y-STRs are characteristics found on the male (Y) chromosome. When Y-STRs are examined, the male components are easily detected since only this portion of the DNA is amplified. Identifying and separating male DNA is helpful when examining homicide evidence where blood is mixed with other blood or with saliva and in sexual-assault evidence when vaginal swabs contain both female and male DNA.

Y-STR analysis cannot pinpoint an individual, but it can identify a family line since male family members have the same Y-STR profile. For example, Y-STR analysis can greatly narrow the suspect pool by showing that the DNA evidence came from someone in a particular family—father, son, grandfather, or uncle. If you cannot obtain a DNA sample from the actual suspect, obtaining one from a male family member is just as effective for this type of analysis.

Most labs require that you have a DNA sample from a suspect or male family member before conducting Y-STR testing. Consult experts at a police or private crime lab for current Y-STR advances and to find out if Y-STR analysis would be helpful in a specific investigation.

PEOPLE ARE A COLD CASE INVESTIGATOR'S BEST RESOURCE.

An event is necessary to revive an old case, and events are triggered by people. A phone call from a family member. A newspaper reporter writing an article. Someone inputting data into a law enforcement database. An investigator looking at old evidence and realizing that new technology could bring the case to life. With technology now virtually limitless, people are still the most valuable investigative resource.

Chapter 5

Investigation 101

Most agencies choose only skilled and experienced officers to serve on cold case squads because the heart of effective cold case investigations is solid police work. Cold case investigators must rely on a base of proven strategies and add innovative approaches tailored to their unique and unpredictable cases. But without the basics, whatever they attempt to build will crumble.

Experienced investigators soon develop their own personal strategies through trial and error, ones that fit their personalities and abilities. But they also rely on standard investigative techniques such as these.

MAKE IT PERSONAL.

"Get to know the victim's loved ones and let the case become personal," suggests investigator Clay Bryant. "If you don't become emotionally attached to a case, you'll never solve it without lab miracles. You have to feel some of the hurt and pain to have the drive to move forward."

Though objectivity may make it easier for an investigator to sleep at night, Bryant believes in caring for the victim and the victim's family. Years after a case is closed, he's still friends with the victim's family because they know that he genuinely cares. No matter how old the case, Bryant knows that every victim is someone's family member, and he treats their memories with respect, always referring to them as Mr./Ms./Mrs. or by first name. He learns all that he can about the victim, not just to analyze his findings for victimology data, but so that he can understand the loss the family suffered and be motivated to find justice for their loved one.

Vieng Phovixay is one of the people Bryant learned to care about decades after she was tortured, raped, and murdered.

When nineteen-year-old Vieng Phovixay went missing in 1987, police were certain foul play was involved. The first break came when Vieng's body was recovered after two years. But by that time, leads had dried up and forensic evidence had diminished. Time was the enemy.

Eventually, time and technology became the tools that closed the case with finality. Early investigators reluctantly filed away the case, hoping that something would eventually happen to rejuvenate the evidence pool. It happened through a series of events over time.

Vieng Phovixay and her family came to the United States in the late seventies as refugees from Laos. Vieng's father, Savang, was a US military advisor during the Vietnam War. He was eventually captured by the North Vietnamese and imprisoned. Vieng's mother,

Murder victim Vieng Phovixay.
Courtesy of Clay Bryant.

Kham, sold all their possessions and used the money to bribe guards and obtain her husband's freedom. The family fled Vietnam at night, eventually taking a raft to a refugee camp.

The family settled in Newnan, Georgia, a quiet town of about twenty-five thousand, located thirty-eight miles southwest of Atlanta. First Baptist Church of Newnan sponsored Vieng's family, which included her three sisters and one brother, and helped them settle into the community, where they were soon known, accepted, and loved. They lived in a small house behind the church. Savang became a maintenance worker for the church, and Kham worked in the church nursery. Church members helped the family learn customs, understand the language, learn to shop, and adjust to their new country in dozens of subtle ways.

Smart, talented, and artistic, Vieng's siblings immediately focused on the American dream, studying hard and making good grades. Vieng's brother became an art teacher, and her sisters became a graphic artist, an accountant, and a court systems employee. Vieng was the free spirit among them, and it took her a little longer to settle down. But by 1987, after a short failed marriage, Vieng was a focused, self-assured nineteen-year-old, excited about life and looking forward to the future. She was employed at a grocery store in downtown Newnan. Her family described her as a sweet, loving, trusting person who had hopes and dreams.

But on October 12, 1987, Vieng's hopes and dreams ended abruptly when her bronze Datsun limped into Gas, Inc., on US Highway 29, south of the I-85 Moreland exit, with a flat tire.

Vieng called her dad, but while she was waiting for him to arrive, a Good Samaritan offered her a ride in his green 1975 Chevrolet El Camino SS, which sported a Confederate flag. The trusting young woman asked the man to drive her to longtime acquaintance Kenneth Baker's mobile home in nearby Moreland, where she could wait until her father fixed her flat. Just as he promised, the Good Samaritan drove Vieng to Baker's, but he returned a little while later, saying he'd found a tire for her. He offered to drive Vieng back to her car, and since he'd taken her safely to her friend's, she trusted him a second time. Baker watched Vieng drive away with a man he later described as a thirty- or forty-year-old Caucasian, heavyset, with brown hair and a beard.

When Vieng's father arrived at the gas station from which Vieng had called, her car was there—still with a flat tire—but Vieng was not. She was never seen alive again by anyone other than her killer.

The community rallied to find a beloved resident. They put up posters with a photo of Vieng.

When a local reporter included Baker's description of the stranger's El Camino in an article about Vieng's disappearance, a probation and parole officer grabbed the phone and called the police. "I have a parolee with a car just like that. And he has an assault record." Charles Travis Manley surfaced as a suspect.

Law enforcement from Coweta County and nearby Harris County, along with the Georgia Bureau of Investigation (GBI), began an intense investigation, including bringing Manley in for questioning. Manley had served two sentences for rape and burglary. Three witnesses stated that they saw Vieng get into a car that fit the description of Manley's car, but two of the witnesses failed to identify Manley in a lineup. Prosecutors were divided about whether they had sufficient evidence to indict Manley, and he was released.

Without a body, without strong evidence tying Manley to Vieng's disappearance, and with other leads and other cases vying for attention, Vieng's case was reluctantly moved to inactive status. Eventually the young woman with dreams of opportunities in America was forgotten by everyone but her family.

Two years later, a timberman was working in a remote wooded area in nearby Harris County, marking trees to be cut. He saw a human skull at the base of one of the trees and reported his finding to authorities. Investigators soon found sixty more bones scattered across a large area, just fifty yards from a relatively untraveled road. They found a wool sweater, a blouse, slacks, and underwear in the same area. The blouse had two slits consistent with knife wounds. Investigators also recovered strips of cloth that appeared to have been cut from the slacks and fashioned into knots.

The bones were tentatively identified as Vieng's, and the family identified the clothing as what Vieng had been wearing when she disappeared.

Investigators pieced together her last hours. She had been tied to a tree with strips of her clothing, raped, and killed. It was two more years before the bones could be officially identified and Vieng's family could bury her.

Soon after the body was found, Manley had his car repainted, although altering the original paint job reduced its value to car enthusiasts.

A few months later, a team of investigators and a forensic anthropologist returned to the crime scene to gather more evidence. They located a pine tree that they believed was the site of the murder. They found threads from the slacks embedded in the tree's bark, and nearby they found more bones and an earring. The soil at the base of the tree contained materials that appeared to be decomposed human remains. Though technology was limited in 1990, the investigators preserved an eight-foot section of the tree as evidence.

Police now had a body and a cause of death. But the case remained cold for sixteen more years until Clay Bryant reopened the investigation.

In March 2005, while working with Bryant on another case, GBI Special Agent Gary Rothwell told Bryant about Vieng's unsolved murder. He said the case had frustrated him since 1987 because he thought it could be solved. It would just take time and dedication from a cold case detective. Bryant decided he would be that detective.

Working with Coweta County DA Pete Skandalakis and Muscogee County DA Grey Conger, who had jurisdiction over Harris County (where Vieng's remains were found), Bryant reinvestigated Vieng's murder.

"Cases that cross county lines can be sticky," says Bryant, "but in this case, everyone's top priority was justice for Vieng. Bob Lines, from Newnan, and lots of others were involved. Once we tackled the case full force, everything sort of fell together."

The investigation led, once again, to Manley, who by now had an additional assault charge. His ex-wife was now willing to testify that Manley had been violent and had raped her during their marriage. Investigators learned that Manley had once worked just two miles from the area where Vieng's body had been found and was familiar with the old logging roads.

This new evidence, along with having a body and cause of death, was enough to encourage Coweta County prosecutors to move forward with the case. Harris County prosecutors were still reluctant to indict, but they gave Coweta County prosecutors permission to try the case.

The investigative team felt that their case could be stronger if they exhumed Vieng's remains. With new technology, they believed they could now positively identify the remains and obtain a more accurate cause of death. Although not legally required to do so, the DA's office approached Vieng's family for permission to exhume her body. Wanting every edge in getting a conviction, the family granted permission.

A forensic archeologist was able to make a more positive identification using mitochondrial DNA and determined the cause of death as strangulation.

"Harris County carefully stored and guarded the evidence in this case," says Bryant. "When we reopened the case in 2005, everything we needed was there."

The trial of Charles Travis Manley began twenty years after Vieng's murder. Coweta Circuit Senior Assistant District Attorney Ray Mayer began his opening arguments by describing Vieng's murder as a cold case that "withered on the vine."

At 11:30 a.m. on September 5, 2007, a jury found then-sixty-year-old Charles Travis Manley guilty of malice murder. He will be ninety before he is eligible for parole.

Vieng's family is still in touch regularly with Clay Bryant, the former investigator for the Coweta Judicial Circuit District Attorney's Office who pieced together the case and arrested Manley. They include Bryant in good news such as pregnancy announcements. He's more than a friend. He's the person who helped their family reach a point where they could observe such celebrations with reasonable peace. Though they'll always be reminded that one special family member is missing when they celebrate, at least now they know that Vieng's killer will never kill again. And for that, they thank Bryant, who made Vieng's case personal....

GATHER AND PROCESS PHYSICAL EVIDENCE.

Many times, investigators are skilled at gathering evidence but not at analyzing it. Once the evidence is collected, take time to figure out what you have, what you want the evidence to tell you, and how technology and tenaciousness can help it speak to you.

Preserve the crime scene with video and still photography. Photograph every corner of every room from every possible angle.

If something is out of place, it's probably significant. You may not have the means to determine that it's significant, but someday someone may. Follow procedure. Preserve evidence. And someone can eventually write the final chapter.

"Collect everything imaginable," says Troy Armstrong, "so a year from now you won't regret not collecting something." Once the home is turned over to the family or the business turned back to the owner, an investigator can't return to gather uncompromised evidence.

FBI Special Agent (ret) Jim Procopio knows what's lost when evidence isn't gathered. In a case as old as the 1946 Moore's Ford Bridge murders, there's no possibility of access to the actual crime scene, usually no crime-scene photos are available, and many witnesses are now dead. Physical evidence is the best chance for solving the case, and if the evidence isn't preserved, it's lost forever. "Hundreds of bullets were fired that day," says Procopio, "and they weren't checked for ballistics."

After analyzing the evidence, store it properly—for the trial or for a future generation of investigators. Cold case detectives have sometimes been disappointed to find that items with DNA were stored in plastic and are now moldy or otherwise unusable. If in doubt about how to store evidence, check with technicians in a forensic lab. They'll know from disappointing experiences what not to do.

GET THE PROSECUTOR ON BOARD.

The prosecutor is a powerful part of the investigation team, and his or her support and advice are crucial. A prosecutor can advise about whether the case is prosecutable, what evidence a jury will need to understand the case, and where the case would fit in the court's priorities.

FORGET TELEVISION.

Very little is as it appears on television. On TV, a single investigator can perform an autopsy, test for DNA, and do a psychological profile of the offender, then strap on a SIG 229, slip into raid gear, bust down a door, and make the arrest. In reality, it takes a team of skilled individuals, each doing his or her part of the work.

No one, including the FBI, has instantaneous access to private and personal data. Much of what television portrays as accessible to law enforcement is either totally protected or available only with a court order or subpoena.

Even with a subpoena, an investigator cannot intercept mail. With proper authorization from the Postal Inspection Service and a solid reason for requiring it, an investigator can obtain a mail cover: a list of return addresses for mail the suspect receives.

Because of the Federal Privacy Act, banks are required to have a subpoena before releasing financial information. Armed with a subpoena, an investigator can find out immediately if a suspect has an account at a particular bank, as well as his or her balance. The investigator can have immediate access to the suspect's safety deposit box. However, a bank can take weeks to comply with a subpoena for details of an account, such as photocopies of canceled checks, checks deposited into the account, deposit tickets, and cashier checks purchased by the suspect.

Hospital records require a subpoena. College transcripts require a subpoena. Employment records require a subpoena unless an employer chooses to supply the information, which in an age of lawsuits is unlikely.

Nothing is as quick as it appears on TV. A computer miracle is a lazy way of solving a crime in under fifty minutes. If the TV detectives had to do an actual investigation, it would be a more complicated story. The writers are trading accuracy for fast-paced drama and crafty investigative skills for segments that can be concluded in time for commercials.

No one gets instant DNA results. A department with its own DNA lab can have results in two or three days. If DNA must be sent to a state crime lab, a six-month wait is not unusual.

Profilers can't narrow the suspect pool as drastically as television proclaims. A recent fictional TV profiler told local police, "We're looking for a disheveled man between the ages of eighteen and twenty-four. He'll be working at a menial job, he'll be driving an American-made truck, and he'll have a severe speech impediment." Of course, in the fictional program, the profiler hit the description dead center. In real life, profilers make a valuable contribution to solving cases, both new and cold, but they cannot paint a surefire, detailed portrait of the perpetrator.

Often a profiler's skills are most valuable when a suspect has been identified. A profiler can affirm that the suspect fits the profile and can advise on ways to successfully interrogate and cross-examine the suspect. Take advantage of a profiler's unique skills, but don't expect television miracles. Calling in a profiler doesn't mean you've solved your case.

GET TO KNOW THE VICTIM.

Even if victims are deceased, a good investigator gets to know them and care about them. Talking to families can give you important, though sometimes overly positive, insights, so it's always wise to ask the family but also to look further. NCIS Special Agent Joe Kennedy warns, "Victimology is crucial in solving a case, but remember that what you hear from the family may be skewed.

"Friends and associates are better resources. Even the trash is better. Find close associates, roommates, lovers, and say to them, 'God bless their soul, but paint me a picture of what really went on. It could help solve the case, so don't hold back.'"

It's wise to talk to coworkers, read diaries, learn the victim's social and work schedules, and otherwise become familiar with the victim's

NCIS Special Agent Joe Kennedy (third from left) with Japanese National Police senior officials, Okinawa.
Courtesy of Joe Kennedy.

personality, possible enemies, and everyone he or she associated with on a regular or occasional basis, both intimately and casually. This information will help you understand what the victim would have done in a particular situation, who might have wanted to harm the victim, and when the victim would have been most vulnerable to attack.

And knowing the victim will help you care about the crime.

STUDY THE CRIME SCENE.

"The crime scene is the heart of the case," says Troy Armstrong, "and the body is the majority of the crime scene. That's where the victim and suspect meet."

Study crime-scene photos from the outside in. It's easy to focus just on the victim, but often items in the background of the photos give clues to what happened before, during, or after the crime.

SECURE THE CRIME SCENE.

Troy Armstrong warns, "Recognize what the crime scene is and secure it. Sometimes when the first officers arrive, they need to realize they're in the middle of the crime scene. If someone is dragged, the entire area becomes the crime scene. First-responding officers need to direct others to protect the entire area.

"You can't let a sexual-assault victim use the restroom," adds Armstrong. "You need to collect the urine. It's part of the crime scene. Drugs are also in urine, and they leave the body quickly. There's nothing wrong with having two or three layers of crime-scene tape.

"Everybody wants to throw up the yellow crime scene tape. Just be sure you throw it up in the right spot," warns Armstrong.

Preserving the crime scene may help an investigator solve the case quickly. If not, it will preserve the evidence for a future cold case investigator.

Cold case investigator Clay Bryant can't stress enough: Preserve the crime scene. Many of his successes are a direct result of plentiful evidence carefully stored decades ago. "Take the time to process the crime scene correctly," says Bryant. "If it takes decades to solve, it will be nearly impossible for a cold case detective to recapture this moment in time unless you preserve it. You never get the crime scene back. You never get that moment in time back. If you don't take the time now to do things right, the case will be a mountain to climb. The new detective will have to start all over again. Preserve what you have because you'll never be at that place in time again."

PRESERVE THE EVIDENCE.

Once evidence is obtained, it must be preserved for testing and for the trial. And in the event that the case goes cold, it must be successfully stored indefinitely.

"The Metro-Dade Police Department had evidence stored in a freezer," recalls retired cold case investigator Greg Smith. "The freezer broke down over a weekend. By Monday, we'd lost evidence dating back to 1984. We learned a valuable and costly lesson: have a back-up generator.

"Preserving witness files is also a key to preserving evidence, and you have to preserve all evidence as carefully as you preserve a crime scene."

Hindsight is always clearer, as the Madisonville (Kentucky) Police Department learned when the sole keeper of their evidence room absconded with thousands of dollars in weapons and drugs, rendering many of its cases unable to be prosecuted. The police chief was later quoted in the local paper as saying, "It's our full intention to correct this so it doesn't happen again." Good, but it's so much better to anticipate such problems and never allow one person to be guardian over an entire evidence room.

"There was no reason in 1974 for a detective to preserve hairs," says Judge Dennis Delano. "All that could have been done at that time was to compare them under a microscope to determine if they were similar

Investigator Dennis Delano.
Courtesy of Dennis Delano.

to other hairs in question. But in the Barbara Lloyd case, the original lead detective, now in his eighties, told me that he kept them because he thought that someday they might be important. And they were."

Simply preserving evidence isn't enough. It has to be preserved properly. "At one point," says Delano, "lab technicians and investigators believed they should put bloody evidence in plastic bags. That evidence has long since molded. Now we hang it out to dry and seal it in paper."

SECURE AND MANAGE VOLUNTEERS, MEDIA, AND EVEN INVESTIGATORS.

Retired US Customs Branch Chief Mike Wewers coordinated the work of reserve deputies in the kidnapping and murder case of eleven-year-old Levi Frady. "Levi was kidnapped in Forsyth County [Georgia] and taken to Dawson County. His body was found in Dawson County. He'd been shot twice in the back and once in the head. There was no indication of sexual molestation. It was not a typical child murder, and a lot of people thought Levi's murderer was taking aim at his family."

Levi's bike was found first, and soon the area where the bike was found was filled with well-meaning volunteers, as well as reserve and regular law enforcement officers. "Even the investigators trampled over the crime scene," recalls Wewers. "Everyone wanted to help, but because the kidnap scene was contaminated, we could never determine exactly where Levi was killed. We couldn't find uncompromised evidence, and Levi's murder was never solved." ...

US Customs Branch Chief Mike Wewers.
Courtesy of Mike Wewers.

PROTECT THE CHAIN OF CUSTODY.

If you can't solve the case, make it possible for someone else to solve it down the road. Protecting evidence includes preserving it properly, documenting where it was extracted, and knowing where it was stored, and by whom, every second after it was collected.

...Hair and carpet fibers were carefully stored and the custody of the evidence was protected for thirty years after Wayne Williams was convicted in the Atlanta child murders case. Williams maintained his innocence, and throughout the years, groups and individuals supported the belief that someone else had murdered nearly thirty Atlanta youths.

Most jurors in Williams's trial had never heard of fiber evidence, and introducing it was tedious. Forensic scientists had found fibers on some of the bodies that could, even in the early eighties, be traced with remarkable accuracy to fibers from Williams's bedroom carpet, his bedspread, a blanket found under his bed, a leather jacket in his closet, and a glove in his station wagon. But in some wild series of coincidences, someone could conceivably have this same combination of fibers on their belongings. The rarity of the carpet tightened the case a little more. The carpet was manufactured only briefly and had limited distribution. But it was impossible to prove that the carpet fibers had definitely come from Williams's house and not one of a handful of other houses in the area that had the same carpet.

Dog hairs were found on some of the bodies, and comparisons under a microscope showed that the hairs could have come from the Williamses' family dog.

On February 13, 1981, the body of eleven-year-old Patrick Baltazar was found at the bottom of a wooded slope behind an office park. Forensic pathologists found fibers and dog hairs on Patrick and on his clothing. But they also found two human scalp hairs inside Patrick's shirt.

In 1981, scientists could say only that the human hairs came from an African American and were similar to those of Wayne Williams. He could not be excluded as the killer, but the evidence wasn't strong enough to say, without question, that he had murdered Patrick. But the hairs were carefully stored for thirty years, their custody guarded, then resubmitted for testing in 2010.

This time, the results were more conclusive, excluding 98 percent of the world's population. Because the hairs were incomplete, only mitochondrial DNA analysis, which traces the maternal line, was possible. Only with nucleic DNA testing, which includes the paternal line, could the results have been 100 percent conclusive.

But the results were powerful enough to silence many of Williams's supporters, and the testing was possible because two hairs had been carefully stored and fiercely protected for three decades.

"The chain of custody of evidence is crucial," stresses Greg Smith. "It's attacked countless times in court. Departments need strict policies for protecting evidence. They need a system to impound and maintain evidence for generations. Metro-Dade has very strict policies in place regarding property and evidence. We have a huge warehouse—a city block long—and the safeguards are stringent.

"When I was a young homicide detective, we were zeroing in on a suspect and we needed a girl as a witness. They arrested her for driving on a suspended license and found cocaine in her possession. We confiscated it, and I locked it in my sergeant's desk over the weekend, assuming he'd impound it on Monday. Needless to say, I found myself in trouble on Monday."

FOLLOW THE EVIDENCE, NOT A THEORY.

Clay Bryant says, "When a lead investigator goes to a crime scene, one of the most heinous things to do is walk in and say, 'I've got this thing figured out.' After that, you just work to prove your theory. Then all you look at is what goes in concert with what you think happened.

"You have to remain open-minded and follow the evidence where it leads. You have to eliminate every suspect. You can't go halfway down the road and say you're there, because you're not there till the case is solved."

Mike Wewers agrees. "When nine-year-old Jimmy Ryce was kidnapped at gunpoint a quarter of a mile from his home in Redlands, Florida, on September 11, 1995, one of our Customs employees ended up being a prime suspect. Ray was a maintenance employee for Customs, and he lived near Jimmy. But ninety sex offenders also lived within ten square miles of Jimmy's home.

"Ray had an interest in law enforcement, and he interjected himself into the investigation. Then one day he called me and said, 'I think I need to talk to an attorney. They have me as the primary suspect in Jimmy's kidnapping.'

"Ray was single, but he didn't have an alternative lifestyle. He was just good to the kids in the neighborhood and police found pictures of him at carnivals and other places with kids. With only those pictures connecting Ray with the kids, they made him a suspect.

"An FBI profiler went to Dade County and agreed with police that Ray was a suspect," says Wewers, "and then everyone turned on him.

"With the focus on Ray, the case might never have been solved. But a lady living nearby owned a nursery. A man named Juan Carlos Chavez worked for her and lived in a mobile home on her property. The lady had reported several items missing, including a handgun, and after Jimmy's disappearance was covered by local media, she became suspicious of Chavez. She let herself into Chavez's mobile home, where she found her handgun and Jimmy's book bag.

"When Chavez was confronted, he readily admitted to stopping Jimmy as he walked the single block from his bus stop to his home, pointing a gun at him, and forcing him into his truck. He said he took Jimmy back to his trailer and sodomized him. About four hours after the kidnapping, a helicopter flew over, searching for Jimmy. Jimmy ran to the door to try to get the helicopter's attention, and Chavez shot him in the back.

"He then dismembered Jimmy's body and placed portions in several large planters on the nursery property.

"But by the time Chavez confessed, Ray's reputation was damaged."

CONDUCT INTERVIEWS AS SOON AFTER THE CRIME AS POSSIBLE.

… That's when "people's memories are sharpest, and they have less time to formulate prepared stories," says Mike Wewers. "I remember going to the Frady family's residence to tell them the sheriff would be coming to talk to them. The family wasn't there. As we were leaving, we saw the father walking down the road, and I suggested that we talk to him while he and his wife were separated. My supervisor said no. Then, before he could be interviewed, the father took off for three weeks. He came back lawyered up."

DO A STRONG INITIAL INTERVIEW, INCLUDING GOOD NOTES.

No investigator wants a case to go cold. But if that happens, you want to be sure you've left a clear story for the next investigator who picks up the file.

"People sometimes laugh about the paperwork federal investigators create," says FBI Special Agent (ret) Art Krinsky, "but there's a reason for it. Another agent can pick up the case at any time and start where you left off.

"The most important things we did in the FBI were to do good initial interviews, turn out a thorough report, analyze information, and keep good records. Good report-writing skills are crucial."

IDENTIFY AND INTERVIEW WITNESSES.

Some witnesses will be present when the police arrive at the initial crime scene. Some will come forward when they hear about the crime. Others will simply wait to be identified and then willingly talk with investigators. And some will deliberately evade law enforcement because they have criminal records themselves, they're in the country illegally, or they're afraid of the perpetrator.

Finding every crucial witness requires time, skill, creativity, and perseverance. The motto used by many law enforcement agencies can pertain to witnesses as well as suspects: "He escapes who is not pursued."

Art Krinsky's FBI training taught him the importance of doing the best interview possible. "You may get one bite at the apple, so do a good interview. Build rapport so you can go back to the person you interview. You get some information out of fear, but you won't be able to go back.

"Don't have the attitude that every person you interview is a bad guy, a loser. Put the person at ease. In new law enforcement, there's a fear factor. Everyone's afraid they're being videotaped or recorded, so don't have a cuff 'em and stuff 'em attitude.

"An interview can lead to other interviews, so build rapport. Try to get information on other criminal activity the person knows about.

"A good investigator is constantly scanning for information, looking at the person as a potential informant."

And good investigators listen more than they talk. "I once worked for someone who checked interview transcripts to see who did the most talking," says retired investigator Dan Tholson. "She said that the interviewer's portion of the transcript should be very small and the person being interviewed should do most of the talking. The interviewer's job is to keep the interviewee talking."

IDENTIFY AND INTERROGATE SUSPECTS.

Suspects will surface through basic questioning: Did the victim have any known enemies? What was the victim's relationship with her ex-husband? Had anyone threatened or stalked the victim?

Sometimes suspects simply hang around crime scenes, grave sites, and other key locations. "Someone looking in the window like a curious bystander when police arrive at a crime scene may be sent on their way," says Troy Armstrong, "and they may later be the prime suspect." Good investigators keep their eyes open, looking not only for crime-scene items that appear out of place, but also for people who appear out of place.

Interrogating a suspect requires careful planning. "You have to be able to understand the behavior of bad guys and be able to manipulate them. You have to know what they like to eat, what they read, everything about them," says Joe Kennedy.

"Use photos of the victim," says Kennedy, "not necessarily crime-scene photos, just everyday photos. You'll learn a lot from a suspect's body language. They either want to relive the crime or they want to suppress it. Either way, you're likely to get a strong reaction.

"Another lost art is charts and graphs. Technology is great, but it can also hamper detectives. People have stopped plotting where various witnesses say they were and at what times. Sometimes a visual, like a timeline, shows what you don't get by just listening."

FIND A SAFE PLACE TO INTERROGATE THE SUSPECT.

Kennedy makes sure the suspect feels safe during an interrogation because there's more likelihood of gaining a confession. And no matter how much physical evidence and how many eyewitnesses you have, a confession can avoid costly trials and painful courtroom experiences for families.

"I usually interrogate by a lake, ocean, or picnic area," says Kennedy. "I act more like a pastor than a cop."

"Get rid of the gun, get rid of the badge," warns Kennedy. "You'll solve a lot more cases if you do."

GET THE INCRIMINATING STATEMENT.

"If you can tell the person how they did the crime, 99 percent of the time, they'll confess," says Kennedy.

A real interrogation seldom plays out like a television program. An attractive Southern lady can rarely trick a sociopath into admitting guilt. And a tough good-cop/bad-cop duo is not likely to bring a seasoned criminal to tears. While a full-blown confession can be a conviction tied with a big red bow, what most investigators are looking for is a slip of the tongue that leads the suspect to incriminate himself. If that doesn't happen, an investigator can be satisfied with body language or expressions that confirm what he already knows about the suspect's guilt.

An investigator is trolling for evidence of any kind. Unless he uncovers additional evidence, he'll probably have only one chance to face the suspect in an interrogation scenario. A wise investigator plans carefully for this one-time event, using psychology and drama to set the scene. And as much as he may find the crime and the suspect distasteful, he feigns camaraderie and creates a comfortable environment for the suspect. Kennedy has become a master of interrogation, and he discounts no trick, no prop, and no scenario that will move the suspect from a declaration of innocence to some degree of confession. And he relies heavily on *Sherman v. Texas* 1973, which gives investigators the right to use trickery and deceit to gain a confession.

Kennedy uses a healthy combination of left brain/right brain strategies throughout all stages of his investigations. He lays out a meticulous plan and then fleshes it out with innovative methods for obtaining evidence and confessions.

When Kennedy is ready to interrogate a suspect, he takes specific steps to ensure the best possibility of success. He starts by assessing the environment for the interrogation. He considers the suspect's personality and mental state, and then creates an environment that is conducive to obtaining a confession or incriminating statement. He uses props, such as photos of the victim, crime-scene photos, autopsy photos, maps and photographs of the area, and newspaper articles, to force the suspect to relive the crime. He plans a theme, or a direction in which he wants the interrogation to go. "Always blame the victim," says Kennedy. "That gives the suspect a way out."

Kennedy makes sure he knows as much about the suspect as possible before the interrogation. He does surveillance to learn the suspect's habits and personality—where he goes, what he does for relaxation, what books and magazines he reads, what music he likes, the type of clothes he wears, what he likes to eat, drink, and smoke. He watches the suspect's body language and the way he treats others. He gets close enough to hear the suspect's accent and speech pattern, sometimes shopping inconspicuously in the same store.

Then Kennedy creates an interrogation environment where the suspect feels relaxed. And he treats the suspect as the suspect treats others.

Before he begins the interrogation, Kennedy decides which questions to ask and which ones to avoid. He determines stimulators for the suspect—what words, questions, or props will be upsetting, what will evoke remorse, what will make the suspect relive the crime. By the time he begins the interrogation, he knows the suspect's hot buttons and he knows when and if to push them.

He chooses a neutral site for the interrogation and strategically places props in the area to elicit a response from the suspect. He may use audio or video recordings. "I try not to act like the police," says Kennedy. "I want to give the suspect a false sense of security."

He uses a nonconfrontational approach, going around and about the subject of the murder instead of approaching it directly. He's empathetic, sometimes downright sympathetic. The crime is never the suspect's fault. If the victim hadn't said or done certain things, it would not have been necessary to become violent. The actual crime was a spontaneous accident, not a premeditated violent act.

Everything is focused on getting the suspect to confess or give an incriminating statement. Getting the interrogation right is so crucial that Kennedy role-plays or rehearses the interrogation beforehand.

GET FEEDBACK FROM OTHER INVESTIGATORS.

To avoid falling into the trap of following a theory instead of following the truth, ask other investigators for their perspective on the case. Then listen with an open mind.

GET FEEDBACK FROM EVERYDAY PEOPLE
WITH APPROPRIATE PERSPECTIVES.

Kentucky Commonwealth's Attorney David Massamore sometimes uses his parents as a sounding board on older cases. He asks the women in his office for a female perspective.

People of certain occupations can give a perspective about the crime scene, the victim, or the perpetrator that's available only to someone highly familiar with the occupation. For example, in the Jon-Benét Ramsey murder case, as soon as investigators learned that Jon-Benét was a regular on the pageant circuit, it would have been reasonable for them to wonder if someone could have become fixated on the attractive little girl after seeing her compete in pageants. Talking with parents of contestants and directors of pageants could have given them quick answers to questions such as: Who is allowed in the audience at pageants? Are the contestants' performances posted on Web sites? Have any of the girls been stalked or harassed in the past?

GET INFORMATION FROM ANYONE WHO OFFERS IT.

Listen to families. Talk to friends and enemies. Ask business associates and social contacts. Listen to snitches. Consider everyone's information as serious until it's proven otherwise. Get information wherever you can. Then filter it. Put every shred of evidence on trial for its life. If it's strong and accurate and reliable, follow the trail. If it's doubtful, file it away in case new leads develop and shine a brighter light on the evidence or its source.

INVESTIGATE.

In spite of recent technological advancements, investigations still require logic and reasoning. "Bottom line," says Kennedy, "basic investigative techniques don't vary, regardless of the age of a case. You keep turning over rocks until you can say, 'Aha. I know what happened.' They're the same techniques Sherlock Holmes used."

One of the most dangerous things an investigator can do is create a paradigm, to draw a box around a case and say, "This is what happened." When an investigator puts himself into a preconceived box, he'll find himself collecting only the evidence that proves his theory.

An investigation is basically answering the question, "What happened?" Pieces of the answer to that question can come from the victim, from witnesses, from the area where the crime occurred, and from physical evidence, both visible and microscopic.

FOLLOW THE MONEY.

Quite often, money is a motive for murder, so if the victim had money, find out who benefited from the murder. If there's any type of financial relationship between the victim and the suspect, look for reasons the victim's death would have protected the suspect or made it easier to cover up illegal transactions. Look for spouses who begin spending freely right after the funeral. Look for sons paying off their gambling debts and business partners taking Mediterranean cruises.

If the victim or someone in the victim's family owed money, remember that, in some circles, murder is a deterrent for anyone who's considering not paying back a loan.

FOLLOW THE HEART.

If murder doesn't involve money, it probably involves romance. Sometimes it involves both. Look for relationships that seem to spring up quickly after a murder. Is the grieving husband dating his coworker before the flowers have faded on his wife's grave? With both parents brutally murdered, is the underage daughter now free to go to the prom with the boy her parents refused to let her date?

FOLLOW THE MOTIVE, MEANS, AND OPPORTUNITY.

It's what Sherlock Holmes would have done, and it still works.

- Did the suspect have a reason to kill the victim?
- Did he or she have a way—a method—to commit the crime?
- Did he or she have the opportunity?

GET OUT THERE AND KNOCK ON DOORS.

Most investigators agree that no technology or psychology beats shoe leather for solving a case. A good investigator may spend hours reading case files and weeks analyzing evidence, but eventually the investigation comes down to talking to the right people. And the only way to find the right people is to talk to plenty of them.

GET AS MUCH TRAINING AS POSSIBLE.

"Good investigators need good communication skills," says retired police sergeant David Rivers. "They need the ability to talk in the language of the people they're interviewing. They need to listen more than they talk. Too often, investigators interrupt before letting people tell their stories. It's important to get as much training as possible in interviewing techniques, then form your own interview style.

"There's a wealth of information available. Join organizations. Go to classes. Read. Talk to more experienced detectives."

GET ON-THE-JOB TRAINING.

Perhaps the best way to learn basic investigative techniques is to study cold case files. You can learn the same procedures by reading about cases that were solved, but studying cold cases has an added benefit: instead of studying history, you may be making it. That's what happened to Dennis Delano.

When the Buffalo, New York, Police Department was short on training funds, then-auto-theft detective Dennis Delano decided to train himself to work homicide cases by studying cold case files. While on sick leave, he spent countless hours reading files from unsolved homicides. Though unable to close their cases, Delano found that most of the investigators had followed proper procedures. They had simply lacked some piece of the puzzle.

Delano learned more about homicide investigations by studying the old files than he could have learned in a classroom. And his efforts provided a surprising bonus. As he read the old files with hindsight, additional information gained through time, and a realization of new techniques and investigative procedures, Delano realized that many of the cases that were unsolvable thirty, ten, or even five years earlier could now be closed.

As he read the reports, Delano realized that the now-dusty file folders represented victims and families still waiting for justice. The faded report pages described crimes that were still fresh and painful to someone somewhere. He returned to work determined to close as many cold cases as possible.

Delano started working cold cases on his own time. When he was successful, he was allowed to work cold cases full time. His early successes soon evolved into a three-person cold case unit.

USE YOUR INGENUITY.

"You usually need physical evidence or witness testimony to solve a case," says Greg Smith. "It's how you get these things that can be a challenge. You're only limited by your own imagination and the confines of the law."

And sometimes ingenuity can not only track down evidence, but it can even get past the chain-of-custody issue. "If you can locate the victim's DNA on a piece of evidence and prove that the evidence was in the killer's possession at the time of the murder, you have usable evidence, even if the evidence changed hands after the murder," says Joe Kennedy. "New owners couldn't have placed the DNA on the evidence because the victim was already dead when they received it. That's how we were able to use Jean Tahan's blood that we found inside the television Michael Palaan sold soon after the murder." ...

"I had someone in one of my classes," recalls Smith, "who worked for a small department. He had a high-profile case, a good case, and this detective was relentless. He found out the suspect sold his car after the murder. He got an undercover cop to approach the guy who bought the car. It was abandoned, and he bought it 'for parts' for $400. The car became the property of the department and they actually found physical evidence in the car that solved the case."

INVESTIGATE OUTSIDE THE BOX.

Cold cases sometimes require a little extra creativity because traditional methods have already failed, so Joe Kennedy and his team developed some innovative techniques that work well with all cases, but sometimes give a cold case the extra boost it needs.

When Kennedy started the NCIS Cold Case Squad, he visited fifteen cold case squads across the nation, gathering ideas and insights. Then his team put together an outside-the-box plan that fits their abilities and the type of cases they investigate. He combines methodical standard investigation techniques with creativity to form investigative techniques like the following.

- The market survey. Kennedy has used this ruse to obtain DNA on several cases. "We print a short survey about regional shopping," explains Kennedy. "Then we go door-to-door in the suspect's neighborhood, offering to pay people to complete the survey. After they complete it, we tell them—for confidentiality—to place their survey in an envelope and seal it. Then we have the suspect's DNA."
- Community policing. "We use a uniformed officer for this strategy," says Kennedy. "We follow a suspect until he goes inside a store. When he comes out, a police officer approaches him and hands him a survey about how they feel local law enforcement are doing. Then again, for confidentiality, he asks them to seal the survey in an envelope and hand it back."
- The water bottle. "When you know you have a good suspect but you need their DNA to prove it, bring the suspect in for a few questions," says Kennedy. "Turn the heat in the interrogation room to eighty-five, then offer the suspect a bottle of water. Once you have their DNA, you can say, 'I have no idea why they brought you in here. You can go.'"
- The cigarette butt. "We find an attractive female agent to set up a promotional display in a pipe-and-tobacco store frequented by a suspect who smokes," says Kennedy. "She invites the suspect to try a couple of cigarette samples and give her his feedback. Each time he tries a cigarette, she takes it back and offers him a new one. Even if he leaves with one of the cigarettes, you have his DNA on the others.

"You can get a warrant for a suspect's DNA," acknowledges Kennedy, "but then they'll know you're on to them and they may try to flee. These tricks also pay off in the interrogation. They know you've set them up and that puts them off balance."

- The envelope. "We use an older female employee, or even a police officer, for this DNA-grabbing trick. We put a bandage over a good portion of their mouth, only leaving them room to speak. They approach the suspect in a public place and tell him that they have a check they need to send to their son immediately and, with their bandage, they can't lick the envelope. If the suspect agrees to lick the envelope, you have their DNA."

- The mail-in survey. "We send a survey in the mail, offering five dollars if it's returned. The instructions tell the survey taker to place the survey in the self-addressed envelope provided, seal it, and return it. If things go right, the suspect mails us his DNA. If the subject doesn't live alone, of course we take the chance on someone else in the residence completing the survey.

  "You can use tricks like these as probable cause in an affidavit," says Kennedy, "and you're not violating the suspect's rights."

- Utility bills. "Everyone pays bills," says Kennedy, "so we've gone to the utility company and asked them to save the envelope when our suspect paid his bill. Then we get DNA from the envelope. Usually we receive good cooperation from utility companies, but we had one where they were apprehensive about helping us. We just told them to let us know when they took out the trash."

- Trash pull. "We just look through the suspect's trash, searching for Q-tips, dental floss—anything with cells. In one case, we sent dental-floss samples to the suspect and then waited for him to discard the used strands."

- Raffle ticket. "We set up in a public setting—a store or business that the suspect normally frequents—and as the suspect walks by, we offer him a free raffle ticket, telling him it's our last ticket and we want to close up and go home. All he has to do is place one portion of the ticket in an envelope, lick it, and seal it."

- Mail cover reversed. For an actual mail cover, an investigator's agency must submit a request to Postal Inspection. Once you've obtained a mail cover, the post office will provide you with a list of return addresses for mail delivered to the suspect. "When we do a reverse mail cover," explains Kennedy, "we intercept mail that the suspect sends out, usually to obtain DNA. We send them surveys and special offers and offer an incentive for returning an envelope. Or we ask a business that the suspect sends regular payments to if they'll give us the envelope the bill was mailed in."
- Traffic stop. "We use this ruse a lot," says Kennedy. "We get a cop with a button camera to stop the suspect for speeding when they weren't exceeding the speed limit. The suspect's reaction tells us how he responds when he's accused of something he didn't do."
- Barbershop. "We've gone into a barbershop where the suspect was getting a haircut and pretended to be a comb distributor. We ask the suspect to try several combs and keep the one he likes best. We have hair samples on the others."
- Newspaper article. "This ruse works when you have multiple suspects, and it requires help from the local newspaper," says Kennedy. "We ask them to print a dummy paper with a fictitious report that one of the suspects has been arrested and that additional arrests are anticipated. It's even more authentic-looking if the newspaper will continue the article onto another page.

  "We bring in another one of the suspects and lay the paper down in front of them. When they see, in black and white, that one of their partners has confessed, nervous suspects say things like, 'I was there, but I didn't pull the trigger.' We've gotten several confessions with fake newspaper articles."
- Videotapes. "This ruse also requires a case with multiple suspects," says Kennedy. "We strategically bring in all the suspects, and we interview one of them and videotape the interview. We ask questions like 'Is your name John Smith?' and 'Do you live at 121 Maple?'

  "Then we splice the suspect's answers with different questions, such as 'Did you kill Mary Brown?' and 'Was Bill Jones also involved in the murder?' Then we show the doctored videotape to the second suspect, but only for a few seconds so he doesn't have time to evaluate it. You're likely to get a confession. This works well with hardcore criminals and gang members because they pride themselves on loyalty. When they think the other suspect has informed on them, they're ready to talk."

Are these carefully planned and sometimes elaborate strategies worth the time, money, and effort? Ask Verle Hartley's family:

In 1981, Pamela Hartley was a twenty-four-year-old newlywed who sometimes approached friends with an unusual request. She asked if they knew how to hire a hit man.

In 1982, Hartley was a widow with at least $35,000 from life-insurance proceeds, annual veteran's benefits, and free military medical benefits.

Hartley's husband, navy lieutenant Verle Lee Hartley, suffered from severe vomiting, abdominal pain, and diarrhea for five months before his death. Doctors treated the symptoms but were unable to diagnose the problem. Verle was assigned to an aircraft carrier, and when he was on his ship, Hartley sent him his favorite homemade snacks. When his ship docked and he was hospitalized, Hartley continued supplying Verle with the homemade foods he loved. When Verle died on November 18, 1982, during his second hospital stay, an autopsy showed arsenic poisoning. The condition is so rare that doctors failed to diagnose it until it was too late.

Investigators believed that Verle's wife was responsible for his death, but they had no way to prove it, and the case went cold.

Fourteen years later, the Naval Criminal Investigative Service's cold case squad reopened Verle's case. They read through the files and came to the same conclusion as the earlier investigators. The prime suspect was Verle's young widow. Joe Kennedy, who headed the cold case squad, was immediately interested when he read the case.

"I recognized the symptoms," he recalls, "because I'd come across a similar case when I was in college in North Carolina." Blanche Taylor Moore was convicted of killing her former boyfriend, and suspected of killing her first husband and attempting to kill her current husband, all with an ant killer with a heavy concentration of arsenic.

Kennedy remembered that the investigators had done an excellent job of pulling together a case, and he patterned his investigation after the Moore case.

First, Kennedy and his team learned all they could about Hartley. They discovered that, at the time of Verle's death, Hartley worked on a wildlife preserve in South Carolina and had access to arsenic, which the preserve used to eliminate deer when they became too plentiful. They questioned Hartley's friends, and with the passage of time, they were ready to admit that she had asked more than once about hiring a hit man.

But Kennedy didn't feel the evidence was strong enough for a conviction. So the cold case squad set out to get a confession, using what Kennedy calls one of the best investigative tools: manipulation.

"People don't like to hear the word 'manipulation,'" says Kennedy, "but a good interrogator is a good manipulator. And by manipulation, I mean getting into the minds of suspects, identifying with them, and making them feel comfortable enough to confess.

"We learned a ton about her background," recalls Kennedy of his investigation of Hartley. "Then we chose interrogators who could connect with her."

They rehearsed the interrogation—several times. "You can't just jump into an interrogation," warns Kennedy. "You have to know as much about the suspect as possible. The suspect has to believe that you have the case under control.

"You have to know what makes your suspect tick. You have to be compassionate and connect with them and tell them how they did the crime."

By now, Hartley was thirty-nine and living in Augusta, Georgia. Investigators questioned her for less than half an hour before she confessed, but the brief interview was a culmination of careful planning and tedious preparation.

The investigators sympathized with Hartley. Of course, she was in a predicament. She wanted out of the marriage and didn't know what else to do. Hartley agreed. She said she still loved Verle. In fact, she killed him because she didn't want to hurt his feelings.

Hartley explained that she enjoyed being the wife of a naval officer, and when Verle talked about leaving the military, she didn't want to be married to him any longer. Her mother had been divorced seven times, and Hartley knew how devastating divorce could be.

As the investigators empathized, Hartley explained that she killed Verle so she wouldn't hurt him by asking for a divorce.

The confession saved Verle's family the trauma of having his body exhumed for further tests, which would have been likely had the case gone to trial. And it gave the family a reason for the crime, however twisted. Hartley received a forty-year sentence.

DON'T STOP THE INVESTIGATION AFTER THE ARREST.

Kennedy knows the importance of following through until he has a conviction. Even after the arrest, he monitors the suspect's written, verbal, telephone, and e-mail communications. He watches the movements of people associated with the suspect and individuals the suspect has been in contact with since the arrest. Often information gathered during this time can be crucial to the prosecution's case.

ULTIMATELY RELY ON OLD-FASHIONED INVESTIGATION TECHNIQUES.

Answer the basic reporter's questions: who, what, where, when, and why.

- Who is the victim? Who are the witnesses? Who are the suspects?
- What exactly happened?
- Where did the crime occur? Often it's not the place where the body was found, so locate the actual crime scene quickly so you can secure it before it's compromised.
- When did the crime occur? Witnesses can help establish a time of death, but witnesses can be mistaken or even lying. Food diges-

tion, surveillance cameras, traffic tickets, and phone records can all help narrow the time span when the crime could have occurred.

- Why would someone commit such a crime? Establish a motive and you've formulated a reasonable suspect pool.

In the end, a skilled investigator uses reasoning, logic, and hard work. For all the new technology, these basic skills will never be replaced. Technology can point a finger, but good old gumshoe efforts place the suspect in the lineup. Never underestimate logical thinking. The computer age has made crimes more solvable and taken away a lot of reasonable doubt, but technology is only as good as the investigator using it.

All investigators want to solve the case, and that's a reasonable goal. But whatever the outcome, a good investigator completes whatever portion of the work that's possible at a particular point in time. Ideally, the case is solved. If not, it's preserved.

"The community and family are cleansed by solving a case," says David Massamore. "If your shift is over, you hand the box to the next person."

Chapter 6

Advanced Cold Case Techniques

THE TECHNIQUE DOESN'T CHANGE.
THE ABILITY TO EMPLOY THE TECHNIQUE CHANGES.
—Kentucky Commonwealth's Attorney David Massamore

T he success in closing naval aviator Dana Bartlett's murder case was a catalyst for NCIS to establish the first permanent federal cold case squad, with Special Agent Joe Kennedy at the helm. Kennedy and his team trained at the Federal Law Enforcement Training Center in Brunswick, Georgia, and they visited more than a dozen cities with local cold case squads, gathering information and studying techniques.

Kennedy observes: "With a new case, you respond to the crime scene. With a cold case, you first have to find out exactly what happened." Boiled down to its most basic structure, Kennedy's equation for solving cold cases is how + why = who. He identifies three variables that can be manipulated: time, technology, and tenacity. Time, which was once the enemy of solving a case, may now be an ally. Technological advancements have changed impossible cases into easy solves. And without the time restraints of dealing with new cases and the accompanying media pressure, a cold case investigator is allowed the freedom of exercising a greater degree of tenacity.

NCIS Special Agent Joe Kennedy.
Courtesy of Joe Kennedy.

CREATING A COLD CASE SQUAD

When Kennedy was assigned to lead the nation's first federal cold case squad, he attacked the assignment with enthusiasm. He gleaned techniques and insights from successful cold case squads across the nation and, adding his own ingenuity, created the effective investigative team that has since solved numerous cases that were once classified as unsolvable.

Kennedy considers these factors crucial to a successful cold case squad:

- Having the support of administration
- Having the freedom to work exclusively on cold cases, without being pulled away to work fresh cases
- Having a wide range of flexibility

Sometimes, of course, situations aren't ideal. Pressure to form a cold case unit comes from outside the agency or department, and administration is far from supportive. Cold case investigations must often be carved out of already overloaded schedules. Some investigators must follow stringent department rules about travel, budget, working with the media, and using trickery to obtain a confession. But a cold case squad with all three of these factors has a high potential for success.

A cold case squad can be part time, full time, a one-person endeavor, or an entirely new unit. What all cold case efforts have in common is a desire to make things right.

Says cold case detective Troy Armstrong, "The Charlotte-Mecklenburg Police Department Cold Case Squad began by pulling two veteran detectives—representing 10 percent of the total homicide squad—into a special unit to investigate cold cases. Their squad received resourcing assistance from the FBI's local office and the National Center for Analysis of Violent Crime. Federal involvement allowed the detectives to become part of the Safe Streets Task Force and be deputized as federal agents, giving them jurisdiction outside Mecklenburg County and the State of North Carolina and making it easier for them to handle interstate fugitives.

"And finally, the department implemented a strategy of using volunteers to help detectives review the huge backlog of cold cases."

When Armstrong hurt his shoulder and was put on light duty, he spent his time going through archives and developing a system for reviewing old cases and submitting evidence to the lab for testing. But in 2006, when Armstrong was assigned to work full time leading a cold case unit dealing strictly with sexual-assault cases, he found it difficult to locate a model. Eventually, Armstrong learned that the Metropolitan Police Service in London had a sexual-assault cold case unit, and he borrowed many of his strategies and techniques from them. The department hired back two retired detectives to help Armstrong review cases and evaluate them for solvability.

SET UP A TRIAGE.

To counteract the time and money crunch and get the most success for your efforts, evaluate each case for resolvability before devoting time to it.

Sometimes media pressure or emotions play a part in where a case is placed in triage, but the more objective a cold case squad can be in prioritizing cases, the more cases the squad can bring to a successful close. "At first, the Metro-Dade cold case unit had a 100 percent resolvability success rate," recalls retired cold case investigator Greg Smith. "One hundred percent closure. We didn't investigate cases we couldn't solve. We reviewed a case and if resolvability was slim, we reluctantly moved to a case with a greater chance of closure.

"The more cases we closed, the more attention we received. As we became successful, we were contacted by more homicide detectives, more family and friends, asking us to look at old cases. Soon we were spending a lot of time reviewing cases instead of working them."

But in spite of strict triage, Smith and his cold case unit refused to give up completely on any case. "We had a case where a nineteen-year-old kid who worked in a convenience store was robbed and shot to death," says Smith. "We had no physical evidence and no eyewitnesses. But we always threw that case in whenever media asked for a story. We tried to keep the case open, and we told the family that we didn't want to give them false hope but we wanted them to know that we hadn't forgotten about the case."

But the cases with the lowest chance of resolvability had to be put on the shelf. Some had no physical evidence, no eyewitnesses, and no reasonable suspects. In a few cases, the body had not been identified. "When we started the cold case unit, we had more than a thousand cases, dating back to 1951," says Smith. "We took a hard look at the 1951 case and even featured it in a magazine article, with no response. Unfortunately, it's still on the shelf. You'd like to solve them all, but you can't."

The Charlotte-Mecklenburg Cold Case Unit uses experienced volunteers to screen and evaluate cold cases. After the original volunteers attempted various methods of reviewing cases, they established a review process that's now used by all volunteers and includes recording information under nine headings, which are based on FBI investigative strategies:

1. Victimology
2. Recap of the crime
3. Crime-scene report summary
4. Evidence/property recovered and lab analysis results
5. Witness information and statement recounts
6. Related investigation
7. Medical examiner's report summation
8. Potential suspects
9. Recommended follow-up

"We attempted to form a cold case unit several times," says Detective David Phillips, whose Charlotte-Mecklenburg Cold Case Unit has won several awards, "and each time our investigators were pulled away to work new cases. In 2003, when the current unit was established, the local FBI field office assigned a special agent to the unit. I believe that commitment assisted in solidifying the squad.

"Our review team includes volunteers, retired law enforcement officers, cold case detectives, an FBI special agent, a sergeant, and a unit captain. Both detectives and squad volunteers have participated in teaching blocks of instructions on developing cold cases through the US Department of Justice and the National Institute of Justice during their annual training seminars."

Volunteers often play an integral part in cold case investigations. "Cold case volunteers can review cases individually," explains David Rivers, who led the Metro-Dade Cold Case Squad before retiring. "They can sort and read all the information in the file. But after they write their reviews, they should meet with the rest of the review team.

"About a week before the group meeting, volunteers should send draft reports of each case to the other team members via e-mail. Then the entire team can provide input and discuss each case extensively. All this information should be incorporated into a final report, to be forwarded to the detectives and the captain for assignment and follow-up.

"The Kansas City Cold Case Squad conducts a similar screening process. In their initial screening, they use only members who were not on the original investigative squad. They consider how much information is available on the case, whether suspects were initially identified or could be easily developed, if there's a known motive, how much witness information is available, whether there's physical or circumstantial evidence that could link a potential suspect to the crime scene, if informants have information, what new forensic technologies can be applied, and the impact—both positive and negative—of the passage of time."

However case review is managed, the key is to decide which cases have potential for prosecution. Every case should be studied, but then comes the tough objective classifications. Some cases have a strong possibility of being solved, and others—though just as important and compelling—have a low probability of being solved, no matter how much money and how many hours of work are invested.

"As I've worked with investigators on choosing cold cases," says Kentucky Commonwealth's Attorney David Massamore, "we've found some that would require a thousand or more hours to get them going. Others would be as simple as just sending off a sample for DNA testing.

"One case we looked at was the 1995 murder of Gary Clark," recalls Massamore. "Black-powder hunters found Gary's frozen body in a wooded area about three miles south of Madisonville, with a 9 millimeter bullet hole in his forehead. He'd been shot execution style, and he'd been shot in another location and his body dumped in the woods. The case went cold quickly, and it remained unsolved for the next twelve years."

Massamore and the Kentucky State Police considered victimology. "Gary was forty-two. We believed him to be associated with the drug cartel, but we could make no solid connection. He was an alcoholic, and his blood alcohol level was .3 at the time of his death. For an alcoholic, that was tolerable.

"Gary had told several people that he didn't trust the Mexican cartel, so we asked ourselves, 'Would he have gotten into a truck with them? Would the drug cartel have known the local area well enough to find the place where Gary's body was dumped?'"

The investigators studied the crime-scene photos and police reports. Two cigarettes had been found under Gary's frozen body. One had been smoked and one was unlit. They checked the stored evidence and found the cigarettes carefully preserved. With strong physical evidence, ripe for DNA testing, the case went to the top of the stack. "The case could be reopened by simply running DNA tests that were unavailable at the time of the murder," says Massamore.

The case became a quick solve when the DNA on the smoked cigarette got a hit on CODIS. The DNA belonged to a local drug dealer. Investigators had nearly ruled out drug dealers through victimology, but the CODIS hit allowed them to build a quick, strong case.

All cases are important, but some aspects move cases up in priority, thus bumping weaker cases. Troy Armstrong uses these criteria to prioritize cases:

- *Is the case still viable?* If the statute of limitations has run out, a case must go to the bottom of the stack. Though identifying a rapist might bring some peace to the victim, justice cannot be served and the perpetrator can't even be taken off the streets if the statute of limitations has run out. Better to concentrate on cases that can be prosecuted if they're solved.

   "Since rapists tend to strike multiple times, efforts can best be served by finding prosecutable cases and getting rapists off the street before they strike again," says Armstrong. "Fortunately, North Carolina does not have a statute of limitations on felonies. Jurisdictions that do can obtain a John Doe Arrest Warrant on a DNA profile or description before the statute of limitations tolls. It takes time and manpower to keep track of cases approaching their statute of limitations, but it's important to watch these cases carefully."

- *Is the case solvable?* Some cases, no matter how worthy, simply lack evidence and leads. With nowhere to start, it may be best to concentrate on stronger cases, hoping that someday a witness will come forward or new technology will illuminate existing evidence.

- *Are new leads available?* Sometimes looking at a case after the passage of time, motive or method is suddenly clearer. If the grieving spouse married her business partner soon after the case was initially closed or the victim's nephew suddenly started living beyond his means, you have new suspects. If the primary suspect's alibi was a dinner with his spouse and the couple is no longer married, you may have a new lead. If you're contacted by a witness who has decided she's no longer afraid to talk, an entirely new investigation can be opened.
- *Are there original leads that were never followed?* Sometimes when looking through cold case files, an investigator will see the names of one or more suspects with no follow-up interviews indicated. Interview records can be lost, but there's also a good chance that an investigator was pulled off a case before he or she had time to follow up on even the strongest leads.
- *Is there DNA or fingerprint evidence that could not have been tested at the time of the crime?* Primary keys to old cases are modern DNA and fingerprint databases and advanced methods of evaluating such evidence. If evidence from an earlier crime was meticulously preserved, you may have a case that was unsolvable thirty years ago but today can be solved by simply submitting forensic evidence to your nearest crime lab.

Retired FBI profiler Steve Mardigian also looks for solvability and prioritizes cases accordingly:

- *Highest potential.* Cases with the highest potential are those with a strong suspect and physical evidence that new technology will illuminate. If you know the suspect, if you have physical evidence, and if you have new technology, then you have the potential for a quick and accurate solve.
- *High potential.* If no suspect is evident, a case can still have high potential if the physical evidence is preserved. With physical evidence, there's potential for linking someone to the crime. If the suspect has committed other crimes, his or her DNA and finger-

prints have likely been added to national databases. When you input information from your case, you could have an immediate hit.

- *Also high potential.* A case can have high potential when you don't know the suspect and you have no physical evidence, but a witness surfaces with new information. Sometimes witnesses remain silent for decades before their consciences start nagging, their relationships with suspects change, or they find out they're dying and they want to set things right. Whatever the cause, consider it a windfall. One new witness can open an entirely new investigation as information dominoes into an entirely new lineup of suspects and evidence.

- *Low potential.* The toughest cases are those that have no suspect, no physical evidence, no new leads, no leads that weren't followed thoroughly the first time, no new witnesses offering new intelligence, and possibly no corpse or no proof of foul play.

- *Also low potential.* Cases that are solely driven by the family's emotion are difficult to solve. Families can be crucial in keeping a case alive, and even in solving it. But often families are subjective. And sometimes victims hid their dark side from their families, or families painted the picture they wanted others to see. When confronted with unpleasant information about the victim, the family may say something like, "Our daughter didn't even have a boyfriend. She certainly wasn't involved in prostitution."

Sometimes a family member comes in with nothing new but a strong desire for closure. The family member may have a theory about what happened, but nothing concrete to back up the theory. If a family has a weak or illogical theory, an investigator's job is to add objectivity and to get the family's theory into a law enforcement framework. A good investigator branches out beyond the family, getting a holistic view of the victim. A family can add crucial information, but an investigator must add objectivity.

Joe Kennedy uses these criteria to screen cases for solvability:

- Has the death been ruled a definite homicide?
- Can the crime scene still be located?
- Has the victim been identified?
- Is there significant physical evidence that can identify a suspect?
- Is the evidence still preserved?
- Are there named suspects in the case file?
- Are there witnesses?
- Are there investigative leads documented in the past six months?
- Can any evidence be processed to yield further clues?

After assigning each of the questions a positive or negative number, Kennedy's team tallies the score to arrive at a solvability rating. They attach a fact sheet to each file, listing the solvability and the who-what-where-when-how of the case. The fact sheets become their triage.

A pattern exists in all these prioritizing methods. An experienced investigator takes an objective look at the strengths of a case before deciding where to place it in triage. If cases are triaged according to

NCIS Special Agent Joe Kennedy with Colonel Pacia of Philippines National Police.
Courtesy of Joe Kennedy.

emotional appeal, promises to families, or political or media pressure, fewer cases will be solved. To accomplish the most good with their time, professionals must take a tough, practical approach to prioritizing cases.

That certainly doesn't exclude an investigator from putting extra time into cases with which he or she feels a personal connection. It simply means maintaining a healthy, realistic balance and possibly allotting personal hours to a case the investigator is passionate about. Many important cold cases have been solved by dedicated investigators on their own time.

CONTACT THE VICTIM OR THE VICTIM'S FAMILY.

When you reopen a case, how do you go about contacting the victim or the victim's family? Investigators differ widely in their approach to when and how to involve a victim or family member. Some cold case detectives contact the family early in the investigation to gain support and cooperation, being careful not to make promises that they can solve the case. Others feel that the family has already been given too much false hope, and they wait until they have at least some positive results before contacting them. And most investigators vary their approach to fit the unique circumstances of the case, having no hard-and-fast rule, but considering all aspects of the case before deciding when to talk to the victim's family.

But at some time, the family will be brought into the case, and an investigator must handle the meeting with sensitivity. While the crime may have occurred decades ago, without closure, the victim's family may respond as though it happened last week. Emotions may be higher than the investigator expected. Or the family may have forced themselves to block out the crime, and they may actually have difficulty remembering details. In either scenario, bringing up the crime may be extremely painful to the family and difficult for the investigator.

Troy Armstrong, who deals with sexual-assault cases, tries not to involve victims or their families until he has tangible and encouraging news. "I don't contact a victim unless I have something to tell them.

There's no reason to bring up a case unless there's something positive happening. If I know I have a case and can make an arrest, I contact the victim by phone. I introduce myself and keep it low-key.

"I say something like, 'I have a cold case unit. I was wondering if I could talk to you about your case.' It gives them the chance to say, 'I have a new life and I want to move on'—though no one's said that yet—or 'I can't believe somebody still cares.' Then I tell them we've made some progress and we think we can do something with the case."

Armstrong tries to be low-key and not give victims false hope. "I located one victim who had moved to Miami," says Armstrong. "I told her I was coming to Miami anyway and asked to meet with her. Actually, I was making the trip to Miami just to talk with her.

"By the time we reopen a case, most of the victims have processed what happened. Now they're more angry than afraid. Someone else controlled their lives for years with fear and now it's their turn to be in control."

INVOLVE THE ORIGINAL INVESTIGATORS.

"Some may be a little defensive at first," says Joe Kennedy, "but 100 percent of the time, it's worth it to involve original investigators. Most prior investigators are excellent to work with and bring a lot to the table." Early investigators have insights that could be gained only from studying the original crime scenes. They may also have relationships with the victims' families and with witnesses.

KNOW YOUR TEAM.

"I investigate the agents I'll be working with, too," says Kennedy. He discovers their strengths and weaknesses. Then he fills in the gaps to create a team with all the necessary skills, backgrounds, and expertise needed to solve the case.

REOPEN THE CASE.

Although David Rivers is a sought-after cold case investigations workshop leader who presents the following twelve-step list and other solid guidelines, he admonishes investigators that there is no all-inclusive paradigm that leads from crime to punishment. Rivers observes, "You can't use a checklist. People tend to check off everything and then think they're finished." Most investigators can benefit from a strong starting point, and checklists are great launch tools. But a skilled investigator adapts every plan to the specific case at hand.

Sergeant David Rivers. *Courtesy of David Rivers.*

Following are Rivers's twelve steps for reopening a case:

Step 1

- Review the case carefully.
- Choose a case that can be successfully worked to a positive conclusion.
- Reorganize the file.

    "A crucial step is organizing the case file," agrees Joe Kennedy. "Homicide cops should do that themselves, not their assistants. You become familiar with the case as you organize the case file. Since you didn't work the case, you need the extra step of putting everything into the files in logical order."

- Get over the "Why didn't they do this?" syndrome. You weren't there. You don't know why, and energy spent analyzing the initial investigation can be put to better use on the reinvestigation.

Step 2

- Review all the physical evidence. Have a detailed list so you'll know what you're looking for.
- Go to the property room and verify that the evidence is still in custody.
- View the evidence personally. You know what you're looking for and you'll be the one to someday present the evidence, so this is another job that should be completed by the investigator and not an assistant.
- Remove the evidence from the old bags and check it to be sure it hasn't deteriorated.
- Place the evidence in new bags using methods outlined by your lab or by your department.
- Include the old evidence bags and the old property receipts in the new bags.

Step 3

- Involve the prosecutor. Present your initial findings to the prosecutor and ask whether the case is prosecutable, whether there will be problems with the statute of limitations, and whether the prosecutor is on board with the case.
- Check for changes in the law since the time of the crime. Certain changes, such as in the Miranda and Search and Seizure laws, could affect a present-day prosecution. The prosecutor is your best source for confirming whether changes in the law will affect prosecution.
- Discuss the future prosecution of the case, and work closely with the prosecutor to plan a successful strategy.
- Make your ultimate goal a conviction. The prosecutor will present the solved puzzle to the jury, but it's the investigator who brings the prosecutor the pieces of the puzzle. While preparing the case, constantly ask yourself: "What will the jury need to know? What will the jury need to see? What will the jury need to hear?"

Step 4

- Ask, "Who benefited the most from the victim's death?"
- Check the victim's will. Individuals who profited financially from the victim's death should at least be considered as initial suspects.
- Check property transfers with the clerk's office to see if any of the victim's property changed hands immediately before or after the murder.
- Follow the money.

Step 5

- Redo all background checks. Don't assume that all initial investigative work was done properly or that backgrounds have remained the same over years or decades.
- Rerun criminal histories. Ask, "Who's the bad guy now?" The answer could be much different than it appeared when the crime occurred. Criminals tend to repeat their crimes, and often their crimes escalate. A suspect with no criminal history twenty years ago may have an extensive one now. A Peeping Tom may now be a brutal rapist.

  Running criminal histories is also an important personal safety measure. Your safety is always an issue. Since petty crimes often escalate over time, know the type of present-day people you're dealing with.
- Check computerized public records. A wealth of new information may now be available, and old information will be more accessible.
- Check with Probation and Parole. Personnel can warn you of dangerous witnesses and help you locate suspects.

Step 6

- Review the medical examiner's file.
- After you're familiar with the file, meet with a medical examiner. If the original doctor is available, ask him or her to go over the

file with you. If that isn't possible, ask another doctor to interpret the report and explain anything that's unclear.

- Check medical notes. If the medical notes in the file are technical, ask a medical examiner to go over them with you.
- Confirm the legal identification. Was there an initial positive identification of the victim? If the identification was tentative, work toward a positive confirmation. Without this confirmation, a defense attorney will argue that there's no way to confirm that the defendant is guilty of murdering the victim.

Step 7

- Contact the victim's family. Be prepared to explain the new activity in the case, but do not unjustly raise their hopes.
- Be cautious of family involvement. Each case has different circumstances, and families have different dynamics. Carefully weigh how involved a particular family should be in an investigation.

Step 8

- Begin witness interviews with peripheral individuals. Sometimes peripheral witnesses can shine light on major witnesses, and since you're likely to have only one shot at interviewing witnesses, be as prepared as possible for the most crucial interviews.
- Involve players in the criminal justice system. No investigator should feel it necessary to be skilled in every area. An entire team of professionals may be needed for a successful investigation, and an investigator should call on other experts as often as necessary.
- Keep in mind that the element of surprise is now gone. Once you begin interviews, your suspect will be alerted that the case has been reopened. If the suspect is a flight risk, try to arrange surveillance. However, you can also use initial interviews to your advantage by filtering information back to the suspect, such as that an arrest is imminent, to evoke a reaction or even a confession.

Step 9

- Play on new relationships. Look for love relations that have cooled, business relationships that have gone sour, and once-threatening relationships in which the witness no longer feels afraid. Use these relationship changes to your advantage.
- Compare old and new interviews. You may find discrepancies because viewpoints have changed over time or early reporting was inaccurate, but you may also find that someone who lied has forgotten exactly what he or she said. Witnesses who are lying often have trouble keeping the story the same, and time only makes it more difficult.
- Utilize the involvement of those within the criminal justice system. It's refreshing to watch how smoothly an investigation can run when various law enforcement personnel work well together. Cases have closed because of professional jealousy and competition, but many more have been solved through cooperation.

Step 10

- Conduct subject/suspect interviews. These interviews are key to a conviction and should be as carefully planned and orchestrated as courtroom testimony.
- Obtain a search warrant first, if possible. To obtain a search warrant, you must have probable cause. If you already have probable cause to search someone's house, business, or vehicle before interviewing them, obtain the search warrant and don't tell the suspect your plans until the interview is complete. The suspect will likely be more cooperative in an interview if he or she does not know that you have plans to conduct the search.

  Immediately after an interview in which a suspect felt threatened, he or she may destroy evidence, so be ready to execute the search warrant as quickly as possible. Interview the suspect in as relaxed an atmosphere as possible and tell him or her about the

search warrant after the interview. Then be ready to conduct your
search before evidence can be destroyed.

- Take your best shot. Often you get only one opportunity to interview a witness or suspect, so prepare as if it's your only shot. Plan
questions, bounce ideas off colleagues, role-play the interview,
plan the interview location carefully, and make use of props to
evoke emotion from the suspect.

Step 11

- Use investigative lead sheets. In order to be thorough and comprehensive, investigations must be organized, especially if more
than one investigator is working on a case. Complete a lead sheet
for each lead that should be followed, and make notations on the
sheet as the investigation progresses. It's much easier to check the
overall progress on a case if you have tangible reminders of leads
that have not been followed and the results of those that have.
- Hold team conferences. It's crucial to touch base with everyone
on the team, to compare notes, adjust strategies, and discuss suspects and new leads.
- Don't be swayed by applause or the lack of it. Along the way, a
career often advances and investigators receive letters of com-
mendation and positive media coverage. But sometimes a case is
simply closed quietly and successfully. And occasionally, the press
picks up on a random quote or small event, and applauds a public
official or the wrong law enforcement agency for solving a case. If
the case was solved, dedicated cold case investigators know
they've reached their goal. President Reagan kept a paperweight
on his desk that said, "There's no limit to what a man can do or
where he can go if he doesn't mind who gets the credit." Promotions are helpful. Accolades feel great. But ultimately, investigators are out to get the bad guys.
- Be limited only by your own imagination. Avoid investigative par-
adigms and simply ask yourself, "What do I need to know, and
how can I discover it?" Brainstorm ideas with other investigators,

and don't discount an idea just because it's elaborate, it's out of the ordinary, or no one's tried it before.

Step 12

- Recognize cases you cannot solve alone. A wealth of human resources is available, so don't hesitate to ask for help when you need it.

Joe Kennedy suggests the following steps for reactivating an old case. Not every step will be applicable in every case, but each step should be carefully considered.

Step 1: Conduct an initial review.

Conduct a complete and thorough initial review of the case file.

It's easy to get psyched up about a case and want to jump in quickly. But understanding the original investigation is crucial to developing an effective reinvestigation strategy. Before moving forward, answer these questions:

- Are all the reports, case notes, and related documentation still available? If not, can they be located? The more documentation, the higher a case moves in triage.
- Are witnesses and suspects still alive, and can they be located?
- Are there complete autopsy files and photographs? Are there crime-scene photos? Photos and files are especially important in reconstructing a crime scene that no longer exists.
- What evidence is still maintained by the law enforcement agency?
- What, if any, technological advances can be applied to the investigation?
- Does the case have a "pulse"? "In some cases," explains Kennedy, "you'll clearly see that the investigative steps were accomplished, so it's easy to access the case. Then you can ask yourself: Does your gut impulse lead you to a suspect or potential suspect? Are witnesses still alive? Will new technology help?"

"Take time to evaluate the case," adds Kennedy. "Is it talking to you? As you read some cases, it's crystal clear who did it and why they did it. A case like that has a strong pulse. Twenty to thirty percent of cases have a pulse as soon as you read them.

"During the initial review," warns Kennedy, "you must get past asking yourself, 'Why didn't they do this?' You were not on the original scene and you do not know what happened then. Proceed with what you have."

Step 2: Confirm the existence of evidence.

Once you have established that there is a statutory case, the very next step should be to contact the evidence custodian and make sure the evidence can be located.

Go to the evidence custodian and personally view the evidence. Make absolutely sure that the evidence is in custody before you go any further.

Step 3: Obtain legal guidance.

Perhaps the most important step is to involve a prosecutor as soon as possible after organizing the file and locating the evidence.

Kennedy notes, "It's much easier if the prosecutor is familiar with cold cases and is interested in working them. It's important to connect right away and find out what you need to get a conviction."

Work with the prosecutor to determine the degree of murder and whether any statute of limitations applies. "In some states," says Kennedy, "second-degree murder has a statute of limitations. A suspect can come in, sit down, and tell you that thirty years ago he killed someone in the heat of the moment. Depending on the state you're in, you may be unable to prosecute. The best thing to do is to sit down with the prosecutor immediately and be sure the case can be prosecuted. You may have to be able to prove first-degree murder."

In addition to determining whether the statute of limitations has run out, find out whether any applicable laws have changed. "New

Supreme Court decisions are handed down almost daily," says Kennedy, "and the Innocence Project has caused changes in state laws. What could have been on the books at the time the crime was committed may be much different than today's law."

Things that may not have been legal issues before may now pose problems, such as privileged conversations and spousal relationships.

"Spousal privilege can be tricky," says Kennedy. "If a husband tells his wife he killed the neighbor, he has spousal privilege. But maybe now the couple is divorced. The lawyers have to consider a lot of criteria to determine whether they still have spousal privilege."

It's always best to check with the prosecutor to confirm state and federal laws, as well as gray areas that could go in your favor. In the trial of Russell Winstead, his ex-wife was allowed to testify that he instructed her in how to provide his alibi. The defense argued that the conversation was spousal privilege, but Kentucky Commonwealth's Attorney David Massamore presented the argument that Winstead had not shared personal information with his wife—spousal privilege—but had instead coached her on how to make a public statement. Since the statement was intended to be public record, it was not protected by spousal privilege.

"Things that were legal issues when the crime occurred are probably more complex now," says Kennedy. "For example, when the crime

Kentucky Commonwealth's Attorney David Massamore and Russell Winstead prosecution team

occurred, the suspect may have been approached by the original investigators and he or she invoked the right to silence and counsel. Can the subject be approached now?

"Different jurisdictions will tell you different things. In some cases, you can approach the subject as long as you re-advise them of their rights. If somewhere, years ago, the subject asked for an attorney, you can't badger him into being re-interrogated. Cases have been lost because the confession was thrown out when the subject confessed in the present day after invoking his right to silence and counsel years ago. If the suspect didn't want to speak to someone then, he probably doesn't want to speak to you now. If you pressure, you've violated his rights."

EVALUATE YOUR OWN ABILITIES AS A COLD CASE DETECTIVE.

"Objectivity is important," says Steve Mardigian. "You have to be open-minded when you come back into a case." No one is skilled in all areas, so know your weak areas and fill in the gaps with other personnel and resources."

GATHER THE TEAM.

Some team members are standard on every case. Some are needed because of unusual circumstances in the specific case. And some should be invited to the team to compensate for skills, training, and abilities the core team lacks. Who's involved in a cold case investigation? Joe Kennedy identifies these possible participants.

- *Agents / Detectives*
- *Medical examiner / Coroner*
- *Prosecutor*
- *Crime scene personnel*
- *Forensic laboratory personnel*
- *Forensic psychologist*

Philippine National Police, Manila
(NCIS Special Agent Joe Kennedy in vest).
Courtesy of Joe Kennedy.

- *Psychological profiler*
- *Forensic consultants*
- *Medical professionals*
- *Blood spatter expert*
- *Firearms/ballistics expert*
- *Forensic anthropologist* (to determine whether skeletal remains are human and to determine gender, approximate age, height, race, and even approximate time of death)
- *Forensic botanist* (to determine, through the presence of various pollens, an approximate time of death, whether the body has been moved since death, and where the body has been recently, and to lead investigators to the actual crime scene if the body was moved)
- *Forensic entomologist* (to determine, by the study of insects on the victim's body, the place and time of infliction of wounds)
- *Criminal justice professionals*
- *Forensic odontologist* (to identify bite marks, identify the body through dental records, and estimate the age of skeletal remains)
- *Arson experts/Bomb experts*

- *Forensic artist* (for sketches of a suspect based on witnesses' recollections, for age-progression sketches and busts, and for postmortem reconstruction by sketch or bust)

WORK AS A TEAM.

In 1979, the Miami Metro-Dade County Police Department formed a pending case squad. They pulled three detectives from regular work and gave them an office, desks, and some unsolved case files. Each detective worked on a different case. They soon learned that effective cold case investigations require time, manpower, and teamwork.

In 1983, they tried a team approach when they formed the first cold case squad, headed by Sgt. Jimmy Ratcliff and completed by investigators Greg Smith and John LeClaire. They soon added a fourth investigator, Steve Sessler. "Everyone sees it a different way," says Smith. "The more hands in the pot the better, as long as everything is coordinated. Get everyone involved. Throw 'who gets the credit' out the window. If you have five guys looking at the case individually and then sitting down as a team and discussing it, you get five perspectives. I've become a great believer in the team approach.

"We had the luxury of our department leaving the cold case squad alone unless it had a manpower shortage for a high-profile case," says Smith. "The cold case squads that also have to work fresh cases find the old cases not getting worked. It's tough now, with budget cuts. All departments have a backlog of unsolved cases."

When Metro-Dade's cold case team was formed, its initial assignment was to investigate the murder of nine-year-old Stacy Weinstein. "Stacy stayed home sick," says Smith. "Her mom had just died of cancer, and her dad had lost his job. When her dad had an interview for a job as a butcher and Stacy was sick, he left her just long enough to go to the interview. He came home to find Stacy murdered.

"Good detectives worked the case. They developed suspects, but they couldn't solve the case. Before long, more murders took their time. But politicians and media didn't let go.

"The cold case squad solved the case. Then the department said, 'Let's keep these guys together.'"

WORK WITH OTHER DEPARTMENTS.

…"Law enforcement agencies can be competitive," admits retired investigator Dan Tholson. "They can be sharks in the water and feed on each other and be critical of each other.

"When we were working the 'Lil Miss' case, we experienced a tremendous amount of infighting that took up time and resources that should have been used on the case. The case was high-profile, and everyone wanted to solve it.

"It's OK to help, but criticism is counterproductive. We even had agencies that wouldn't share information." …

Cooperating with other law enforcement agencies is crucial when working cold cases. Because of the time lapse between the crime and the reinvestigation, it's common to discover that the suspect has moved from the area. When time and money make it difficult to travel to the area where the suspect has moved, cold case investigators often rely on local law enforcement to locate, apprehend, and even interrogate suspects.

"In one 1967 case," recalls Greg Smith, "we received a tip that one of the three men who had robbed and murdered an elderly lady was working for a land developer in Las Vegas. We asked the Las Vegas Metro PD to stop him. He was cool when they talked to him, but when they mentioned the murder, he was visibly shaken. We wanted to work out a deal for him to testify against the other two, and the Vegas police talked with him. Within two weeks, he pled guilty and was on board to testify."

INVESTIGATE.

"When you get an active case, compare it to a puzzle," says Troy Armstrong. "Regardless of how illusive the suspect, you pretty much have an entire puzzle. You have responding officers, hospital personnel, the crime scene, the victim—you might be missing your suspect and some MO. But you have a pretty good idea of what happened."

When you have a cold case, finding those puzzle pieces is harder.

"For cold cases, you have to put the puzzle back together with a lot less pieces," says Armstrong. "You may go to the crime scene and discover that it's now a Walmart. The original responding officers and detectives may have retired and died. The ER nurse, doctor, and crime-scene people may be anywhere in the world—who knows. You may or may not have the original notes, photos, or critical pieces of evidence.

"The chain of custody may have gaps, and if you can't show how evidence got to your lab, you have nothing. You can't just go to a courtroom with a piece of bloody cloth with the suspect's DNA. It means nothing unless you have a whole chain of custody throughout the years.

"With homicide cases, you don't have a victim who can be questioned. In sexual-assault cases, when victims die, it's like rolling the dice because the suspect has the right to face his accuser in a court of law.

"You may have the biggest part of your puzzle—the suspect—but you need all the other pieces, too. You have to look at all the witness statements and see if anything was missed. You have to re-interview witnesses. But sometimes people remember things years later that they didn't remember then.

"Look for evidence that wasn't tested with new technology. Look for ways to use up-to-date technology on crime-scene photos. Reinvestigate the case from start to finish. Ask the right questions based on what you know now."

"Sometimes when you re-interview, you hear new information," says David Rivers. "When you ask why witnesses didn't tell the original detective, they'll say, 'They never asked.'"

Greg Smith suggests broadening the list of witnesses: "Deal with families, deal with snitches. Deal with anyone who may have information."

Joe Kennedy divides his investigations into four phases, which he says are "almost backwards" to what's done on a fresh case: (1) analysis, (2) programming, (3) fact finding, and (4) evaluation and verification. Kennedy suggests these investigative steps:

Analyze.

- Organize/reorganize case file. Use this work as an opportunity to become more familiar with the case. An investigator should do this, not an assistant.
- Set up five three-ring binders for the following information:
  + Complete Case File
  + Key Individuals
  + Case Notes
  + Evidentiary Items and Photographs
  + Legal Considerations
- Conduct an analytical review to:
  + Determine the focus of the original investigation.
  + Identify investigative leads.
  + Identify potential witnesses and suspects.
  + Link analyses.
- Make use of visual aids such as:
  + Comparison graphs and charts
  + Timelines
  + Time correlation charts
  + Statement time-check charts
  + Statement and information cross-check charts
- Develop a list of inconsistencies.
  + Place all inconsistencies into a written format.
  + Refocus the investigation based on suspects and witnesses whose information is inconsistent over time or compared with the statements of others.

Program.

- Contact the original investigator.
  + The original investigator will be able to answer existing questions and clarify issues about the first investigation.
  + The original investigator can explain the initial crime theory.
- Reconstruct the crime scene.

- ✦ Update the crime theory, based on new information, technology, and insights.
- ✦ Establish a final crime theory.
- ✦ Study the original crime-scene examination—all photographs, autopsy protocol, interviews, interrogations, statements, police reports, case notes, and any other related documentation.
- ✦ Revisit the crime scene.

Conduct fact finding.

- • Conduct interviews.
  - ✦ Interview all the original investigators, crime-scene technicians, and the medical examiner.
- • Brainstorm.
  - ✦ Consult with forensic experts and psychological experts.
  - ✦ Conduct team conferences to coordinate information.
  - ✦ Conduct brainstorming sessions to be sure every theory, every idea, and every possible approach is considered.
  - ✦ Use the equation: what, how, why, and when = who.
- • Reconstruct the crime.
  - ✦ Role-play situations to see if theories and witness statements are feasible and to practice for key interviews and interrogations.
  - ✦ Use live models or dummies to reconstruct the crime.
  - ✦ Build graphic displays of the reconstruction to help investigators and prosecutors understand the crime and for use during the trial.
  - ✦ Photograph or videotape the reconstruction.

Evaluate and verify.

- • Evaluate the evidence.
  - ✦ Resubmit all evidence to the forensic laboratory for additional examinations and/or reexaminations. Obtain contemporary evaluations for the original analyses.

- ✦ Conduct scientific experiments to prove or disprove theories and to see if things could have happened as a suspect or witness said.
- ✦ Resubmit all evidence to the forensic laboratory for additional examinations and/or reexaminations. Obtain contemporary evaluations for the original analysis.
- Conduct background checks.
  - ✦ Redo all the background checks on suspects, witnesses, and anyone else involved in the case.
  - ✦ Look for criminal arrests.
  - ✦ Identify changes in associations and personal relationships.
  - ✦ Document changing relationships.
- Review the medical evidence.
  - ✦ Carefully review the medical examiner's file and make sure it's complete.
  - ✦ Identify and locate the doctor who did the original autopsy.
  - ✦ Establish contact with the person who made the legal identification of the body.
- Re-contact the victim's family.
  - ✦ Be especially careful at this point not to unjustly raise their hopes.
  - ✦ Explain what has brought about the new, or continuing, interest in the case and try to involve them (unless, of course, they are suspects).

Kennedy also suggests these investigative strategies:

Create a plan of action. Formulate an investigative plan of action, utilizing as many of the following methods as are applicable to the case:

- The element of surprise. This is more crucial in some cases than others, but if the suspect could become violent or flee, plan each action with that in mind.
- Mail cover. To do a mail cover, a law enforcement agency sends a request to Postal Inspection, specifying the felony case they're

working on. The request must be approved by the Postal Inspection Field Office. A mail cover lasts for thirty days, and the investigator receives a report at the end of that time, consisting of the return address information on any mail the suspect received during the time period covered by the mail cover.

- Trash pull. This is usually not a favorite strategy for investigators, but a suspect's trash often contains a great deal of helpful information, including DNA, financial records, and correspondence.
- Telephone records (toll, local, and cellular). Obtaining these records requires a subpoena. You can specify the time segment for which you need records.
- Subpoena. A subpoena is a court order to produce whatever information is stated on the subpoena. Subpoenas are obtained through the prosecutor.
- Forthwith subpoena. This type of subpoena requires that the information be produced immediately. If you're afraid the suspect may skip out or you're afraid a business may shred its evidence, you'll want a forthwith subpoena.
- Cellmate informants. Constitutional rights must be protected, so check with the prosecutor before enlisting cellmate informants.
- Prison escorts, correctional staff (e.g., nurses, counselors). It's also wise to check with the prosecutor before approaching prison staff.
- Psychological profile. The more you know about the suspect, the easier it will be to conduct a successful interrogation. For instance, if you know the suspect harbors extreme guilt for the crime, placing in the room photos of the victim or even a map of the area where the body was dumped could evoke a confession.
- Forensic opinions. Gather information from as many experts as you have available.
- Computer databases. These are discussed in chapter 4.
- Judgments, wills, lawsuits. Probate and civil courts make these records available to the public.
- Case validation. When you feel your case is as strong as you can make it, ask someone outside your department to critique it and provide feedback.

- Sources of information. Verify the sources of all information. Be ready to be challenged in the courtroom.

Conduct interviews and inquiries.

- Begin your interviews with peripheral witnesses and associates. These witnesses may provide information you need for key interviews. However, keep in mind that the early interviews may alert your suspect, so weigh this factor heavily.
- These early peripheral interviews will also give you insight into the changing relationships and associations with the suspect, and this knowledge can help you better prepare for your crucial meeting with the suspect.
- Start thinking of ways you can use the changes in relationships to your advantage.
- Look for changes of all kinds, including changes in daily routines, religious activities, social functions and where they're held, hangouts, hobbies, social services, finances, creditors, jobs, living arrangements, landlords, arrest records, probation/parole officers, relatives, and adversaries.
- Look for changing relationships among friends, associates, coworkers, supervisors, neighbors, current and former cellmates, clubs, organizations, spouses, ex-spouses, girlfriends, and boyfriends.

"The biggest change that occurs over time is in relationships," says Kennedy. "I had a case where a man murdered a girl who lived next door to him. He came home with blood on his jeans, and when his girlfriend saw the blood, he told her he'd been playing with the dog and the dog bit him.

"Police interviewed him about the murder, but they couldn't prove anything. The girlfriend suspected he'd killed the neighbor, but she said nothing.

"Fifteen years later, they interviewed the girlfriend again, but by then she was the ex-girlfriend, and she was willing to talk. She said she didn't want to tell anyone at the time of the murder because she didn't want to believe her boyfriend did it.

"When we interrogated the suspect and told him about the blood on his jeans, he wondered what else we knew."

Conduct major witness interviews.

Before interviewing major witnesses, find out if they are in new situations since the time when the crime occurred. They may be in jail, be on probation, or need help with another aspect of the judicial system. They may have straightened up their lives, gotten married, or become religious. These changes will affect how you conduct the interviews.

Interviews should be accomplished in a strategic and orderly fashion. Plan questions and role-play strategic interviews in advance.

Maintain control and direction of reactivated cases.

- Evaluate the information from the interviews with peripheral and major witnesses.
- Create an active file.
- Create and maintain an investigative lead sheet on each witness.
- Use lead-tracking devices, software, and methods, as well as computer databases. Stay up-to-date on new methods and new resources. An investigator can now accomplish in half an hour's computer time what investigators of past generations would have found impossible or too time-consuming to consider.

Get evidence and statements that will convict.

Many cases go cold because the evidence is all circumstantial. Investigators knew who committed the crimes years, even decades, ago, but they couldn't prove it. A cold case detective may see the suspect's name surfacing over and over in the investigation files and realize how obvious the solution was at the time of the crime. New methods and new technology may finally produce the evidence necessary to close the case. But it's just as likely that the convicting evidence will come from the suspect's own words.

Without solid evidence or powerful witness testimonies, a cold case investigator needs incriminating statements before getting an arrest warrant or taking the case before a grand jury, and getting such statements sometimes requires a creative, nontraditional approach. Joe Kennedy and his team have developed one of the most comprehensive and creative cold case investigation plans in the nation, some of which is outlined in chapter 5. Kennedy summarizes the goal of his work: "Our ultimate goal is the successful prosecution of guilty individuals. Evidence is not always enough. We need to be able to recognize cases that cannot be solved by evidence alone. If witnesses cannot be located or suspects refuse to talk, then go to the next case until something develops or someone decides to talk."

HURRY UP AND WAIT.

The Charlotte (North Carolina) Police Department has a rare and valuable asset: its own DNA lab. "We have the advantage of getting evidence processed quickly," says Troy Armstrong. "Charlotte can put resources immediately on a high-priority case instead of waiting in line behind every other law enforcement agency in the state. Because of this, results can be measured in weeks instead of months. We have four or five analysts at work. Payroll is not cheap, and equipment is not cheap. But when you rely on the state lab, you get in line. Other departments can expect to wait six months for DNA results. They have to prioritize what they send to get their most crucial cases solved.

"Charlotte used federal grant money to start its lab, and now we're using National Institute of Justice grants for personnel and equipment. We see a big difference, and the more success we have with our cases, the more successful other grants for other departments will be."

MAKE USE OF EXPERTS.

An investigator cannot be expected to possess every skill needed for a successful investigation, and good investigators take advantage of their strengths and compensate for areas where they're not as strong. Experts should be chosen to complement the skills of the investigative team and to answer the questions on a specific case. However, some experts, such as profilers, can almost always add strength to an investigation.

Steve Mardigian stresses the benefits of enlisting a profiler. "Profilers look at old cases by going right back to the beginning. They look at the dynamic interaction between the victim and offender and can develop a profile about who the suspect could be. A profile of a suspect is basically a description of the characteristics and traits that suspect is likely to possess.

"But profiling the offender is only one aspect. Profilers deal with the crime scene and crime reconstruction. They look for motivation—was it a stranger or someone the victim knew? When they've gathered that information, they look at how the case could or should be investigated and make recommendations to the investigative team.

"They do crime analysis. They advise on how to engage the media, and they can provide resources for getting information to the public and even to the offender.

"Profilers do indirect assessments of suspects. They look at the suspect's strengths and weaknesses. Once someone's been charged, a profiler can help with how to interview them and how to deal with them in court."

MAKE USE OF MEDIA.

Media can be friend or foe, often depending on the relationship investigators develop. Law enforcement agencies usually have stories of misquotes that gave the public the wrong idea of how an investigation was going, media leaks that caused a suspect to flee, and other struggles with media. But most seasoned investigators agree that it's wise to develop media contacts. Media can help get crucial information to the public and provide positive publicity when cases are solved. And many reporters are eager to help solve a case if they're given the opportunity.

Joe Kennedy appreciates the power of media in cold cases. "First, media that depict a positive image of a police agency are always welcomed by administrators," says Kennedy. "Second, media coverage makes others in society realize that we as police officers do care about the old cases. And finally, media coverage generates calls on other cold cases."

Retired FBI special agent Jim Procopio suggests maintaining a good relationship with media representatives so an investigator can have easy access to past media. "The newspaper morgue—now available in online archives—and television news channel footage can give an investigator a good background on a cold case."

"Media can be helpful if the relationship is good," says Steve Mardigian. "In one case we worked on, a newborn baby girl's body was found floating in a pond in Maryland. She still had the placenta attached. She'd been stabbed to death. The local community rallied. They paid for Baby Jane Doe's funeral.

"As I looked at the case from a profiler's perspective, I suggested a way the media could help us lure the suspect to the grave site. The media were eager to help solve the case and more than willing to help."

PREPARE FOR PROSECUTION.

Kennedy considers the following as he prepares a case for prosecution.

- *Sell the case.* An investigator must sell the case to the prosecutor, and the prosecutor must sell the case to the jury. Look for angles, rationales, timelines, visuals, and testimonies that will help the jury understand what happened, who did it, and why.
- *Make the case visual.* Help jurors understand what happened by showing them crime-scene photos, photos of the victim, weapons, and articles of clothing. Use charts, presentation boards, graphs, slideshow presentations, and timelines. Remember that

jurors must become familiar with the case quickly and without the benefit of a law enforcement or legal background, without the emotional commitment you have made to the case, and without the luxury of having visited the crime scene or having talked one-on-one with witnesses. Try to bring all these aspects to jurors through visual aids.

- *Visit prosecutors outside their work environment.* It's good for an investigator and prosecutor to talk without a mahogany desk between them. Meet over coffee or on the golf course. Develop a relaxed relationship in which you both feel comfortable expressing frustrations and making suggestions. Get to know what approaches are most helpful to a prosecutor—written or verbal reports, phone calls, or e-mails.

  "I always approach the prosecutor outside his office," says Kennedy. "If he plays golf, I go to the pro shop. Or I go to his house. I let the prosecutor know how important the case is. I always present the case with a PowerPoint. Before PowerPoints, I did storyboards. The visual presentation gives the case life. Getting prosecutors involved at the beginning is critical."

- *Anticipate an initial negative response.* Prosecutors are busy with new, high-profile cases and are often getting political pressure to complete these cases quickly. Don't be surprised if a prosecutor is not as excited about your case as you are. It's your job to convince the prosecutor that a cold case not only brings closure to a long-suffering family, but also stops a perpetrator from committing additional crimes and sends a strong and reassuring message to the community that victims are not forgotten and crime—no matter when it occurred—will not be tolerated.

- *Be prepared to gather extra evidence.* "Prosecutors want twice as much evidence in a cold case," says Kennedy. Because jurors may be less confident in the decades-old testimonies of witnesses and may be impressed that the suspect has lived a stellar life since the crime, more evidence may be necessary for them to convict. A prosecutor who requires additional evidence may be wisely anticipating what jurors will need to find the suspect guilty.

- *Take a team approach.* Everyone's goal must be to get a conviction. It's not a time for any individual or agency to shine. Share information. Offer help. Support the team.

TESTIFY FOR THE ENTIRE TEAM.

"Testifying at a cold case trial is much more difficult than testifying at a new murder trial," says David Rivers. "In addition to your own testimony, you have to answer for what the original detectives did or didn't do."

Sometimes while going over old files, an investigator realizes that leads weren't followed and evidence wasn't preserved. But whatever *was* carried out, documented, preserved, or filed away was the catalyst the new investigator needed. And whatever a new investigator finds was there because an investigator placed it there years before.

When a cold case finally goes to trial, a present-day investigator can consider it a privilege and a responsibility to speak not only for the victim but also for the original investigators who, because of time and budget restraints, the information and technology of the time, or a million other reasons, were forced to file the case away. And if a present-day investigator hears a guilty verdict, it might be nice to quietly whisper back through past decades, "We got 'em."

WATCH FOR PITFALLS.

A pit is only dangerous if you fall in. And if you're watching carefully, you can usually avoid the fall. After working dozens of cold cases, Kennedy knows that certain situations can derail an investigation, so he anticipates them and tries to deal with them before they control a case's destiny. Kennedy watches out for the following.

- *Focusing on what you lack can make you afraid to get started.* Few investigators have all the personnel and other resources they need to investigate a case. They simply go with what they have.

Perhaps the greatest handicap is a lack of evidence. "One of the most discouraging things often found lacking in a cold case is usable evidence," says Steve Mardigian. "In a small department, sometimes you find the entire file, including the evidence, in someone's garage. Then you have chain-of-custody issues." But even with compromised or missing evidence, an investigator must focus on the evidence that is available.

- *Believing the case will be too time-consuming can discourage investigators.* Most cases will be time-consuming, whether they're new or old ones, so concentrate on the positives. With old cases, you have the advantage of fewer deadlines and less media pressure. You often have the luxury of stretching out the investigation if necessary. Time is on your side.

  "One way to counteract the feeling that you won't have time to investigate a cold case," says Steve Mardigian, "is to allow cold case investigators to focus only on older, unsolved cases. Don't overload investigators. If they're doing cold cases, they shouldn't have to deal with new cases that come up. They're going to need time and resources." Decisions on time and resources usually begin with an investigator's direct supervisor, so make sure your supervisor is on board and willing to work on your behalf.

- *Facing the "I don't know why they" syndrome wastes energy.* Instead of placing the blame on earlier investigators, why not use that energy to solve the case today?

- *Encountering a prima donna can lower everyone's morale.* Prima donnas can surface from just about any group. Detectives, city officials, the prosecutor's office, family of the victim, witnesses, lab technicians to name a few. But when the case becomes what one person wants or demands, the focus is lost. Prima donnas can be confronted or ignored, but they can't be allowed to change the direction of the investigation.

  And be sure the prima donna is not you. It's easy for investigators to get so involved in cases that they resent the prosecutor or even a family member being interviewed by the media. In order to "own" a case, some investigators keep information close, refusing to update prosecutors or supervisors. When an investigator struggles too hard to own a case, he or she may find that the case becomes something that's not worth owning.

Steve Mardigian warns: "Failing to involve the prosecutor and your management will hinder the investigation. You need support and input from the top down. You may need to know about court decisions, laws at the time the crime was committed, statute of limitation issues, people who invoked their right to an attorney years ago. Prosecutors know these things."

- *Believing that the older the case, the harder it will be to solve can make you feel defeated before you start.* It may or may not be true that an older case will be harder to solve. Evidence may be missing. Witnesses may have died. Crime scenes may no longer exist. But time is now on your side. Technology is leading the way. And changes in relationships can be the boost that turns once-silent witnesses into prosecution allies.

- *Finding that references and points of reference have changed can be discouraging.* Decades ago, it was more tedious to take and develop photos, so cold case investigators sometimes find few if any photos of the neighborhood or shots from various angles of the room where the crime occurred. When the investigator attempts to visit the crime scene, the vacant lot is now a department store or office complex. The investigator can no longer mark off the distance between two points described in the police report, and reenacting the crime with accuracy becomes difficult. In some ways, it's as though the crime never happened, and the investigator has to be sure jurors never have those feelings. It's a challenge to make the crime real and horrific to the jury without tangible points of reference.

  Reconstructing the crime scene and reenacting the crime can put the events back together in a tangible way. Reconstructions can be videotaped to help demonstrate the crime to department superiors, prosecutors, and jurors.

- *Locating witnesses becomes costly.* With an increasingly mobile society, locating witnesses and suspects has become costly in both time and money. Building rapport with law enforcement agencies in other parts of the country can save resources if local officers are willing to locate and possibly interview witnesses and suspects.

LEARN FROM OTHERS.

No one has all the answers, but most of the answers are available to a team player. "Review the process with more than one person," suggests Greg Smith. "The team concept is powerful. If several detectives review the case separately and prepare lead sheets and then sit down together and discuss their findings, you always get different perspectives."

STUDY ORIGINAL REPORTS THOROUGHLY AND CAUTIOUSLY.

Original reports hold powerful information if a present-day investigator knows what to look for and how to filter the information.

Suspects can usually be found in the old case report. "Suspects usually surface early," says Kennedy, "often in the first 10 to 15 percent of the case report pages."

Investigative leads completed within the first thirty days often are the key to solving the case. Even if no one followed up on these leads, the fact that they surfaced quickly could mean they were important. Look first at early leads when revisiting a case.

Suspects may have passed polygraphs. Kennedy doesn't let a passed polygraph sway his decision to list someone as a suspect. In past generations, polygraphs were much more subjective than today's computerized analyses, so it was much easier to fool the box.

Too many investigators may have worked on the original investigation. Especially if a case was high-profile, too many investigators may have created information overload or caused information not to be assimilated and distributed to everyone. When each investigator holds a different piece of the puzzle and those pieces aren't laid on the table and methodically assembled, separate theories can develop, which are supported by weak and incomplete evidence.

Witness testimonies may not have been verified or evaluated. What you read in an original report may simply be one witness's version of what happened. Unless the file contains documentation that the testimony was verified, verify it yourself. Compare the testimony to timelines and to the testimonies of other witnesses. Re-interview the witness. Talk to others with similar knowledge. Evaluate all testimonies, considering the witness's relationship with the victim and the suspect, his or her past history of reliability, and any changes in relationships since the time of the crime.

The original investigators may not have prepared well for witness interviews or for the interrogation of the suspect. In past decades, fewer investigators had formal training. They were less likely to be skilled in psychology or to use profiling to plan an effective interrogation. The most innovative props they may have considered were photos. They would not have rehearsed or role-played the interrogation and may not have planned questions in advance. The lack of planning is not a reflection on the earlier investigators. It's a reflection of the era in which the crime was committed.

Crime-scene photos may contain valuable information that was overlooked. The focus of crime-scene photos is, of course, the victim, but an investigator should also look for items out of place in the background of photos. Ask someone familiar with the crime location if any items are missing or moved. Two glasses on a table may tell you that the victim knew the perpetrator and that they had been having a congenial visit before violence erupted. A cigarette butt in the home of a victim who didn't smoke could tell you that the perpetrator talked with the victim before the crime or lingered afterward. Let the photos take you back to the crime scene that no longer exists, and let them tell you not only about the crime but also about what happened before and after the crime.

A victim's status in society may determine the amount of police resources dedicated to the case. This is often difficult for an investigator to accept. But take advantage of the resources available, and tackle a high-profile case head-on. Media- and politically driven cases are important, too. And the quicker you solve them, the more time you'll have available for other cases. Solving a high-profile case can bring strong media coverage, which can result in more personnel and resources for future cases.

FOLLOW EVERY STEP.

An appliance, toy, or piece of furniture that arrives in a flat box evokes dread for most of us. As we lay a hundred pieces of plastic or wood beside ten plastic bags of screws, nuts, and bolts, all numbered to match the various pieces of wood or plastic, we scramble to the bottom of the box to find the instructions: the steps to assembling the object.

Some of us are more inclined to connect two pieces that obviously go together, even when we haven't reached that stage of construction. When we do that, we often come to a point where we realize that we can't move forward until we take apart the pieces, go back to the instructions, and follow the steps in the order they're given.

It's easy for cold case investigators to read case files and think they see the solution. If they jump into the investigation at that point, they may later discover that the early evidence was unsubstantiated, that the theory falls apart when held up against indisputable evidence, or that a step was left out of the original investigation that, if taken, would have disproved the theory decades ago. It's tempting, when the entire early case is before you, to assume that whatever is written is fact. The only way to be sure of facts is to check them yourself, and that requires starting at the beginning and following every step. If the theory still holds true, you have the evidence you'll need to back it up for a prosecutor or jury. If it no longer holds, you're free to move on and discover the truth.

LOOK FOR EVIDENCE THAT WASN'T TESTED WITH NEW TECHNOLOGY.

Once-useless evidence can now be the key to solving a case, and the solve may be a couple of mouse clicks away. Know what new technology is available. Know who has access to it and how you can gain access. If you're not up-to-date on databases and technological advancements, you could easily file away usable evidence.

The best way to stay current with new investigative tools is to attend workshops, search the Internet, talk with medical examiners and lab technicians, and share ideas with other law enforcement officers. A good rule of thumb is don't return anything to the evidence box untested until you've checked every possible source to see if new testing can be done.

ASK.

"People don't normally come forward," says FBI Special Agent (ret) Art Krinsky. "You have to find them and ask them the right questions.

"Go back and talk to witnesses. Something may have happened in the life of a witness that will make them more willing to talk. Sometimes they've gotten divorced from the suspect. The crime may have bothered them for years. And sometimes they're just waiting to be asked."

WORK FROM THE OUTSIDE TOWARD THE CENTER.

Interview minor witnesses first. Start on the outside of crime-scene photos and work your way to the middle. Eliminate the least likely theories and suspects first. "Sometimes you have to start on the peripheral," explains investigator Clay Bryant. "Innuendos. Urban legends. A lot of things can be totally backward from a fresh case. If you work from the outside going to the center, you'll find people who are finally able to speak."

STUDY RELATIONSHIPS.

Often the key to solving a cold case is identifying relationships that have changed and using these changes to your benefit. Look for relationships that changed after the crime or over time. Did the spouse remarry immediately after the murder? Did the suspect's wife divorce him soon after the crime? "Keep digging up history and look at relationships," suggests retired US Customs Branch Chief Mike Wewers. "Build a dossier on everyone involved in the case."

TAKE ADVANTAGE OF HINDSIGHT.

"One thing that helps in cold cases is for the new investigator to go over every shred of evidence again," says Wewers. "Things can be missed the first time around or, in hindsight, evidence has new meaning. This can be time-consuming, but it often brings results."

And a cold case investigator has the advantage of looking back, not just to the crime but to all the years between the crime and the present day. If similar crimes occurred after the case was filed away, an investigator can look for physical evidence, relationships, and MOs that tie the crimes together. The investigator may find the offender already in prison, just waiting for new charges to be filed against him.

LOOK FOR THEN-AND-NOW DISCREPANCIES.

Some discrepancies nearly always occur between original reports and current interviews. "After doing your own investigation," suggests Wewers, "read the original depositions and compare them with interviews from then and now." Look for discrepancies and follow up on them. Witnesses telling the truth will probably have fewer discrepancies. The truth of a traumatic event is often etched in a person's mind forever. While a witness may not remember the weather, conversations, or clothing from an average day ten years ago, he or she may remember the events of the crime with vivid details.

. . . "I interviewed a man who had watched from his front porch as Gwendolyn Moore was savagely beaten by her husband," recalls Clay Bryant. "He was fifteen at the time, and he reported the beating to his mother. The woman visiting his mother, who later married Ms. Moore's husband, told them that what was happening in the house next door was none of their business."

The boy had watched Ms. Moore get beaten many times before that night, but the next day she was found dead in a well not far from her house, so the day was etched in his mind forever.

"I asked him how he could remember so many details that happened thirty years ago," recalls Bryant. "He told me, 'Clay, you don't understand. I didn't see this thirty years ago. I've seen it every day for thirty years.'" ...

TIME TRAVEL.

"Younger detectives need to understand the language of years gone by," says Joe Kennedy. Yesterday's language can include phrasing, slang, word meanings, and even gestures and body language that have changed over time.

Some products that were standard at the time of the crime are unfamiliar to younger detectives and will also be unfamiliar to younger jurors. It's up to the investigator to research and understand, then be certain the information that goes to the prosecutor includes photos or descriptions of items younger jurors may be unfamiliar with.

Clothing and hairstyles change, too, and these subtle differences can make it difficult for younger jurors to see solving the crime as urgent. Skilled prosecutors can describe victims in terms younger jurors will relate to, portraying them as individuals with the same dreams and same feelings as the jurors.

Reference points change, too. An investigator can no longer visit many crime scenes, and photos may not be available. Recreating a room or area in miniature or in full-size can help investigators and juries understand the logistics of how the crime occurred.

UTILIZE GOVERNMENT ARCHIVES AND HISTORICAL COMMISSIONS.

"If you have a local archive or historical commission, they'll have county records and newspaper articles," says Bryant. "Troup County, Georgia, has one of the best government archives for its size. They keep the history of every aspect of life in the county, and everything's indexed. Every case I've had, I've found everything I needed loaded on the computer. They have legal documents; newspaper articles; birth, marriage, divorce, and death records.

…"Vieng Phovixay was kidnapped in 1987, and her skeletal remains were found in 1989. When I reopened the case in 2005, I found all the information in government archives. And the ladies in charge of the archives found a similar case where the offender didn't kill the victim. We were able to solve Vieng's case based on evidence from the second case that the archives ladies found."…

MAKE USE OF COMPUTERIZED DATABASES.

Probably the greatest advancements in investigative tools, besides DNA, are the databases that share DNA and other forensic evidence. It's crucial for an investigator to stay current on what databases are available.

KNOW THE CASE.

"Technology is great," observes Joe Kennedy, "but you have to know the case file to use it. You have to pay attention to every piece of information that's put before you.

"When you respond to a hot homicide, you get to go to the crime scene and it's in your memory. When you're working a cold case, you lack the ability to appreciate the crime scene, so you have to make the case come alive through analysis, programming, fact finding, verification, and evaluation. In cold cases, you can't take any shortcuts. I go to the library where I'll have no interruptions, and I read every piece of paper in the case file a minimum of seven times. I have to know that file inside and out."

WRITE GOOD REPORTS.

"The facts never change," says David Massamore, "but sometimes you don't know their significance until years later." Including as much information as possible in your reports helps another detective pick up the case a week or ten years from now. Report-writing skills are crucial if a case goes cold, but they're also vital when an investigator turns over the report to the prosecutor.

Reports don't have to be elegantly worded, but they must be thorough and accurate. Classes are frequently available to train investigators on report-writing, and such classes are usually time well spent.

DON'T MINIMIZE THE IMPORTANCE OF SIMPLE LEGWORK.

"Don't exclude anything or anybody," warns Clay Bryant. "You can't count on lab miracles. You may need good old-fashioned investigation. There's no substitution for that. Explore every possibility. You should know everybody who could bring something to the table."

APPRECIATE THE PAST.

Most cold case investigators can tell nightmare stories about compromised evidence and entire files with only one sheet of paper. But for every case that was filed carelessly, dozens were preserved carefully and their reports were written with copious details. Most early investigators did it right. They went beyond the rules and guidelines of their eras and stored garments with no obvious bodily fluids, smeared prints, blurry photos, and tiny blood spatters they could not conceive of someday providing a DNA fingerprint of the assailant.

These early detectives built the foundation for modern-day cold case investigators. The hound dog followed the path until the scent was gone. But he left the trail intact, so another hound dog could pick up the scent long after the first hound's hunting days. And sometimes the second hound can follow the path only so far before he also preserves the trail for some time in the future when the scent will be easier to follow.

WAIT, WHEN THAT'S ALL YOU CAN DO.

... "You have to do everything right at the beginning," says Dan Tholson, "but even then the case doesn't always come together quickly.

"We did it right in the 'Lil Miss' case. We followed thousands of leads, but the suspect never surfaced in any part of the investigation. But we collected plenty of DNA. And fourteen years later, the suspect was sent to the Wyoming State Penitentiary on an unrelated charge. That's when they took a blood sample." ...

DON'T GIVE UP.

"You have to be tenacious," says Bryant. "Cold cases have picked up baggage, so they're seldom quick solves."

When Dennis Delano first started working on cold cases, his colleagues called him a pit bull. "I wouldn't let the case go," explains Delano. "Most cases can be solved. The answer may be right in front of you. Sometimes on the third or fourth read through an old report, it may hit you like a brick."

Chapter 7

Why Colder Can Be Hotter

Time is the enemy in fresh cases, but the ally in cold cases.
—Sgt. David Rivers (ret), Miami Metro-Dade County Police Department

When a cold case is solved, the tendency may be to wonder why a new investigator succeeded where others failed. Sometimes, it's true that a new detective has more determination, more passion for the case, or better investigative skills. But just as often, the answer is simply that new evidence surfaced, witnesses came forward for the first time, or technological advancements made a once-difficult case easier to solve. Sometimes looking back through the lens of time or considering events since the crime occurred gives a new detective a different perspective. For many reasons, cold case detectives often succeed where earlier detectives failed. It's important for these detectives to understand why they've had success over earlier investigators so they can keep a healthy perspective on their work and an appreciation of the original work done on the case.

TIME BECOMES AN ALLY.

"Time can be an effective tool and a cold case investigator's ally," observes retired FBI profiler Steve Mardigian. "Relationships change. Coworkers no longer work together. Cellmates turn on each other. Ex-spouses no longer feel loyalty. Friendships and relationships falter. All that can be helpful to new investigators."

NCIS Special Agent Joe Kennedy agrees. "Time and technology are both on the cold case investigator's side. Concentrate on relationships and friendships. With time, the boyfriend and girlfriend of yesterday may be a thing of the past. What was a friendship in 1970 may have become adversarial by 1990.

"And over time, people tend to talk. Suspects confide in friends with vague comments like, 'The police think I killed her because I was the last person with her that night.'"

FEELINGS CHANGE OVER TIME.

"Sometimes people feel remorse for their crimes," says retired police sergeant David Rivers, "and sometimes they feel less protective of a suspect. Marriages and relationships end, and the 'man or woman scorned' can work to your advantage."

… The murder of Atlanta police officer Sam Guy went cold not because no one knew what happened but because no one was willing to talk in 1975.

But in 1982, FBI Special Agent Art Krinsky got a tip from an informant that Abner Wilkinson and Terry Jackson were the men who gunned down Sam Guy. Krinsky contacted the Atlanta Police Department with the information and also provided it to Sam's son, Sergeant David Guy, who by this time had transferred from the Atlanta Police Department to the newly formed Fulton County Police Department. The two began reinvestigating.

The Fulton County Police Department removed David from the case, stating that they wanted the investigation carried out by someone who was not emotionally involved and that the Atlanta Police Department had primary jurisdiction.

David was off the case. Krinsky transferred to the Cleveland Division of the FBI. And though the identities of the killers remained in the files, the case went cold again.

But through the years, one woman knew the truth: Myrtle Wilkinson. Her husband confessed his part in the murder to his then eighteen-year-old wife. She kept the secret, even after they divorced. But in 1999, when Wilkinson fell behind in his child-support payments, Myrtle called the Atlanta Police Department and told her story. The case was reopened.

When Wilkinson learned that the case was being reinvestigated, he turned himself in. He offered to testify against his partner, Terry Jackson, in exchange for a reduced sentence. He stated that he and Jackson had been heroin addicts in 1975, and the night they robbed the motel, they were desperate for a fix.

The trial had to be postponed for three months because of Jackson's medical problems. When Guy's seventy-five-year-old widow entered the courtroom, the men she saw sitting at the defense table looked like two tired grandfathers.

When the bailiff sent word that the jury had reached a verdict, Mrs. Guy took a nitroglycerine tablet from her purse to counteract the stress from a possible not-guilty verdict. But as she heard the verdict, she placed the tablet back in her purse.

PEOPLE CHANGE OVER TIME.

"People sometimes have genuine religious experiences and want to set things right," says Rivers. "I've had two suspects come in and confess, and they now lead Bible studies in prison."

In 1990, Paul McKeen Jr. owed a $200 debt to a local cocaine dealer. One Friday, the dealer sent three men—Charles Bulloch, Johnny Phillips, and Randy Ragan—to confront McKeen: either pay the debt or suffer the consequences. The men pistol-whipped McKeen, but he could not pay the $200.

Murder victim Paul McKeen Jr.
Courtesy of Clay Bryant.

On Tuesday, they abducted McKeen from a pub in Pine Mountain, Georgia, and drove him to Harris County. He still could not come up with the money, so they beat him to death, drove him to Meriwether County, and threw him from a moving pickup truck.

The next morning, motorists found McKeen on the side of Georgia Highway 190, the apparent victim of a hit-and-run. But the coroner examined McKeen's multiple contusions and quickly ruled his death a homicide.

When the men threw McKeen from the vehicle, Ragan fell out, too. He suffered a broken arm and severely burned skin. Two days later, the men staged an accident to explain the injuries and allow Ragan to seek medical treatment. His injuries were inconsistent with his story, and medical personnel notified police.

Agents from the Georgia Bureau of Investigation interviewed Ragan at the hospital, but they could not link him to McKeen's murder.

The GBI's investigation led them to the pub where McKeen was abducted. The pub had been crowded that night, but the three killers were known for their violent behavior, and witnesses were afraid to speak. With no strong leads, the case went cold.

Years passed. Occasionally, a new lead surfaced, and agents followed it. But investigators never grew close to solving the case.

In 2007, GBI Special Agent Walter Davis, who investigated the original case, told investigator Clay Bryant that he'd always felt bad about leaving the case. He asked if Bryant would reopen it. With clearance from the district attorney's office, Bryant focused on finding the link that would put the three men at the scene of McKeen's death.

Within weeks, Bryant had confessions from all three men, primarily because people were finally willing to talk.

"We just meant to whup that boy," said Bulloch during his confession, "but Johnny knocked his brains out with a tire tool before we could stop him."

"That's the kind of men they were," explains Bryant. "The local people were scared to death of them. They knew at the time what happened. They just wouldn't talk.

"Twenty years later, when I started re-interviewing people, I found that some of the people had changed their lives. They'd become Christians. They led me to people who led me to people, and the case was solved quickly.

"Time can be your friend. People's values and what they're willing to talk about can change for the better over time."

GUILT INCREASES OVER TIME.

Sometimes just a press release on the crime brings back guilty memories, and when the suspect is re-interviewed, he readily confesses. He may even turn himself in when he realizes the investigation has been reopened.

Family, coworkers, and investigators may notice personality and behavior changes over time, and when they're re-interviewed they may quickly respond, "He was never the same after the murder." At that point, just bringing the suspect in for questioning may be enough to trigger a confession.

PEOPLE TALK OVER TIME.

Most people have trouble keeping something as monumental as a murder to themselves. Most perpetrators have told someone over the years. The investigator just has to find these confidants.

FRIENDS BECOME ENEMIES OVER TIME.

… When Julie Love's fiancé, Mark Kaplan, covered Atlanta with posters about Julie's disappearance, he did so in part to appeal to the innate kindness of someone who might have information. Kaplan, a marketer who owned a chain of thirty regional ice cream stores, did what he did best. He created a powerful marketing campaign to find Julie. His goal was to help people understand the loss he and the others who loved Julie were feeling. He told reporters that he believed if anyone had information on Julie and understood their loss, chances were good that the person would be motivated to take action.

Thirteen months after Julie's disappearance, a woman came forward. Not because she understood the family's and friends' loss. Not out of guilt or compassion. Not to give the family closure. Not even for the $20,000 reward. She came forward because now Emmanuel Hammond's violence was directed at her. She came forward for spite.

In August 1989, Hammond attempted to strangle his girlfriend, thirty-four-year-old stripper Janice Weldon, and she had him arrested on aggravated assault charges. While he was in jail on these charges, Weldon told police that Hammond and his cousin Maurice Porter had kidnapped and murdered Julie Love. She agreed, after thirteen months, to cooperate with police, who wired her and monitored her conversations with Porter. After Porter made incriminating statements while talking to Weldon, police arrested him and Hammond.

Porter confessed to rape and to his part in the kidnapping, but he stated that Hammond had actually killed Julie. He led police to skeletal remains and Julie's childhood dentist identified the remains as Julie's. Porter and Weldon testified at Hammond's trial.

Weldon was with Hammond and Porter when they attempted to lure Julie into their car and later forced her in at gunpoint. She was with them when they drove Julie to Grove Park Elementary School and when they searched Julie's purse for money and credit cards. It was Weldon and Porter who took Julie's bank cards to the ATM and attempted to withdraw money while Hammond remained at the school with his sawed-off shotgun pointed at Julie.

When Weldon and Porter returned, saying the PIN Julie had given them was incorrect, Weldon watched as Hammond struck Julie repeatedly with the shotgun. She was there when Porter raped Julie.

Weldon heard Julie plead with Hammond and Porter not to hurt her, saying she had more cards at her apartment complex. She drove with Julie, Hammond, and Porter to Julie's apartment to get more cards, but when they saw the security guard at the entrance of the apartment complex, they left.

It was only at this point that Weldon told Hammond to take her home. Weldon saw Hammond the next morning at 7:00 and asked what happened to Julie. Hammond refused to talk at that time, but he later told Weldon clearly that he shot Julie in the head, dumped her body in a trash pile, and covered her with a board. He gave Weldon a pair of earrings he'd taken off Julie's body and told her to pawn them.

Knowing everything she knew, Weldon continued to live with Hammond and keep the information about Julie's murder to herself—until Hammond became violent with her.

After twenty-six-year-old Hammond was arrested, he offered to pay a fellow inmate $20,000 to kill Weldon. He knew he had a lot to lose by going to trial. His defense counsel would have a difficult time making him appear innocent as the prosecution presented a history of violent behavior.

While still a juvenile, Hammond had kidnapped a woman, driven her to an ATM to withdraw money, and raped her twice. Also while a juvenile, Hammond had kidnapped a man at gunpoint and driven him around in the man's car before releasing him. Later, Hammond kidnapped, raped, and sodomized a woman at gunpoint, then slit her throat, stabbed her five times in the chest, and left her for dead in a pile of trash. He then kidnapped another woman at gunpoint, drove her around in her car, and threatened to rape and kill her. She escaped before he could carry out his threats. Soon after that, he broke into a woman's home while she slept, fondled her, and stole cash and merchandise.

Hammond served less than three-and-a-half years for these crimes. He had been free from custody for seven months when he chose Julie

Love as his sixth victim. But it was his seventh victim, Janice Weldon, who stopped his rampage of violence when lovers became enemies.

While Hammond was in jail awaiting trial, he taunted a guard by grabbing his crotch and describing what he'd done to Julie. Both Porter and Weldon testified against Hammond, and Hammond received a death sentence. He was executed on January 25, 2011.

"Over time, relationships dissolve," says cold case detective Troy Armstrong. "Friends become enemies, and enemies become friends. Someone who was afraid isn't afraid any longer." Sometimes a case just needs time.

With all the excellent and conscientious work on Jean Tahan's murder investigation, the most powerful piece of evidence resulted from a changed relationship. Someone once willing to cover for the killer was no longer willing to do so.

In 1989, twenty-four-year-old Jean Marie Tahan was struck more than fifty times in the head with a tire iron, dumped into a drainage ditch in Jasper County, South Carolina, doused with gasoline, and set afire. Her body could not be identified, and she became another Jane Doe. But local investigators didn't give up. They enlisted forensic specialists to reconstruct Jean's skull and create a sketch of what she may have looked like before she was beaten and burned beyond recognition.

Years passed with no break in the case. Meanwhile, Jean was listed as a missing person.

Then in 1995, investigators matched Jean's picture with the forensic sketch. Though several of Jean's teeth were knocked out during her brutal beating, specialists were able to confirm a match with her dental records. Now Jane Doe became Jean Tahan, and with the identification of the body, a primary suspect surfaced. NCIS was called into the investigation.

Navy petty officer Michael Palaan had fathered Jean's child a year before the murder, but by the time Jean was killed, he had a new girl-friend. NCIS investigators questioned the girlfriend. Once again, time proved to be an ally for the cold case investigators. The girlfriend was now an ex-girlfriend, and she readily admitted that she knew Palaan had killed Jean. In fact, she had helped him clean up the crime scene and dispose of the body. She said they had cleaned blood spatters from the walls and from a television set and repainted the walls. They rented a steam cleaner to remove the blood and brain matter that had seeped into the carpet.

Identifying the body led to a suspect. Time changed a witness's interest in covering for the suspect. And technology confirmed the witness's story. Forensic specialists found blood beneath the paint on the walls, but it had deteriorated too much to provide a positive identification. The television set became a star witness.

Palaan had sold the TV, but agents used apartment rental records to locate it. They opened the back and found Jean's blood. Palaan was arrested in Long Beach, California, two weeks before he was scheduled to retire from the navy.

"The suspect didn't confess," says Kennedy, "but he received a life sentence. We got a conviction purely because of the tenacity of the agents. They reconstructed the crime scene and tracked down the evidence. They recovered enough blood from the apartment to prove that someone died there, so they kept investigating.

"The TV tipped the case. We recreated the crime scene and showed that the blood that entered the TV was clearly caused by high-velocity blood spatter from blunt-force trauma."

Though the chain of custody of the evidence—the television— had been broken, the investigators could prove that the blood spatters had been made while Palaan owned the television. "We proved when Jean died and when Palaan sold the television. Jean's blood had to have been put on the television while it was in Palaan's possession."

PEOPLE ARE LESS FEARFUL OVER TIME.

Witnesses are sometimes less fearful after time has passed. Perpetrators may age enough that they no longer seem threatening. A woman who witnessed a crime at a young age may feel more confident now because she's more mature or because she's now married and lives far away. The only way to know whether witnesses are ready to talk is to re-interview them.

PEOPLE ARE LESS PROTECTIVE OVER TIME.

Someone may have been protecting the perpetrator and no longer has a reason to do so. The guilt of not coming forward or realizing how the victim's family has suffered may now be stronger than the desire to protect a friend or family member.

CRIMINALS CONTINUE TO BE CRIMINALS.

It was the day after Thanksgiving, 1992, and the Gastonia (North Carolina) Eastridge Mall was overflowing with shoppers. As a mother and her two daughters struggled toward the door with a stack of packages, one daughter, sixteen-year-old "Sonya," volunteered to take the packages to her mom's van. She had parked her own car beside her mother's vehicle.

Sonya's mother and sister took their time maneuvering through the crowd toward the van and Sonya hurried through the parking lot with the packages. To a casual observer, she appeared to be alone.

She opened the back of the van and scooted the packages inside. Suddenly, a man shoved her inside the van and slammed the door shut.

The man held a gun on Sonya as he assaulted her. He was still in the van when Sonya's mother and sister approached, and he ran when he saw them. A young businessman standing nearby chased the assailant. When he saw that the assailant had a gun, he decided to follow him in his car. Sonya's sister jumped into the car with him and they headed after the assailant.

Few people had cell phones in 1992, but the businessman had one. As he followed the assailant, Sonya's sister called the police and told them the direction the car was heading and gave descriptions of the assailant and the car and provided the car's license plate number. They finally lost the car, but by then they'd given police enough information to issue a BOLO.

Detectives Phil Firrantello and Cindy Isenhour responded at the scene. After Sonya was taken to the hospital, they obtained statements from several witnesses and hoped that an alert officer would locate the suspect's car.

Just two hours after the assault, another police department notified Gastonia that they'd apprehended the suspect. Firrantello and Isenhour drove the hour and twenty minutes to pick him up.

The suspect had a briefcase in his car when he was apprehended and Firrantello and Isenhour inventoried it: a role of paper towels, duct tape, a lubricant gel, and a pornographic magazine with many of the pages stuck together.

Captain Cindy Isenhour.
Courtesy of Cindy Isenhour.

The assailant was identified as Darryl Lippard of Bakersville. He was married with three young children. He stated that his occupation was Baptist minister.

"When we picked up Lippard," recalls Isenhour, "he was belligerent and hateful. But we thought it was odd that he slept during the entire ride back to Gastonia."

"The case received a lot of media attention," says Isenhour, "and Lippard's photo was on the news. A lady called us from the Greensboro area and said, 'That's the man who raped me.' Her case had never been solved.

"She came to Gastonia and identified Lippard in a photo lineup. I noticed that, though she was older than our victim, the two resembled each other. They both had shoulder-length brown hair.

"She'd also been shopping when Lippard got into her car and forced her to drive to a secluded area, where he raped her. Seeing Lippard's photo was an extremely emotional time for her."

Though the first victim identified Lippard, with the Gastonia case so strong against him, he wasn't charged in the original rape.

The parishioners in Lippard's church in the small mountain town of Bakersville tried to put up their homes as property bond, but since their property was in another county, they weren't able to bail him out. So Lippard languished in jail until the trial. While awaiting trial, Lippard was also charged with attempting to make wine in his jail cell from sweeteners and juices he'd saved.

The trial ended in a hung jury. "I was a younger detective, and that trial taught me to never second-guess a jury," says Isenhour. "Sometimes they make their decisions based on personal bias. The prosecutors talked to the jurors after the trial and learned that one juror refused to find Lippard guilty because they couldn't believe a minister could be guilty of sexual assault.

"Lippard's wife had shoulder-length brown hair, just like the two victims. His wife and their three young sons were visible during the entire first trial," says Isenhour. "A lot of his church members were there, too. They heard from eyewitnesses. They saw the contents of his briefcase. I guess they finally realized that he was guilty because they weren't nearly as supportive during the second trial. I don't recall seeing any of them in the courtroom."

The second trial, held less than a year later, ended in a guilty verdict. When Lippard was sent to prison, his DNA was entered into CODIS.

When Lippard was released from prison, he moved to the greater Charlotte area and found another unsuspecting congregation. He may have harmed more women in the future if it had not been for a cold case reinvestigation.

In 2006, Troy Armstrong opened a nineteen-year-old sexual-assault cold case file, ran the DNA through CODIS, and got a hit. Darryl Lippard had another victim.

Armstrong contacted the Gastonia Police Department and talked about the case. Isenhour told him that Sonya had been devastated by the assault and had been unable to finish high school with her class. She eventually got her degree in night school and then moved away. Armstrong located Sonya, and Isenhour was pleased that with the passing of fifteen years, Sonya was strong enough to participate in another trial for Lippard.

TECHNOLOGY SHEDS NEW LIGHT.

Technological advancements in the past few years have surpassed most 1940s science fiction. DNA and new techniques such as the Integrated Automated Fingerprint Information System (IAFIS) make it possible for cold case detectives to search nationally for perpetrators. Labs can now illuminate fibers under special lights and make instant identifications. Forensic technicians are now as involved in a case as the hands-on investigator.

MEDIA BECOME FRIENDS.

Because they don't often work under the media spotlight, cold case detectives can take their time and approach a case in a more comprehensive way. Then, when they need media coverage to draw out a suspect or announce an indictment, reporters are usually happy to cover the story.

HINDSIGHT CREATES CLEARER VISION.

Ten years after a crime, a detective may look back and see that several cases were related. The first detectives didn't have the benefit of the cases that followed. The first crime in a series is worked as a single case and then sometimes closed. When you can look back and tie cases together, you may have a quick solve.

Hindsight is also an advantage as you look at changing relationships and situations. When suspects know they're under scrutiny, most will wait until the case is closed to remarry, move away, or spend a large amount of money. During a reinvestigation, a detective sometimes learns that these types of changes occurred soon after the case was closed.

PERSPECTIVES BROADEN.

Your fresh perspective can show an entirely new picture of the crime if you don't get caught up in the previous detectives' theories.

"When I open a case file and see a folder of suspects, I put it aside," says Troy Armstrong. "I start from scratch and take my own notes. It's easy for the initial detectives to get tunnel vision. They can form a theory or choose a suspect and refuse to let go. If that happened in the original case, viable suspects may have been ignored. When you're in the middle of tunnel vision, it's hard to get out, so I try not to step into the middle of someone else's tunnel vision.

"The advantage of homicide cases over sexual-assault cases is that you usually have more detectives working on the initial case. When you go back to an old homicide case, nine out of ten times you'll find that the offender is mentioned somewhere in the file. Sometimes it's just a name written in a detective's notes or a criminal history printed out with no notes. The chances of finding the assailant's name in an old sexual-assault file is about fifty-fifty, but those are still pretty good odds."

INTERROGATION TECHNIQUES IMPROVE.

Today's investigators realize that an interrogation is not a lengthy impromptu meeting where the suspect becomes so exhausted and confused that he confesses to anything the investigator suggests. It's a carefully planned and orchestrated meeting, with the investigator in control of the direction of the meeting.

Art Krinsky says, "The purpose isn't to get a confession. Someone will always confess. The purpose of an interview is to get the truth. Richard Jewel would have been exonerated if the interview had continued."

In some agencies, getting at the truth has become more elaborate and creative than a rerun of *Law & Order*. Scriptwriters could learn new tricks from the actual interrogation techniques of today's skilled professionals.

A successful interrogation requires planning, psychology, and even theatrics. Citing *Sherman v. Texas* 1973, Joe Kennedy explains that investigators are now free to get a confession through trickery or deceit. For Kennedy, this freedom often leads to elaborate stories and hoaxes to convince the suspect that he's already been found out, that his partner being questioned in the next room just informed on him, or that a victim he thought he'd killed is actually still alive and has named him as the assailant.

NEW ENERGY COMES TO A CASE.

When an investigator strikes out multiple times and new, simpler-to-solve cases are available, it's easy to shelve a difficult case. Years later, a cold case detective—backed by new technology, more time and resources, and an improved perspective—opens the case and sees possibilities the initial detective could not have seen. The present-day investigator can tackle the case with new energy.

MORE RESOURCES ARE AVAILABLE.

"It's not a matter of being a better detective," acknowledges retired cold case investigator Greg Smith. "You just have more resources and more time. Time is one of the most important resources you have. Unless absolutely necessary, a cold case squad shouldn't be utilized for anything other than cold cases."

Chapter 8

How Cases Ice Over

F ishing in cold water can be difficult, but fishing through solid ice requires more time, more skill, and more resources. It's the same with the degree of coldness in a case.

Most cases go cold when an investigator loses the scent and there's simply no more trail to follow. These cases can easily be picked up later when the scent becomes clearer. But other cases ice over because of certain mind-sets or actions on the part of law enforcement personnel, and picking these cases up later requires more time, more skills, and more resources.

"Cold cases require the most energy and resources," says NCIS Special Agent Joe Kennedy. And those that have iced over need the most time and resources from a cold case investigator. When prioritizing cold cases, it's wise to consider their temperature. And when working a new case, it's prudent to do what you can to keep the temperature as high as possible in case you have to eventually file it away. Some circumstances that cause a case to ice over are beyond an investigator's control, but a prudent investigator guards against avoidable pitfalls.

CASES ICE OVER WHEN EVIDENCE IS NOT PRESERVED.

Evidence can be lost, compromised, carelessly stored, or carelessly preserved. Many cold case detectives have been disheartened to find that none of the evidence listed in the first report is still available. Or they find that the evidence has been stored in an unofficial location. Or it's been stored in such a way that it's now unusable.

"Sometimes," says investigator Clay Bryant, "before law enforcement officers were trained as well, evidence wasn't preserved.

"We had a lady in Meriwether County [Georgia] who was found wandering down the street after she'd been raped. They did a rape kit, which was sent to the crime lab. When the crime lab moved, they sent out a letter saying if evidence wasn't picked up it would be destroyed. The originating investigator never picked it up, so the case now has very little chance of ever being solved.

..."A cold case investigator needs to be able to put his hands on the evidence. In Harris County, they had all of the evidence from Vieng's murder carefully stored and guarded. They even had an eight-foot piece of the tree that she was tied to. When we opened the case in 2005, it was all there. Everything we needed to convict Charles Travis Manley had been preserved....

"Every time you change the man at the head of the dam, it changes the way the water flows," says Bryant. "But there has to be continuity in the way evidence and records are kept and stored, especially in cases that haven't been solved."

"It's easy for evidence to be destroyed," says retired police sergeant David Rivers. "Sometimes it happens through an administrative error. If one of the suspects is convicted, the case can accidentally be closed. If one suspect is convicted, watch that evidence.

"If they need space in the property room, watch the evidence. Evidence can be lost, misfiled, or stored in a place that breaks the chain of custody."

CASES ICE OVER WHEN EVIDENCE IS NOT EVALUATED.

"One of the biggest flaws in homicide investigations and I believe one of the main reasons cases go cold is that detectives don't evaluate what they have at the time of the murder," says Rivers. "Sometimes they're just too busy with other cases, or media pressures pull them away from taking time to evaluate.

"Sometimes, as detectives, we're good at collecting evidence but not evaluating it. Evidence gets stored without being evaluated, and then it's forgotten. You'll find rape kits with vaginal swabs that have never been tested. I'd like to think that all these cases have been cleared from shelves around the country by now, but I'm sure some are still there."

CASES ICE OVER WHEN EVIDENCE DETERIORATES.

When investigating a cold case, it's impossible to predict, or even imagine, the circumstances in which you may find evidence. And even in a murder investigation, people of lower economic status can have less opportunity for justice simply because of their financial circumstances. It may have been, at least in part, Chris Stanback's modest burial that allowed his killer to go free.

It was summer in Muscle Shoals, Alabama, 1994, and the temperatures were predictably in the nineties. Seventeen-year-old Chris Stanback had recently arrived from Idaho to spend the summer with his mother, Teresa, his brother Harold, and his sister Tara. When Chris didn't come home the evening of August 1, his frightened mother reported him missing the next day. His body wasn't found until four sweltering sun-drenched days later when children playing in a wooded area near the Carver Heights housing project smelled and saw something that bore little resemblance to a healthy teen.

Four days in the Alabama heat and humidity made it difficult to identify the body, but word spread quickly in the projects that the body the children had discovered was Chris's.

"The police put up tape and did their best to secure the crime scene," says Mike Wewers, an ALERT volunteer with the National Center for Missing and Exploited Children. But not much was left of Chris's body. "The heat had deteriorated the body, and what was left was blackened."

A crowd of about a hundred people gathered, mostly young boys, and they threw rocks at the police as they tried to remove the body and secure the crime scene. Carver Heights wasn't an area where police were normally welcome. Their presence often meant that they were doing a drug raid. Most of the onlookers resented the police and assumed they'd do nothing to find out who killed a poor black boy.

"They took the body to the morgue, and it remained there from Friday to Monday before an autopsy was performed. All this time, larvae from maggots were creating body heat," says Wewers. About all that was left of the body was a terrible stench.

"The initial autopsy stated that Chris had been beaten and mutilated, and he died of head trauma," says Wewers. "Police had a cause of death, but still no motive or killer. Chris's brother Harold was a known drug dealer, and the brothers bore a strong family resemblance. Some wondered if Chris's murder was a case of mistaken identity.

"That area of Muscle Shoals had major racial tensions at the time," says Wewers, "and a rumor started that the body was burned. Chris was supposedly dating a white girl—the daughter of a high-ranking city employee—and word spread that the police had been instructed to get rid of Chris. And everyone was sure that his 'mutilation' included castration." With the racial tension, the rumors of police involvement, and the community's distrust of law enforcement, few people in Carver Heights expected that Chris's killer would be found.

Time proved them right. Local city officials offered a $10,000 reward for information that would solve Chris's murder, and Chris's uncle promised a matching amount. But even a $20,000 reward generated no viable leads.

The FBI was eventually invited into the investigation on the premise that Chris's murder was a hate crime. The FBI was also unable to solve the case.

Years passed. Chris was forgotten by many, but not by his family.

When they learned that his age classified the crime as a child murder, they contacted the National Center for Missing and Exploited Children.

"The Center sent me to work with two detectives assigned to the case. When we entered the case, we felt that our best hope of getting a conviction was to start at the beginning," explains Wewers. "The medical examiner we worked with was in shock when he saw the initial autopsy report. It was only a page and a half long. We went over the files and re-interviewed witnesses. Our final hope was to do a second autopsy and find evidence overlooked in the first one.

"So in April 2003, we exhumed Chris's body and did a second autopsy. I had a long career in law enforcement, but the day we exhumed Chris's body is one I'll never forget.

"The family was low income, the burial was modest, and the body had not been embalmed. They used a backhoe to try to get the casket out of the vault. The casket was full of water, and it was so heavy that the front of the truck came off the ground as they attempted to pull it out. They had to knock the vault open with sledgehammers. We were dismayed at the condition of the body."

The body had been in the ground for less than ten years. Bodies are exhumed in much older cold cases with more promising results. But poverty was again a handicap for the Stanback family. The vault had leaked. When they opened the casket, they found a body bag. And when they pulled it out, the bag split.

"Chris's remains were just slush from all the water," remembers Wewers. "And the stench was unbearable.

"The chief said to bring everything, casket and all, to his office," says Wewers. "A local funeral home loaned us one of their old hearses, hoping we could bring in the body with as much dignity as possible. They lined it in plywood and heavy black plastic and put the casket into the hearse. A rookie detective volunteered to drive the hearse. He had to wear an oxygen mask.

"As we drove down the road, cars were passing as soon as they had a clear space. The odor was so bad from the hearse and the truck that drivers could smell it inside their cars.

"They unloaded the remains onto a gurney and carried them to the lab. The condition of the body—the four days Chris was outside before his body was discovered, the delay in the first autopsy, the inexpensive vault, and the lack of embalming—made it impossible to gather new evidence in the second autopsy.

"We sent the bones to Kentucky State University to a pathologist, expecting and getting no new information. A local radio station offered us free airtime to remind people of the reward. Several police officers passed polygraphs. We had no witnesses.

"But we had a suspect, and we were pretty sure he was the one. We brought him in and interrogated him, but just as he was about to confess, the police let his mother into the room. She told him not to talk, and that was it. We turned our information over to the FBI and I came home."

The Alabama Bureau of Investigation eventually took charge of Chris's case, and Chris's mother, Teresa, still asks local businesses to display reward posters. And investigators can't help but wonder if Chris's killer may have been convicted if the body had been more carefully preserved.

CASES ICE OVER WHEN INFORMATION IS NOT ENTERED INTO DATABASES.

In 1982, a woman's skeleton was found in Natrona County in Wyoming. "The sheriff's department made plans to submit bone and dental records to NCIC," says Dan Tholson, a retired investigator with the department, "but it was an election year and with people transferring in and out of office, the records were never entered into the system.

"The new officers assumed the information was in the system, and they, along with a mother who thought the remains might belong to her daughter, waited for a hit."

With advanced technology and national databases bringing resolution to many older cases, the mother wondered why the sheriff's department was receiving no information on the 1982 case. In 1994, the mother asked a friend in law enforcement to check NCIC, and that's when the omission was discovered. Soon after entering the data, they got a hit, and the victim was identified. It was not this mother's child, but it was someone's child.

"It's time-consuming to enter data," observes Dan Tholson, "but it's crucial to get physical evidence entered into national databases. If everyone in the next year got all the information into the same systems, we'd have all sorts of hits."

Tholson recalls another case where an investigation was slowed because information wasn't entered into national databases.

..."We had several unsolved murders, which we expected were connected with the 'Lil Miss' case, and we collected data for comparison. In 1986, two years before Lisa Kimmell was murdered, someone abducted a young woman, took her out in the country, and ran over her with a car.

"We didn't get a match with Lisa's case, but in 2005, one of our investigators read the case over a weekend and identified a suspect. The man the investigator thought did the killing was in prison. DNA should have been collected when he entered the prison system, but it wasn't." The prison ran the DNA, and the suspect was confirmed.

CASES ICE OVER WHEN MEMORIES BECOME HAZY.

Time works for you and against you. Getting people to remember things is difficult. Time makes memories crystal clear for some. For others, time fades recollections. "When you go into court after solving a cold case, it's good to hit witnesses with 'What do you remember?'" says retired cold case investigator Greg Smith. "Don't give them anything to trigger their memory.

"We worked the case of a girl who had been gang-raped," recalls Smith. "I asked her to tell what she remembered, and she told the story with amazing detail. Obviously, she'd been remembering it every day. I had her statement from 1971, and it was the same.

"If you use things to trigger witnesses' memories, you'll get hammered in court by the defense. Just let them recall."

CASES ICE OVER WHEN WORK PILES UP.

When investigators work both cold and fresh cases, the workload can be overwhelming, and, naturally, older cases begin to pile up. "The fresh cases have to be worked on," concedes Clay Bryant. "Then the investigator leaves or is transferred, and his stack of cold cases goes to the bottom of someone else's stack. This can happen more than once over time. The person most involved, the one with the most baggage, is gone and the next detective knows nothing about the case.

… "Vieng's case should have been solved in a matter of days. They started off with the wrong premise—that the boyfriend did it. Then the investigator was promoted, and the case went to the bottom of someone else's stack. When GBI agent Gary Rothwell talked to me about the case, he said, 'This case is solvable.'"

CASES ICE OVER WHEN POLICE RECORDS BECOME DIFFICULT TO LOCATE.

When Dennis Delano worked auto-theft cases in Buffalo's major crimes unit, a thirty-something woman came into the station one day and asked about her mother's 1974 unsolved murder. The woman had been nineteen months old when her mother, Barbara Ann Lloyd, was raped and stabbed to death. Delano agreed to give the case another look.

Delano asked more seasoned investigators where old homicide files were kept, and many didn't know. He eventually found some file cabinets in the boiler room. Though it took three weeks of searching through the old cabinets to find the file on the young mother's murder, he only had to study Barbara's case briefly to realize that "this one should have been solved."

Delano opened the dusty file and studied the faded police reports: On March 15, 1974, Galan Lloyd arrived at his Riverside home in Buffalo, New York. He checked his three-year-old son, Joseph, and his nineteen-month-old daughter, Kimberly. Both children were sleeping. He went to the bedroom he shared with his wife, Barbara. Barbara was lying on the bed, but Galan knew immediately that she wasn't sleeping. Blood covered her dress and seeped onto the bedclothes and, as he approached Barbara's body, he could see that she'd been stabbed multiple times—the medical examiner later determined she'd been raped, then stabbed twenty times.

Police immediately focused on Galan, interviewing him for twenty-three hours. His alibi was airtight: he'd been working, and many people saw him throughout his work shift. But police still suspected he had something to do with Barbara's death, and that focus may have kept them from looking seriously at other suspects. Delano studied the evidence and quickly identified other suspects.

He learned to appreciate the need to locate and study cold case evidence. "I later found that a lot of evidence was stored in a woman's cell block in a prison," says Delano. "They built wooden shelves in a catwalk behind the cell block where they stored old evidence. I had to hand-search those shelves and ended up reading a lot of the material. As I worked, I became aware of what evidence was there. When others worked cold cases, I could sometimes help them find evidence."

CASES ICE OVER WHEN PEOPLE MOVE.

Delano read through the reports on Barbara's murder, making notes of everyone who had been questioned and every man whose name was mentioned during the initial investigation. The name Leon "Rusty" Chatt was one that he added to his list for follow-up. Chatt had been married to Barbara's stepsister. Delano asked around and found that Chatt fancied himself a ladies' man and that he'd left town soon after Barbara's murder. It wasn't enough to point a finger at Chatt, but it was certainly enough to point one in his direction.

Delano began following Chatt's thirty-year trail. He'd moved to Georgia shortly after the homicide, he and Barbara's stepsister divorced, and he was arrested for armed robbery and served time. But the trail eventually led back to Buffalo, and Delano found Chatt living just a mile from the original crime scene.

CASES ICE OVER WHEN EVIDENCE BECOMES DIFFICULT TO FIND.

When Delano asked to interview Chatt, he resisted. "That made me suspicious," remembers Delano, "so I started searching for any evidence that might have been preserved from the crime. The concrete room where much of the evidence was stored was so crowded I couldn't walk inside. After filling that room, investigators had stored evidence in various places in the police department. Some was stored in boxes and some in garbage bags. It was all in disarray.

"We had to clean the evidence room before I would find the one box of evidence, but the evidence that had been collected thirty years earlier was a powerful key to solving the case." ...

CASES ICE OVER WHEN EVIDENCE IS USED UP.

"Sometimes you take chances with evidence," says Detective Troy Armstrong. "You use up a small stain. You take the shot. But then the evidence is destroyed by processing. Maybe ten years from now there would be new technology that would be better. You always think you're on the cutting edge of technology, but something new is always in the near future."

CASES ICE OVER WHEN INVESTIGATIONS ARE EXPENSIVE AND COMPLICATED.

... "When we finally found the evidence in the Barbara Ann Lloyd murder case, the box contained the dress Barbara was wearing when she was killed," says Delano. "I sent it to the lab to check for DNA. They told me that DNA tests were so expensive that they could only perform a few. I let the lab technicians decide which tests to run."

A month after submitting the dress for DNA tests, Delano checked on the lab's progress. They had sent the dress back to the administrator's office without testing because the county district attorney hadn't authorized the testing. "That was their rule because of the cost," explains Delano, "but no one told me."

Delano approached the district attorney's office, asking for approval for DNA testing. "I was told that I had enough new cases to work on," recalls Delano. "I asked, 'What makes a new case more important than an old one?' The DA agreed and gave me permission to do the testing."

The efforts proved futile. Because of costs, the lab did only blood typing and found that all the blood on the dress belonged to Barbara.

But the evidence box also contained a small manila envelope. Inside was a business envelope labeled "Hairs."

"I went back to the lab," says Delano. "I handed them the unopened envelope and asked if they could find DNA. Tests showed that the envelope contained three pubic hairs that did not belong to Barbara."

It took nine months to get the DNA report back, and again, the report was discouraging. The hairs had deteriorated, and the lab could isolate only three of the thirteen markers.

"All we knew at that point was that the hairs belonged to an unknown male. It was our job to narrow the search."

Delano approached Barbara's husband for a DNA sample, and he quickly cooperated.

Next Delano attempted to visit Barbara's brother-in-law. Chatt dodged him for several weeks, but Delano finally caught him at home. Chatt refused to let Delano into his house, so the detective interviewed him on the porch.

"I told him I was eliminating suspects," says Delano. "I asked for his DNA so he could be eliminated and we could move on with the investigation and find Barbara's killer. He refused.

"But I got him to sign a statement that he'd never been in Barbara's bedroom and never had sexual relations with her. Eventually, that statement ended up hanging him."

The three markers identified in the DNA testing were present in one out of 100,000 people. It wasn't enough for a solid indictment, but it certainly narrowed the suspect pool. Delano knew he needed Chatt's DNA, so he conducted a trash cover.

He found a razor in Chatt's garbage and obtained DNA from it. Chatt had the three markers. Delano sent Chatt's DNA and the pubic hairs found on Barbara's body to Quantico for additional testing. The match between Chatt's DNA and the hairs boosted the odds to one in 800,000. That was good enough for Delano but not good enough for the DA.

The Buffalo lab had saved enough of the hair samples to do further tests, and their technician got certified in DNA testing. The additional tests boosted the odds to one in several million.

CASES REMAIN ICED OVER WHEN JURIES ARE HESITANT TO CONVICT ON OLD CASES.

Delano interviewed some of Barbara's friends and learned that Chatt had tried to sexually assault five of them. Only one filed a formal complaint, and she dropped the charges before the case went to trial. "In the seventies," explains Delano, "women didn't normally come forward for sexual attacks because they didn't want to go to court and have to tell their stories." But with the passage of time, the women were ready to talk.

Even with strong DNA odds and the women's testimonies, the first trial resulted in a hung jury. Delano and the prosecutors pressed forward, and the second trial resulted in a twenty-five-to-life sentence.

Evidence had been difficult to find. The primary suspect had moved. The cost of the investigation grew daily. Jurors were hesitant to convict someone for a crime that seemed as if it had happened in another lifetime. But the evidence was found. The suspect was located. And twelve peers decided that Chatt had murdered Barbara Ann Lloyd thirty-three years earlier, and her murder was just as heinous as one reported in today's newspaper.

Joe Kennedy believes that a strong jury selection is key to a cold case conviction, and he feels that older jurors are often more concerned for older crimes and have no learning curve when lawyers introduce old evidence. "I encourage prosecutors to select older jury members," says Kennedy. "Younger people seem to feel like the crime is in the past, so who cares now. I've found that older jurors are better for cold cases.

Another advantage is that when older jurors look at crime-scene photos and see things like shag carpeting and a Rolodex, they resonate."

CASES ICE OVER WHEN INVESTIGATORS
FAIL TO KEEP THE FAMILY INVOLVED.

Most investigators find that maintaining a relationship with the family keeps a case from icing over. Violent crimes never go away for the family, and often family members can be the strongest advocates for keeping a case alive. An investigator needs to understand who the victim was, and the family can be an invaluable resource. While a family's viewpoint may be rose-colored, their picture can help the investigator care about the victim. Soon after the crime, an investigator may hear only the positive aspects of who the victim was, but time sometimes makes even family memories more accurate.

CASES ICE OVER WHEN EVIDENCE SIMPLY ISN'T THERE.

"Sometimes suspects weren't entered into databases or they've died," says Troy Armstrong. "They have to be in databases to get a hit. So you have to wait.

"Every once in a while, you have to get humble. With all the new tools, sometimes the leads and the evidence just aren't there."

Chapter 9

Keeping Up the Heat

I magine being a 1960s cutting-edge detective. As you gather evidence and dust for fingerprints at a murder scene, someone suggests that you save a piece of clothing because someday fingerprints will be able to be lifted from fabric. After having blood drops the size of a nickel typed to eliminate certain suspects, a lab technician suggests that you save the tiny spatters of blood barely visible to the naked eye, suggesting that someday those tiny dots of blood will be as accurate as fingerprints in telling you exactly who committed the crime.

If you heard those things in 1960, you'd feel as if you'd stepped into a science fiction movie. But because many investigators saved evidence that seemed, at the time, useless, cold case squads across the country are solving cases today.

We stand on the shoulders of investigators who refused to submit to the limits of technology. When advancements we now take for granted were inconceivable, these investigators simply collected everything. They didn't just follow the rules; they went far beyond what they were required to do.

In many cases, the investigators of past decades knew "who did it." But without sufficient evidence, they reluctantly filed away cases, remembering them from time to time, but—out of necessity—moving on. Many of these investigators didn't live to see enhanced fingerprint techniques, touch DNA, and CODIS. A good investigator may need the satisfaction of solving the crime, but a great investigator cares only that eventually the bad guy is caught.

Great investigators refuse to limit future technology. They collect evidence that has no use to them, hoping someday it will be the key that unlocks the case. Today's great investigators have only to squint into the future to see remarkable advances. Their job is to prepare currently unsolvable cases for their day in court, whenever that day comes.

ADVANCES IN DNA ANALYSIS WILL CONTINUE.

Near-future advances may make solving today's unsolvable cases a simple task. At one time, identifying a criminal by DNA was unimaginable. Yet one day soon, scientists may be able to use DNA to create a visual likeness of the person from which it came.

FACIAL RECOGNITION WILL BE USED TO SOLVE CRIMES.

New technology may soon allow investigators to drastically enhance surveillance videos and create a facial recognition database as accurate as the databases for DNA and fingerprints.

NATIONAL AND INTERNATIONAL DATABASES WILL CONTINUE TO IMPROVE.

States cooperate with each other more now than just a few years ago. They make DMV photos more available. Databases talk to each other better, which increases an investigator's evidence and suspect pools.

Personal information must always be protected and respected, but when someone commits a crime, their information is no longer their own. As new databases are developed and current ones are improved, we may someday catch up with fictional television programs that have led citizens to believe that complicated cases can be solved in under fifty minutes.

INVESTIGATORS WILL MAKE BETTER USE OF EVER-IMPROVING COMPUTER TECHNOLOGY.

Soon after the introduction of the World Wide Web, Google became a verb. Not long after that, grandmothers began Googling to find phone numbers and checking Facebook to locate old high school friends. Even an amateur sleuth can now find an amazing amount of information by simply using search engines such as Google and Bing.

"We now have tire-tread identification based on Google Maps," says retired police sergeant David Rivers.

"We've identified suspects on Facebook," says Detective Troy Armstrong. "We go to a friend of a friend on Facebook and get a suspect's photo. We've done lineups with Facebook photos. You almost feel more like a librarian at times when you're doing all the searches, but many cases are solved by someone working at the computer." As computer technology advances, more and more suspects will be identified by information they posted on social networking sites years earlier.

SATELLITE INFORMATION WILL BE USED MORE EFFECTIVELY.

Using satellite information is routine for Armstrong. "If I want to zero in on a suspect," explains Armstrong, "I do a Google map and find a creek or railroad track near their house."

Retired cold case investigator Greg Smith's team once pursued what they called the Sputnik Lead. "A seven-year-old girl was murdered near Homestead Air Force Base," recalls Smith. "One detective made a suggestion that got a lot of laughter, but we ended up pursuing it. The detective said that maybe the Russians had a satellite up there watching the Air Force base at the time the body was dumped. Maybe they had a photograph.

"We contacted the Russian Embassy and explained that a young girl's body had been dumped just outside Homestead Air Force Base, and we asked if they had a photograph from that night. It took several months to get a response, but the embassy acknowledged that they had Russian satellites photographing the area on that date. Their photographs didn't produce anything to help the case, but they could have. And at least we tried. In the future, this may be a common method of identifying suspects. They may be able to zoom in on a license plate."

ENHANCED FIBER EVIDENCE WILL CLOSE CASES QUICKLY.

The Atlanta child murders was the first major case to use hair fibers as evidence, so this method was foreign to the jury. And the O. J. Simpson case was probably the first time most people heard of DNA, including the jury. In just a few years, such evidence has become accepted and understood by the majority of people. Someday lab technicians may be able to state definitively that a fiber came from a suspect's clothing or household by first identifying the fibers as coming from the same batch of fabric or carpet and then matching minuscule DNA traces found on the fibers.

For future advanced technologies to be applied, the next generation of cold case detectives will need carefully preserved evidence. "If you do your job the right way," says David Rivers, "even if you can't solve the case now, someone else can come along ten or fifteen years later and solve it. But you only get one chance to preserve the case."

SO PROTECT THE CHAIN OF CUSTODY.

Too many cold case investigators find evidence stored in someone's garage or even taken with a detective when he retires. That's a defense attorney's dream but not something you want to tell a prosecutor.

BE FORWARD-THINKING.

Imagine what you would want to have if you were investigating the case thirty years forward. Summarize facts: what was done, what wasn't done, and why. Create an accurate and detailed record of what happened in a case.

Think future, and let the sky be the limit. Save all evidence, and assume that someday someone, somewhere, will somehow extract something important from it. "We can now swab a steering wheel to get DNA," says Greg Smith. "It will get more refined."

PROTECT EVIDENCE FROM BEING DESTROYED.

Laws now protect evidence. "Because of the Innocence Project, it's a felony in North Carolina to destroy evidence, whether there's a conviction or not," says Troy Armstrong. "The law was originally made to protect those in prison, but it also helps cold cases. With the new law, anything with potential for biological evidence can't be destroyed.

"Departments have limited space, so it's understandable that someone's always trying to free up space. The bean counters can't justify having climate-controlled warehouses to store evidence. But it's frustrating in cold cases that once you start looking at horrific cases and believe they're solvable, you find that all the evidence has been destroyed. You have a constant battle between storing evidence and time and money."

KEEP TRACK OF TECHNOLOGICAL ADVANCEMENTS.

What was useless evidence last week may be the key to solving a case today. And what was useful yesterday may be obsolete tomorrow. "Keep track of changes in technology," suggests retired investigator Dan Tholson. "When the FBI changed DNA formats in CODIS, everything had to be redone. If it wasn't, the evidence entered earlier was useless."

Go to conferences. Read books. Do Internet searches. Know the latest techniques and resources. If no one says a resource is possible, ask, "Why not?" As Greg Smith learned with the Sputnik Lead, information may be available for the asking.

PRACTICE THE GOLDEN RULE.

"Document everything," says Tholson. "If someone else has to pick up the investigation later, you don't want them using your scribbled notes." Ask yourself what information you'd need if you were picking up the case and apply the Golden Rule to the investigation: do for the future investigator what you would have liked a past investigator to have done for you.

KNOW WHAT'S AVAILABLE RIGHT NOW.

NCIS Special Agent Joe Kennedy has a healthy respect for basic investigative techniques, but he also uses cutting-edge technology to bring historically successful methods up-to-date. The navy uses technology that only a few years ago would have been considered impossible, and they combine this cutting-edge technology with proven investigative methods. It was a combination of forensic advancements, psychology, and good old-fashioned detective work that helped Kennedy solve the cold case murder of Pamela Kimbrue.

On a foggy March evening in 1982, Radioman Seaman Pamela Kimbrue stopped by the Norfolk (Virginia) Naval Base Communication Center to pick up top-secret documents. For this naval courier working the graveyard shift, transporting important documents was a common assignment. But this night was special. It was Pamela's last night at the base. The next day she was scheduled to ship out to Greece.

Pamela said her good-byes at the Breezy Point Communications Center, then at 3:40 a.m. she stepped outside. In the deep fog, Pamela didn't see the fist that punched her in the mouth. She didn't see the man who dragged her to her Camaro and shoved her in the backseat.

Once inside the car, Pamela saw that her assailant was wearing a forest-green arctic ski mask and makeshift mittens made with stapled pieces of a T-shirt. For 1982 technology, he had covered all his bases by disguising his face and eliminating fingerprints. If Pamela had not pulled off her assailant's ski mask, she may have survived her ordeal. But impulse must have overtaken her. She had to know her attacker.

When she pulled off the mask, she blurted out, "I know you! You're a courier, too!"

Anger and panic gripped the unmasked man. He tied Pamela's hands with a rope, beat her with a glass Tab (soft drink) bottle until she was unconscious, and raped her.

Now the rapist could see only one way out of his escalating situation. His victim had recognized him, so he had to be sure she could never testify against him. He checked Pamela's pulse to be sure her heart was still beating. Then, with Pamela battered but still alive, he fastened a seatbelt around her neck, put her car into gear, and pushed it down a seaplane ramp into ten feet of water in Willoughby Bay.

The next day, when word spread around base that Pamela was missing, witnesses stated that they'd seen headlights disappear over the seawall the night before. Divers searched for Pamela's car, but it had floated farther than estimated, and the car remained submerged for forty-eight hours.

The navy initiated a full-fledged investigation, interviewing more than a thousand people. They collected evidence, including vaginal swabs and thirty-one hairs imbedded in the discarded ski mask. They preserved the documents Pamela had clutched as her assailant dragged her to the car. Though all the items had been submerged in water for two days, navy personnel had the foresight to preserve what was, at the time, worthless evidence.

A group of about a dozen suspects surfaced: boyfriends, former boyfriends, and a young fellow courier whom witnesses claimed was infatuated with Pamela.

Investigators had no physical proof to place any of the suspects with Pamela in her last moments. And with another theory getting attention, it was easy to change focus. In the mid-eighties, it wasn't unusual to identify and capture a navy spy. Since Pamela had been carrying classified information the night she was killed, many people assumed a spy had killed her. When that theory surfaced, investigators thought less and less about boyfriends and coworkers. Eventually the case grew cold.

Nearly thirteen years later, in January 1995, NCIS started its first cold case squad, with Special Agent Joe Kennedy appointed as its supervisor. Pamela's was one of the first cases investigated.

"I read the entire case file," remembers Kennedy, "several times. I studied each crime-scene photo. I examined the evidence to determine if technological advancements could give new meaning to any of it."

Since the top-secret documents had been pushed into the bay with Pamela, Kennedy prioritized the spy theory as low and concentrated instead on people Pamela knew.

Pamela had been hit so hard with the Tab bottle that the insignia from the bottle was pressed into her face. Since most of the damage was done to the right side of Pamela's head, police surmised the killer was left-handed. Kennedy checked navy records and learned that Pamela's fellow courier, Richard Hugh Whittle, was left-handed. The investigative reports quoted witnesses as saying that Whittle had stalked Pamela. One witness said Whittle told him that he was the last person to see Pamela alive. Whittle's interviews included a number of inconsistent statements.

In spite of Pamela's car being submerged in water for two days, advanced technology retrieved multiple fingerprints from the documents and a partial print from the car. They had DNA samples from the vaginal swabs and from hairs caught in the ski mask.

Hindsight shed more light on Whittle's behavior. After Pamela's murder, he was administratively discharged from the navy for drug use. With each bit of information he uncovered, Kennedy became more convinced that Whittle was his prime suspect.

Kennedy traced Whittle to an area just outside Burbank, California, where he was married with a child and working in the film industry providing lighting for a movie studio.

"We were pretty sure Whittle killed her," recalls Kennedy, "but we didn't want to alert him. People we interviewed described him as 'weird,' and he'd been convicted as a Peeping Tom. Considering his psychological state, we thought we might be able to get a full confession if we took our time and handled him just right."

Kennedy asked a forensic psychologist for input before approaching Whittle. The psychologist said that Whittle did not like police and should be approached in a friendly environment away from uniforms, guns, and badges.

Kennedy and his team found out as much about Whittle as they could—what he ate, how he talked, what sort of women he preferred. He seemed to have a fixation on brunettes with long, straight hair, like Pamela's. Kennedy decided to create an environment that might force Whittle to relive Pamela's murder.

"When you can get a guilty person to relive the crime, either through photos or conversation," observes Kennedy, "you're likely to get one of two strong reactions. He'll either demonstrate extreme remorse, or you'll see by his body language that he enjoys reliving the crime."

Kennedy created an elaborate plan to bring back memories of the crime. He enlisted the help of a young female agent who fit Pamela's physical description. They printed a simple five-sentence survey about shopping at the nearby Walmart. The survey included instructions at the bottom of the page: to ensure confidentiality, the person completing the survey should fold the completed survey, insert it in the envelope provided, and seal the envelope.

The undercover agent went door-to-door down Whittle's street, offering to pay residents to take the survey. When she knocked on Whittle's door, he answered. She asked if he'd take the survey, and he agreed. As he was filling it out, she mentioned that she'd just moved to California from Virginia.

The agent watched as Whittle licked the flap and handed the DNA-laden envelope back to her. It seemed as though Whittle was reacting to the agent and her story, so the investigators decided to push a little further.

The undercover agent knocked on Whittle's door again, explaining that she'd locked her keys in her car and asking if she could call a friend to pick her up. Whittle invited her inside, and his wife offered to let the agent stay in their house until her friend arrived. The brunette wife had long, curly hair, but family photos showed that it had been long and straight in the early years of their marriage.

The undercover agent stayed with Whittle and his wife for nearly two hours, talking about Virginia and even getting Whittle to complete a second survey to help her reach her quota. When she left, the agent wrote a phone number on the back of a card and told Whittle and his wife to call her at home if they had questions about the survey. In the next two weeks, Whittle placed fourteen calls to the number, which was answered with a recording.

Kennedy sent the sealed envelopes to the crime lab in Virginia and waited. After three weeks, he received the report he'd expected: Whittle's DNA matched the DNA found on Pamela's body.

"We got an immediate arrest warrant for Whittle," says Kennedy, "but we still wanted a confession."

Kennedy contacted Whittle and told him casually that he was one of several suspects in a cold case investigation, and Kennedy wanted to talk to him to clear him so he could move on. Before their meeting, Kennedy followed Whittle to a nearby Home Depot, staying just out of visual contact but listening to his speech patterns so he could adjust his own speech to Whittle's and make him feel more comfortable.

Kennedy asked Whittle to meet him at a local hotel instead of a police station. He had a Mountain Dew and a Snickers bar—Whittle's favorite snacks—waiting for him. He offered to let him order room service and call his wife. He helped relax Whittle by matching his speech patterns.

Then he described the crime, using all the details the cold case squad had pieced together.

"I've found that if you tell a suspect how he did the crime, he'll confess," says Kennedy. He told Whittle that the killer was left-handed. He told him exactly how the killer dragged Pamela to the car, how she pulled off his ski mask, how the killer beat her with a glass bottle until she was unconscious, and how he raped her. Then he'd rifled through her purse and taken her money.

Kennedy opened the door for a confession by acknowledging that the killer had no choice after Pamela pulled off his ski mask. He *had* to get rid of her. But now they'd recovered hairs from the ski mask and DNA from the body. They would easily identify the killer.

Within seventy-five minutes, Whittle confessed on video. Though he tried to recant his confession, it held. Whittle is now serving a life sentence in the Federal Correctional Complex in California.

Chapter 10

Speaking for the Victims

WHEN I LEARNED THE RAPIST HAD BEEN IDENTIFIED, IT FELT SO GOOD
TO KNOW THAT NO OTHER GIRL WOULD HAVE TO LOSE WHAT I LOST.
—Jessica, a rape victim

W hen a criminal case goes unsolved, does grief eventually end for the family? Does time erase the desire for justice from the gut of the investigator? Does it eliminate the need for the guilty to pay for the crime? Ask the family member if she still remembers. Ask the investigator if he's put the case behind him. Ask the justice system if the case is marked closed.

Only when a case is solved can justice be served and healing begin. Only then does the final chapter begin to be written for victims and their families. Sometimes that final chapter is never written in its entirety. Often it's written slowly. Occasionally it's written with suddenness and finality. But with few exceptions, justice is the ink that writes the final chapter.

JUSTICE FOR GWENDOLYN

..."My earliest memories of my mother and the abuse she took started when I was very small," Gwendolyn Moore's oldest son, Allen Moore, told Detective Clay Bryant thirty-two years after his mother's violent death at the hands of his father, Marshall. "I remember myself and my brother Ricky being in bed one night and listening to the fighting and screaming: my father screaming, hollering, and cussing at the top of his voice; my mother screaming and crying for him not to hit her anymore.

Murder victim Gwendolyn Moore.
Courtesy of Clay Bryant.

"All I could think of doing was to cover my head with my pillow and cry, but the noise was still loud.

"The next morning, when I saw my mother, both her eyes were swollen shut. Her entire face was black and blue. She had dark black and blue bruises all over her body. You could see where some of her hair had been pulled out. Looking on the floor, I seen where her clothes and bra had been literally torn off of her and ripped into pieces. Little did I know that my father's behavior would become a way of life.

"Daddy could always find a reason to beat Momma. If supper was cold, Momma got beat. If supper was wrong, Momma got beat. If Daddy overslept, Momma got beat. If Momma woke him up too early, she got beat. Once I saw Momma get beat for not ironing fast enough to suit him.

"The thing that haunts me to this day is that when Daddy would work himself into a rage with one of us kids, Momma would step in and let him take it out on her to keep him from beating us.

"Daddy never just slapped her or hit her once. He beat her to the ground or until she was out cold. He enjoyed it, and he had kind of a ritual about it. He'd tear her clothes off, I guess so he could see the damage he was doing. Or maybe it was just to degrade her. Then he would hit her with his fists. When she would go down, he'd pick her up by the hair and hit her again.

"Momma wouldn't try to fight back. Sometimes she would beg him to not hit her anymore, but it seemed like that made him even worse."

Allen lived most of his childhood dreading his own beatings and trying to protect his mother and younger brothers from theirs. Allen would have had another sibling, but in 1960, when his mother was twenty years old and pregnant with her third child, his father claimed the baby wasn't his and beat Gwendolyn and stomped on her stomach until she started to miscarry. Then he left her lying on the floor, bleeding and crying. He did not return until long after the baby was buried in a donated coffin. No birth certificate was filed, and the baby's gender was not even recorded.

The doctor who treated Gwendolyn told her mother that if she continued to be subjected to such violent beatings, she'd have permanent brain damage. In 1960, a doctor had no obligation to do or say more.

Allen knew that his father was capable of the worst kind of violence imaginable. He beat Allen with a pipe, a bicycle chain, a tree limb, a wrench, a shoe, and his fists. When Allen was ten, his father told him to wait in the car with his little brother, Ricky, while he ran an errand. Ricky got bored and began playing with the blinker switch. It broke in his hand. The boys were terrified as they anticipated their father's reaction. Allen was afraid his father would kill Ricky, so he took the blame for breaking the switch.

When they got home, Marshall jumped from the car, stomped to the front porch, and grabbed a heavy chain made of cut and twisted steel wire, barbed where the links were joined. He beat Allen until he was unconscious. When Allen woke up, his wounds had begun scabbing and his body was stuck to the sheets of his bed. Gwendolyn quietly slipped into the dark room, cautioning Allen to be quiet so Daddy didn't hear. She soaked his scabs with a warm cloth to soften the blood that was stuck to the sheets, whispering comforting words as she soothed his open sores.

Suddenly, they heard Marshall's slurred voice: "I'm sick of you goin' behind my back with these young'uns." Marshall grabbed Gwendolyn by the hair and pummeled her with his fists until she collapsed on the floor. He ripped off her clothing and beat her repeatedly, pulling her up by her hair and beating her in the face until her eyes swelled shut.

After Marshall's rage subsided, he left the room. Allen rushed to his mother to make sure she was alive. She was, but she remained unconscious for three days.

When Gwendolyn regained consciousness, she attempted to file for divorce. A lawyer in Carroll County helped her prepare the paperwork, but he told her she had to take it back to DeKalb County to file. For reasons only Gwendolyn knew, she instead returned to the house where her sons looked to her for security and her husband savagely beat her.

The beatings continued, and each time Allen wondered if his mother would survive. When finally she didn't, Allen blamed himself.

"The night my mother died, I remember seeing her under the back porch of Mrs. Turner's house. Her face was black and blue. Her eyes was swollen shut and her lips, as well as her left jaw, was really swollen. She asked me not to tell my dad where she was because she was afraid he would kill her and that as soon as she could get to the police and get help she would be back for me and my brothers.

"Since August 4, 1970, I have felt my mother's death was my fault. I didn't want her hurt anymore, so I didn't tell anyone, and I didn't go back to her."

Detective Clay Bryant was a fifteen-year-old kid when Marshall Moore killed Gwendolyn Moore. He lived in the same Georgia town, and he was one of Allen's classmates. He was also the son of the police chief, and on August 4, 1970, he went with his father to investigate a body found in a well.

"The well was on property adjacent to the Turner property, the neighbor whose porch Mrs. Moore usually hid under when her husband beat her," recalls Bryant. "The well had once been curbed to the side of a house with no running water, but the house had burned down years ago. The hand-dug well was uncovered and level with the ground, and its opening was about four feet across.

"I peered down into the well and saw a woman's body, facedown, on her hands and knees. Her head was inside a box, as if the impact had caused a discarded box to topple on top of her. All I could see was her back. She was wearing yellow shorts and a white blouse.

Gwendolyn and Marshall Moore with three oldest sons.
Courtesy of Clay Bryant.

"By now, a small crowd had gathered—twenty or twenty-five neighbors. It was a time before police collected forensic evidence, so the neighbors pressed close to the well, stepping on potential evidence and obliterating footprints and fingerprints.

"The three oldest Moore children stood in a row, like stair steps, away from the rest of the crowd. All three boys were barefoot and wore cut-off jeans and no shirts. They just stared quietly as the rest of us crowded around the well. I don't remember seeing Marshall Moore—Gwendolyn's husband.

"The wrecker arrived a few minutes later, and Larry Webb agreed to be lowered into the well to help bring up the body. Mr. Knight lowered him down on the cable from the wrecker, Webb attached the hook around the body, and Mr. Knight pulled it up.

"When the cable reached the top of the well, the body began spinning. I looked over toward the Moore children. Allen was not quite fourteen. His brothers Ricky and Larry were thirteen and ten. They also had a baby brother, Dean, who was a year old.

"The boys just watched, expressionless. They didn't cry. They didn't look away. They just observed the scene, numb. It was as if Gwendolyn Moore's sons were simply watching the inevitable played out, a scene they'd been expecting all their lives."

Decades passed, but Bryant remembered Gwendolyn's murder. When he had the opportunity to investigate the case after it had iced over for more than thirty years, he went hard after Marshall Moore, pulling together a powerful case against him. Moore claimed his wife had simply fallen into the well, but when Bryant had Gwendolyn's body exhumed, a second examination revealed that Gwendolyn had been strangled.

In 1970, Marshall Moore was questioned but never indicted. At that time, the GBI was not the elite crime-fighting organization of today. In 1970, GBI agents were assigned counties, and they basically worked under the direction of the local sheriffs. Understandably, this system resulted in some cases losing momentum for political reasons. Bryant's police chief father suspected Gwendolyn's murder investigation had numerous flaws. "Daddy always believed that the Troup County Sheriff used his influence with the GBI to quietly close Gwendolyn's case—a case that would have created problems for him with the Phenix City Mafia, which was prevalent in the town. When outraged citizens asked about the case, all [Sheriff] Bailey had to say was, 'GBI is handling it.' And GBI did as little or as much as the sheriff told them to do."

Marshall volunteered to take a polygraph, and the sheriff arranged for the test to be administered by the GBI. Marshall passed.

Exhuming Gwendolyn Moore's body.
Courtesy of Clay Bryant.

Murder victim
Gwendolyn Moore's
bones after body
was exhumed.
Courtesy of Clay Bryant.

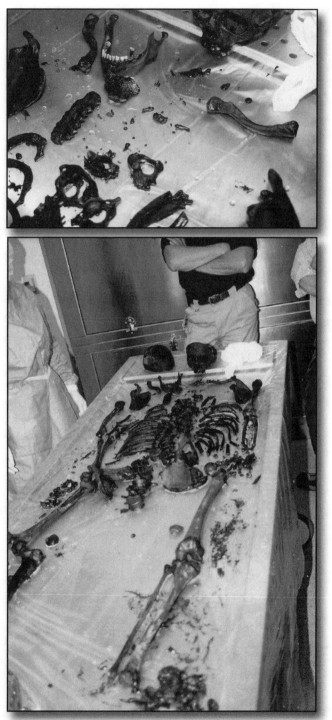

Murder victim
Gwendolyn Moore's
bones at autopsy.
Courtesy of Clay Bryant.

At best, the polygraph of the 1960s and 1970s was highly subjective, and some operators could be persuaded to produce the results the person who hired them wanted. Bryant's father always feared that was the case for Marshall's polygraph.

But when Marshall passed the polygraph, he was quickly dismissed as a suspect. With no new witnesses and no new leads, the sheriff's department ruled Gwendolyn's murder an accidental death and the case was unofficially closed. Clay Bryant and his father considered the case dormant but certainly not solved. Gwendolyn's body had been found just four-tenths of a mile outside the city limits, so Bryant's father could only watch as the sheriff led what seemed to him to be a surface investigation.

Time only weakened the case. Over the years, police reports disappeared. Polygraph results were lost. People stopped talking about the case. It was as if Gwendolyn Moore had never existed. For most of Hogansville, Gwendolyn's life closed with the case.

But not for Gwendolyn's oldest son, whose only source of love and security died with his mother. Four months after Gwendolyn's death, Moore married Priscilla, the woman many people assumed he'd long had a relationship with, and he moved her into the house he'd shared with Gwendolyn.

Townspeople whispered that Marshall was still far from docile, and the rumors were fed each time Priscilla wore large sunglasses and kept them on indoors in the winter. But for the most part, the house on Mobley Bridge Road was now quiet.

Allen blamed both his father and himself for his mother's death, and their relationship became even more strained.

Six months after Gwendolyn's death, Allen followed his father up to the hill where he was working on the carburetor of the family car. Most of his friends knew how to do basic car repairs, and he hoped to watch quietly and try to learn what his friends' fathers willingly taught them.

As Allen quietly watched his father work, Marshall suddenly turned, full of rage, and shouted, "Don't ever cuss me again!" Allen swore that he hadn't said a cuss word, but his father attacked him with his fists and with the wrench he'd been working with. He beat him and dragged him down the hill to the front porch of his house. He grabbed him by the ears and banged his head against the door frame until Allen passed out. When he regained consciousness, Marshall was beating him with his shoe.

When his father's rage subsided, Allen broke free and bolted toward the Turners' house, diving over the short fence between the houses.

Ronnie Turner and Mike Thrower, both fifteen-year-old friends of Allen, were talking in the Turners' yard when Allen ran toward them, begging for help. Cursing Allen from the fence, Marshall ordered him back to his yard, promising him an even rougher beating if he didn't come immediately.

Mike went inside the house, got his father's shotgun and propped it against the porch. Ronnie stepped in front of Allen.

"If you put one foot in our yard, I'm gonna shoot you," Mike told Marshall calmly. Marshall retreated to his house, and the boys called the sheriff's department. When deputies arrived, Allen was lying, beaten and bloody, on the Turners' floor. They photographed his wounds, took a statement, and arrested Marshall.

At the hearing, Allen asked the judge to let him leave fifteen minutes before his father so he could get away from him. At fourteen, Allen left Hogansville, walking.

His aunt lived in LaGrange, and though Allen was sore from his recent beating, he walked the thirteen miles to her house in three hours. Aunt Siene was Joe Moore's ex-wife. She'd experienced domestic violence at the hands of Marshall's brother and she'd known and loved Gwendolyn, so she opened her home to Allen for as long as he attended school or worked.

Allen decided to work. He ordered a copy of his birth certificate, altered his birthdate, and applied for a job at the Dixie Cotton Mill in LaGrange. He worked in the mill for three years, earning a reputation as a hard worker and an honest young man.

In 1973, with Aunt Siene's support, Allen joined the navy and quickly earned his high school equivalency diploma. He served in the navy twenty years, retiring as a full Chief Petty Officer, the highest enlisted rank. Though others saw him as hardworking and accomplished, his childhood nightmares never ceased. When he closed his eyes late at night, he'd see his mother, bloody and battered, cowering under the Turners' house. Over and over, he'd relive the night she died, never able to save her from his father's wrath.

Allen struggled in his relationships. With no healthy role model, Allen moved in and out of marriages, never allowing himself to continue the family violence but never able to establish a healthy family. Decade after decade, Allen's violent past shadowed his life. Knowing his father was living a new life and raising a new family while his mother's life had ended far too early robbed Allen of the closure he needed to move forward.

His father wasn't prosecuted in 1970, so Allen wasn't safe in his own hometown. Because no one was punished for his mother's death, Allen spent his life punishing himself. He cooperated fully when Bryant reopened the investigation, standing ready to testify against his father if the case went to trial.

But the years of abuse, coupled with the guilt that he was unable to help his mother, took a lifetime toll on Allen, and even finding eventual justice hasn't fully healed his emotional scars. Though his father died before he could stand trial for the atrocities he committed against the woman he once vowed to love and honor, participating in his father's investigation had a certain healing quality for Allen. What happened to Gwendolyn Moore for half of her young life cried out for justice.

Even Marshall Moore's sister wanted justice for her sister-in-law. She understood the environment that gave her brother only a brutal role model of what a husband could be, yet she knew that Gwendolyn deserved justice. Torn by loyalty to her brother and justice for Gwendolyn, she chose justice.

Marshall's sister told Bryant that she and Marshall knew only violence as they were growing up, and their family had lived in violence for as long as anyone could remember.

The Moore family was from the northeastern corner of Georgia, in the poverty-stricken foothills region of the Great Smokey Mountains known as Appalachia. They'd lived there since before the Civil War, and for generations, they attempted to chisel out a living from the rough terrain surrounding Bogg's Mountain. Local educational, law enforcement, and social services programs were inadequate in the area, so most Appalachian families lived by the "Code of the Hills"—a homespun social system in which a man ruled his family at his discretion, and no one interfered with another man's sovereignty.

On a cool autumn day in 1924, J. P. Moore and his sister, Mary, played in the yard of the old house at the foot of Bogg's Mountain. They heard familiar sounds from inside the house: their momma, Sara Jane, screaming for their father, Joseph, to stop beating her. Then Sara Jane, battered and bloody, bolted out the door and ran crying up the hill toward the mountain. Joseph screamed at his children to go to their grandfather's house down the road. "I'm gonna kill yer maw," he shouted as the terrified children ran to their grandfather's.

The parents didn't come home that evening, but from their grandfather's house on Bogg's Mountain, the children could see a fire glowing on the side of the mountain. As the smoke settled on the valley, the unforgettable smell of burning flesh floated down with it. The next day, Joseph picked up his children and told them their momma would not be returning. Human remains were later found in a fire pit on the mountain.

No one questioned what happened to Sara Jane. According to the Code of the Hills, Joseph's family was his property to do with as he pleased.

After their mother's death, J. P. and Mary were raised by the father they knew had killed their mother. Mary became a child bride and J. P. took a child bride as his own. J. P. and his young wife, Maude, married in 1936. Their son Marshall, the first of six children, was born March 18, 1937. Marshall had four brothers and one sister.

"Memories of our childhood were more like nightmares," his sister remembers. "One of the first memories that I can vividly recall was Daddy coming in the house. I was just three or four years old, but I remember it like it was yesterday. I was on Momma's lap, sitting by the wood stove, when he came in. We were dirt poor, and he had his boots tied with wire because he couldn't afford store-bought laces. As he pulled his overalls over the boots, the wire snagged the denim and ripped a hole in his pants leg.

"Daddy went into a rage, threw the overalls into the fire, and spun around and slapped Momma, knocking her and me out of the chair. He slapped her several times and made her sit in the chair while he cussed and beat her. He got the kerosene jug we used to start the fire and threatened to set her on fire. He continued to beat and slap Momma until he got tired of it. Then Daddy gave the kerosene jug to my brother, Joe, who was twelve or thirteen at the time. He told him to burn Momma if she moved. Joe stood guard, not knowing what to do, until Daddy finally calmed down.

"Ordeals like this were regular throughout our childhood," Marshall's sister shared with Bryant. "Momma finally got some relief in 1955 when Daddy got caught burglarizing a place in Banks County. Daddy made Joe drive the car during the burglary, so when he went to the chain gang, poor Joe got sent to reform school.

"When Daddy got out of prison, he came home to Momma.

"As soon as he got home, he started beating Momma again. After an extra-bad beating, he told her to get out. By that time, it was just me and Ray left at home. Momma filed for divorce and started a new life, and Ray and me got to live the rest of our lives in peace. But it was too late for Marshall. He'd already left home."

Marshall's sister grieves for what her brother could have been if he'd had a decent home life. But she also grieves for her gentle sister-in-law and the four boys she loved so much that she lived an unspeakable life rather than risk her tyrannical husband carrying out his threats to take the children if she tried to leave. When Bryant reinvestigated Gwendolyn's murder, Marshall's sister's first reaction was, "Let it rest." By the time Bryant was assigned the case, Marshall Moore was old and sick. In fact, he died before he could be brought to trial. But justice delayed would still be justice and at least, before Moore died, the town where he committed his unspeakable crimes would have to admit what most already knew: Marshall Moore was a cruel and vicious coward who took out his rage on his petite wife and his young sons. The weeks and months that Moore was under investigation brought long-awaited satisfaction to those who loved Gwendolyn, and that list included his own sister.

THE HEALING POWER OF JUSTICE

"You can tell families that they need to get over it," observes Clay Bryant. "But how do you tell a mom to get over her child? She shouldn't have to. She should not be willing to accept that her child's murder has become a cold case. She has the right to stir the pot.

"Like in the Gwendolyn Moore case, families never find total closure, but not knowing, or knowing and not being able to substantiate it, makes the suffering worse. The most satisfying experiences I've had in this life were bringing cold cases to a conclusion."

…When Connie Quedens was arrested for the murder of Fred Wilkerson, Fred's family, friends, and neighbors lined the street, cheering and applauding, as the Troup County Sheriff's Department squad car drove Quedens to jail. Sometimes there are few family members or friends to care, but there's still a healing that needs to take place, even if it's just a quiet victory in honor of a victim who can no longer speak.

The status of the victim makes no difference to a dedicated cold case detective, and whether or not the courtroom will be full of family and friends, and the media area crammed with reporters, has no bearing on how hard a case is worked.

All cases are treated with the same passion. "We had one case that involved a national celebrity," says retired investigator Greg Smith. "The case was high-profile, and the extra media coverage made the investigation a nightmare. But we worked on the case for ten years.

"We had another case where a bartender was robbed and killed in 1979. No media were pressing for us to solve it, but we worked on it for six years. The case involved a lot of expensive travel. It involved investigating a Puerto Rican terrorist group and a scared witness who disappeared.

"The witness was on probation, and we finally located her in Hartford, Connecticut. I flew from Miami to Connecticut the day after Thanksgiving. It was snowing when I arrived.

"The witness was a heroin addict, so I located the methadone clinics in the area. They have strict privacy laws, but I was finally able to find the witness in a flophouse in Hartford. It was before everyone carried cell phones, and the only telephone in the two-story building was a payphone on the first floor.

"I called my supervisor and then the state attorney. Then I turned around to see a guy holding a knife, trying to rob me. I pulled out my 9 millimeter and he dropped the knife and said, 'This isn't my knife.' Then he ran."

The case brought closure to the witness, and she asked Smith to call her after the trial.

"I called the payphone on the first floor of her building," recalls Smith. "A man answered, and I asked him to go get Candy in number five. He said he was too busy, so I told him it was important. He asked if I was the detective who had come to see Candy. When I said I was, he said, 'I'm the guy who tried to rob you.'"

Sometimes cold case detectives receive the accolades they well deserve. When NCIS Special Agent Joe Kennedy was instrumental in bringing Dana Bartlett's killers to justice, he received the following letter from Mike Mullen, Captain of the USS *Yorktown*, who later became a four-star admiral and chairman of the Joint Chiefs of Staff:

> Just a short note of boundless thanks to you for finally succeeding in arresting the individual allegedly responsible for the murder of Dana Bartlett. I was the Commanding Officer of USS YORKTOWN (CG48) at the time and the events of that night will forever be seared into my being. Dana was a superb young man whom I had only known for a brief period of time. But what a grand naval officer he was with unerring focus and rare sparkle in his every look. Why the good Lord would see fit to have him depart this earth at that point in his life is one of those questions which will remain unanswered. That the criminal justice system was able to finally apprehend the alleged perpetrator brought great joy to all of us who were involved in the tragic circumstances surrounding Dana's death.
>
> I know from just the time alone, as well as the obvious political sensitivity of this case, that you expended an incredible number of days, weeks, months, and even years, and there is still I imagine a great deal left to be done. You clearly proceeded professionally on all

fronts and for that I extend a hearty congratulations. I have spoken to the Director and shared these feelings with him as well. You have my heartfelt thanks for a job incredibly well done. You have served your nation, your service, and humanity exceptionally well and at a level "beyond the call" in this case.

Again, Joe, my deepest appreciation to you and all of your team. You have truly been brilliant and have brought to a close for many of us an open wound. We are all indebted to you.

When a supervisor or commanding officer applauds, an investigator tucks the note in a file marked "personal" and pulls it out to reread on days when no one is there to notice an equally important victory. Because by the time some cases are solved, the victim is only a faded photograph in an old family album. The family and friends who could recognize the photo are also dead.

Sometimes, families prefer to put the case behind them and are less than grateful for the renewed publicity that a conviction brings. And sometimes the victim is an obscure person, and the courtroom is nearly empty when the verdict is announced. At those times, the reward comes from validating a life by bringing justice to the one who took it away.

JUSTICE FOR CYNTHIA

A dedicated detective doesn't stick with a case for media acclaim or promotions. He doesn't follow through because the victim was well-known or influential. He does his job because it's the right thing to do.

Cynthia Henry was *just* a thirty-six-year-old woman who lived under a bridge in downtown Anchorage. She was *just* one of the many homeless people who pepper the streets of nearly every major city. She didn't carry a cell phone. She didn't go Christmas shopping or bake a Thanksgiving turkey. Her name never appeared in the *Anchorage Daily News* for participating in a breast cancer walk or serving on a school committee. Few people knew she existed. If they noticed her sleeping on the ground or foraging for food, they didn't make eye contact, and they didn't ask her name. She was one of the people most of us prefer to ignore.

Then one morning in September 2002, Cynthia could no longer be ignored. The brutality of her death was the reason Cynthia Henry made the newspaper and the reason she became a part of Detective Glen Klinkhart's life. That morning, police found her naked body, facedown in a pool of blood, under the A Street Bridge that once sheltered her.

Detective Klinkhart was assigned to the case, and as he studied the crime scene, he could piece together Cynthia's last hours. The previous evening had been cold and rainy. Cynthia had curled up on a flattened cardboard box under the A Street Bridge to shield herself from the rain and get a little sleep. She had no blanket, so she pulled her worn jacket as tightly around her as possible.

Sometime while she slept, her killer crept under the bridge and stabbed Cynthia in the back with such brutality that the four stab wounds penetrated five inches into her body, severing arteries and puncturing a lung. Then, as she struggled for her last breaths, her killer raped her with a plastic Gilbey's Vodka bottle. The bottle lay nearby, covered with Cynthia's blood.

No public outcry kept the case going. No celebrities appeared on national television demanding that Cynthia's killer be found. But Klinkhart investigated the case with the same passion he applied to his other cases. He spent months talking to hundreds of people in homeless camps, following even the vaguest leads.

The homeless people cooperated because they were afraid for themselves and their friends. But Klinkhart found it difficult to secure detailed information. Most witnesses can say, "I remember it was Wednesday because that's when I take the kids to dance lessons" or "It was Thursday the twenty-first because that's when I had my teeth cleaned," but for these willing witnesses, every day was the same. They could tell Klinkhart if something they'd witnessed occurred when it was cold or rainy, dark or light. Other than those broad differentiations, they had little concept of time.

Despite Cynthia's friends offering minimal concrete evidence, they painted a picture of Cynthia that caused Klinkhart to appreciate her value. Though Cynthia lived without many of the comforts most people consider necessities, her friends described her as a gentle person who willingly shared the few possessions she had.

Klinkhart's best evidence was a bloody partial palm print left in Cynthia's blood on the vodka bottle. Lab reports confirmed that someone hadn't left the print when they picked up the bloody bottle. It was a transfer print, left by a hand already covered with Cynthia's blood.

Unfortunately, the print meant nothing until Klinkhart could connect it with the killer, and for two years, the print remained unmatched. But Cynthia deserved justice, and Klinkhart continued his investigation.

Cynthia was murdered under a downtown bridge frequented by homeless people, so Klinkhart suspected she'd been killed by someone who was also homeless. He knew that finding Cynthia's killer would not only bring her justice but also protect the many vulnerable people who took refuge in the homeless camps of Anchorage, many of whom he'd gotten to know and appreciate during his hundreds of interviews for Cynthia's case. He spent months collecting prints from homeless people. Though none matched, Klinkhart continued searching.

After two years, Klinkhart had exhausted all available leads. He turned to the media for help. On the second anniversary of Cynthia's murder, Klinkhart held a press conference under the A Street Bridge, and media shared the story again.

This time, an anonymous caller phoned the police department, suggesting that they check out Roger Wade McKinley. Klinkhart was cautious about an informant who refused to give his name, but he described facts of the case that had not been released to the media. And he offered a suspect's name. It was a name that had not surfaced previously. When asked why he'd waited two years to notify police, the anonymous caller said he'd assumed the case had already been solved.

With McKinley as their focus, police soon understood why the caller would assume the case was solved. Numerous people had witnessed McKinley's suspicious behavior the night of Cynthia's murder, but until now, no one had come forward. The informant's call was all Klinkhart needed to revive Cynthia's case.

"After the informant called in," remembers prosecutor Alan

Goodwin, "Mr. McKinley was on Glen [Klinkhart]'s radar. Glen got a warrant for Mr. McKinley's prints and also located people who had been with Mr. McKinley the night he killed Cynthia. They recalled having seen Mr. McKinley wearing bloody clothes and his having explained that he had been attacked by two men near the A Street bridge and had stabbed them. These people saw Mr. McKinley dispose of his clothing, and one recalled his having acted nervous when Cynthia's murder was reported on the evening news."

Klinkhart located McKinley and secured a palm print. It matched. He continued his investigation.

Witnesses said McKinley had been drinking at the Avenue Bar on Fourth Street the night Cynthia was murdered. When he left, he told friends he was going to find some marijuana. He had a hunting knife with him.

When he returned to the bar later that night, the sleeves of his white button-down shirt were stained with blood from his mid-forearm to his wrists.

Klinkhart ran a criminal background check and learned that as a teenager, McKinley had kidnapped a sixteen-year-old girl at knife-point. In 1995, he was sentenced to six years in prison for stabbing a Juneau woman.

Prosecutor Alan Goodwin, who built the prosecution's case with the vodka bottle as the key piece of the story, wanted the jury to see that raping Cynthia as she lay dying was the ultimate cruelty and humiliation. And when McKinley tossed the bloody bottle aside and left the crime scene, he signed his guilt in Cynthia's blood.

In his closing remarks in the nearly empty courtroom, Goodwin told the jury, "As Cynthia Henry lay dying under the A Street Bridge from the stab wounds he had inflicted on her, Roger Wade McKinley— literally with Cynthia's blood on his hands—picked up a vodka bottle and sexually assaulted her with it. Although he didn't know it yet, when he sexually assaulted Cynthia…when he pressed this vodka bottle against Cynthia with so much force that he left his palm print, in Cynthia's blood, down in the concave recess of the bottom of the bottle, Roger Wade McKinley signed his name to his crime.

"When the APD Crime Scene Team collected the bottle, it had the identity of Cynthia's murderer. The only thing that remained was finding the person, the identity of the person who left his print in Cynthia's blood. Fortunately for Cynthia Henry's family and fortunately for the people of Anchorage, Detective Glen Klinkhart would not let this case go unsolved. Fortunately, he beat the streets month after month, year after year, until he finally, at long last, found the man who, quite literally, signed his name to the crime in Cynthia's blood. That man sits before you here today, and his name is Roger Wade McKinley."

The judge and jury agreed. Judge Eric Aarseth declared that he could not find in McKinley a "glimmer of a chance of rehabilitation," and though McKinley walked free for years after murdering and brutalizing Cynthia, he'll pay for the crime for the rest of his life. Aarseth sentenced McKinley to 129 years in prison with no chance of parole for 86 years. He was 37 at the time of his conviction.

After the trial, Goodwin talked with jurors and learned that Klinkhart's determination had impacted them. "The jury was impressed by Glen Klinkhart's thoroughness and dedication to the case. After the verdict, one of the jurors told me she was comforted to know that detectives like Glen were working in her city.

"They were also impressed by Mark Halterman's testimony. Mark was the latent print expert who analyzed all of the prints in the case. Mark was able to explain to the jury that the print was recessed in the concave part of the bottom of the bottle. The portion of McKinley's palm that made the print does not reach into that concave area without pressure being applied to both the top and bottom of the bottle. Using the prints, Mark was able to demonstrate the way in which McKinley would have been holding the bottle when he left the print. This is not the natural way a person would carry or hold a bottle unless they were using it to jab or press against something or someone.

"Mark also explained that McKinley's hand had Cynthia's blood on it *before* he touched the bottle, and he transferred her blood to the bottle when he left the print, as opposed to his hand leaving a print by removing blood that was already present on the bottle before he touched it. This convinced the jury that the bottle was the instrument with which Mr. McKinley had sexually assaulted Cynthia after he had mortally wounded her."

Goodwin recalls that Cynthia's father and stepmother attended most of the trial. Mr. Henry acknowledged that Cynthia had lived a hard life, but he and his wife loved her. "He's a man of few words," observes Goodwin, "but he thanked us for not giving up on Cynthia, shook our hands, and left the courtroom." It was all the thanks the prosecution and investigative teams needed.

Cynthia's was a case that could easily have remained unsolved, and Goodwin knows why that didn't happen. "This case was solved because Glen Klinkhart refused to let it go unsolved," declares Goodwin.

JUSTICE FOR JESSICA

Jessica, a rape victim, speaks firsthand of the impact cold case investigators have:

"When I left St. Louis, I was twenty-five, and I was seeking a safe place away from a college boyfriend-turned-stalker. I decided to stay with my aunt in Charlotte, North Carolina, and take a year off to recover from the trauma.

"After the year, I felt renewed and enthusiastic. I enjoyed the relaxed Southern atmosphere, so I decided to stay in Charlotte a while longer. A friend and I found an apartment complex in a neighborhood where lots of young people lived. When we checked out the apartment, one of the first questions we asked was, 'Is this a safe area?' We were assured that it was, so we moved in and started furnishing our new home.

Rape victim Jessica with daughter.
Courtesy of Jessica.

"Two weeks later, my roommate went out for the night, and I found myself alone for one of the first times since we'd moved in. After watching a movie, I realized how tired I was. It was getting late, and I decided to turn out the lights and go to bed.

"About fifteen minutes later, I heard a noise that sounded like my front door opening. *It's just Lori,* I thought. *I guess she's back earlier than she planned.* I got out of bed and walked to the door. Someone was opening the door, and I could tell it was a male. *He must be one of Lori's friends looking for a bathroom,* I thought. My first thought was to tell him he was at the wrong door.

"When I tried to open the door, I knew immediately that something was wrong. Someone was holding the door—tight. I felt an uneasy chill.

"Before I could consider what to do next, he rushed into the room, tackled me and beat me in the face with his fists. My nose was bleeding profusely and blood was filling my throat as he dragged me into my bedroom, pushing me hard against the bed where a few minutes earlier I'd had the last peaceful sleep I'd have for many years to come.

"He covered my face with my pillow, and I was sure I was going to die. I remembered that I had spoken to my friend earlier that evening and I thought that if I could reach my phone and hit speed dial, my friend might pick up and figure out what was going on and send help. I managed to reach the phone, knock it off the hook, and hit speed dial but instantly realized that I'd called for a voicemail after my call to my friend, so I heard a recording instead of a friendly welcoming voice. I struggled to breathe and blood continued to fill my throat. I stopped struggling when I realized I was suffocating.

"He was rough and frenzied as he turned me over and bound my hands, gagged and blindfolded me, using items of clothing he found in the room. The room was dark, and even before he covered my eyes, I couldn't see the intruder well. I could only tell he was a tall black man with shaved head and a strangely shaped head with a lump on top.

"He dragged me into the living room and made me kneel while he cut off my nightgown. Then I heard him walk to the kitchen.

"I could hear him rummaging through the silverware drawer, and I assumed he was looking for a knife. I'd always had a phobia about leaving knives lying around, and all our knives were hidden.

"I called out to the intruder as well as I could through the gag: 'Please, take anything, but please don't rape me.'

"I could hear him moving back toward me, and his voice was rough and guttural. 'I didn't come to rape you. I just came here to rob you. But you had to struggle and now I am turned on.' Even in my panicked state, I sensed he was manipulating me to be passive and trying to put the guilt for what was about to happen on me.

"He then pulled me up, grabbing my bound wrists behind me and led me back into my bedroom. Bound, gagged, and blindfolded, I struggled to keep my balance. As we reached the bed, he laid me face down and began raping me. Somehow I managed to let him know I could not breathe, he switched momentarily to a strange mode that seemed almost kind, though I know now that he was simply making sure I didn't die until he was finished with me. He unbound my hands so I could hold my head up to keep my breathing passage clear.

"For the next couple of hours, he alternated raping and sodomizing me, all the while taunting me by toying with whether or not he should kill me and by calling me filthy names.

"When he finished, he made me promise on my mother's life that I wouldn't go to the police. At that point, I was emotionally destroyed. That promise seemed overwhelming to me. I was horrified to repeat it, but with my throat still filled with blood, I meekly voiced the promise.

"'If you go to the hospital,' he said with a trace of satisfaction, 'they'll do a rape kit and it'll just sit on the shelf.'

"Then he commented that he'd done this before and that he'd only had to kill one person. *Kill one person.*

"He took me to the bathroom. I was still blindfolded, and he led me into the tub. He told me I had to get rid of the evidence. As he ran the water, he asked me if the temperature was right.

"He forced me to wash, and I numbly followed his directions. The room was quiet except for an occasional choking sound as I continued to try to clear the blood from my throat. Then he said quietly, 'I'm still here.'

"A few minutes later, he said it again: 'I'm still here.' He continued repeating those three words, each time with longer intervals in between.

"Eventually, I heard his voice for the last time. I waited, still terrified to move, convinced that if I tried to get up, he'd kill me.

"I waited at least fifteen minutes after hearing his voice for the last time before getting out of the tub. I was still blindfolded, but I was afraid to uncover my eyes. I felt my way back to my bedroom, locked the door, shoved my bed against the door and finally removed the blindfold.

"Every inch of my body ached, and I wasn't sure I had the strength to call for help. I gathered the tiny bit of strength I had remaining and dialed my friend. I told him what happened and said I was coming to his house. I asked him to stay on the line to be sure I got out of the house safely. I pulled on a raincoat, wearing only my towel underneath, and ran to the front door and out to my car. It was the middle of the night, no one was out, and I didn't know where the assailant had gone.

"I drove the five minutes to my friend's apartment. When he saw me, he told me I needed to call the police. 'I can't,' I told him. 'I'm too afraid.' I had left my purse in my apartment, and I didn't know if he'd stolen my driver's license. He could know my name. He could come back. I'd promised on my mother's life not to call the police. Though my mother was almost a thousand miles away, in my fragile state, I was sure he would kill her if I didn't keep my promise.

"My friend said something that had more power than the rapist's threats: 'If you don't do something, he's going to do this to somebody else.' At that moment I knew that I'd do anything I could to keep another girl from experiencing what I'd been through that night. I called the police.

"The police took me to Carolina Medical Center, and I once again became a victim.

"I'm an extremely private person. I'd always had a female OB/GYN. Even people who tried to help seemed invasive.

"It's hard to imagine the feelings of violation involved in a rape exam. After giving the police my statement, medical personnel took me to an examination room and had me stand over a large plastic bag and drop my jacket and towel into the bag. They took many photos. I knew the photos were necessary to prove the brutality of the crime, but it was hard to comprehend that these photos would be filed away somewhere for anyone to see, that copies could be made without my knowledge.

"My body was no longer my own. It was evidence; a crime scene.

"A male doctor ordered the photos and examined me. The exam was extremely painful because of the trauma my body had been through. It would have been impossible to endure if I hadn't kept reminding myself that the evidence the doctor collected would help convict the rapist.

"A police officer drove me back to my apartment. As we pulled up, I saw my bed being taken out. 'Evidence,' explained the officer.

"As quickly as possible, I gathered my belongings. By now it was 9:00 a.m. That morning, I flew home to my parents in St. Louis.

"From that day in May 1998, I was a different person. No matter how hard you try, rape changes you.

"Since I didn't get a clear look at the assailant, everyone who fit my limited description created a quiet panic. Countless times, I asked myself, *Could* he *be the one?*

"Every night the rape crept into my mind. I went to sleep worrying that another woman might be going to bed peacefully and waking up to horror.

"I decided I needed a dog for protection, so I bought a Rottweiler puppy while in St. Louis. My mother, the puppy, and I traveled back to Charlotte to begin piecing back my life. As it turned out, the puppy had serious aggression issues. In retrospect, I think she was most likely reacting to my mental state.

"My mother signed me up for a puppy training class at a local pet store. On the first night, the instructor warned, 'If your dog bites, it's out of the class.' Mine bit him the very first day, but we were not thrown out of class. A friendship developed between my instructor and me. He was understanding, and he empathized with what I'd been through. After several years of friendship, we fell in love. He's now my husband.

"At first, I expected every day to hear that the rapist had been caught. But as time went by with no arrest, I began to feel as if the rape didn't matter anymore, that my case had dropped off the radar. I felt that everyone had given up.

"I know some rape victims want to put the crime behind them, and I understand. But I was driven to find the attacker. I talked to the Charlotte detectives. They took my information, but I wasn't much help. I didn't know what he looked like. I didn't know how he found me or why he chose me. The police suggested that the rapist might be someone I knew. I was certain he wasn't, but I told them anyway, 'If it's someone I knew, I still want them caught. Get DNA on anyone you consider suspicious.'

"I moved into another apartment in Charlotte and began my life again. I continued checking regularly with the police. I kept up with DNA advances, always asking if the rapist's DNA had been entered into new databases.

"The Charlotte rapes continued, and police suspected a serial rapist. They sought help from the FBI. It took six months to get the rapist's DNA analyzed and even longer to get it entered into local, state, and national databases. I constantly followed up for ten years.

"I got discouraged. I remembered what the rapist said would happen if they did a rape kit. I didn't put myself through the exam for the evidence to sit on the shelf. But that's where it stayed for ten years.

"In the meantime, my husband and I had a daughter. When I found out I was pregnant, I was thrilled. But when I learned that the baby was a girl, I broke down. I didn't want to bring a girl into this world.

"Though discouraged, I never gave up that the rapist would be caught. I eventually moved far from Charlotte, but I faithfully read the online edition of the Charlotte newspaper. One day I read that the Charlotte Police Department had created a new sexual assault cold case unit. I immediately sent them an e-mail, but I didn't receive an immediate response.

"Then one day, I received a call from a cold case detective named Troy Armstrong. He said he wanted to talk to me, and he could drive to St. Louis as early as the next day. My case wasn't forgotten! Somebody knew my name! Somebody cared about what happened, and he was willing to drive halfway across the country to talk to me.

"When I met Troy, I immediately felt confident. He was genuinely kind and caring. And he had the news I'd waited a decade for. He told me, 'We got a match on the DNA. The rapist is Darrell Boyd, and he's in jail in Ohio on a fairly minor charge. He's scheduled to be released in six months, but he'll be coming straight back to Charlotte.'

"That night was the first time in ten years that I hadn't gone to sleep thinking, 'He could be out there tonight. Another woman could be going through what I went through.' When I learned the rapist had been identified, it felt so good to know that no other girl would have to lose what I lost. It was a highlight of my life.

"But the nightmare wasn't over. The trial was worse than I could have imagined. The day before, I met with the district attorney. They prepared me as much as possible for what to expect, but nothing could have prepared me for seeing the rapist. I'd never seen his face, but being in the courtroom with him brought back the rape. He had a twin brother, and he was in the courtroom, too. When I walked in and saw both men, I panicked. But I kept moving forward and sat down on the prosecution side. I later learned that I should not have gone straight into the courtroom and was taken to the witness room while the defense attorney argued that the DNA should not be allowed as evidence. To our relief, the judge allowed the DNA to be admitted.

"Telling about the rape to a crowded courtroom of strangers wasn't too difficult. That's probably because I don't, and never have, felt one molecule of guilt or responsibility for the rape. I simply told the jury about the deranged behavior of a sick individual named Darrell Boyd.

"But after my testimony, the defense attorney attacked me, claiming that I'd invited the rapist into my apartment and willingly had sex with him. She tried to convince the jury that I'd asked the rapist to kill my ex-boyfriend. Those humiliating photos taken ten years ago that I had agonized over were a powerful witness that what I experienced was not consensual sex. I will forever be grateful to the emergency-room physician for making the decision to order those pictures.

"I was not the only victim to testify. Another woman told her story, and it was similar to mine. The attorneys asked us both if the rapist spoke with a northern or southern accent. We both said he had no accent at all. When the rapist took the stand, he attempted to speak with a Jamaican accent. The prosecutor kept him on the stand until he dropped the accent briefly, but the point was made.

"During the trial, I was terrified that he'd be set free. How could the jury know who was telling the truth and who wasn't? We had strong DNA evidence, and I kept thinking about the trials where DNA hadn't been collected or preserved. Their chances of a conviction were much slimmer. I continue to feel for women who have had to testify in these cases with only their memory for evidence.

"I sensed that the jury was made up of strong people who saw through the charades, and I was right. Darrell Boyd was found guilty on all accounts. The defense insisted that each juror be polled, and that experience was very healing for me. One by one, the jurors repeated the charges and affirmed his guilt. At one time I'd felt that no one remembered or cared. Now twelve men and women were telling the judge, the attorneys, the rapist, the media, the people in the courtroom—and me—that they knew what he had done and that his crime was worthy of punishment.

"But for me, the desire to find the rapist had nothing to do with seeing him punished. My whole concern was that he not hurt anyone again.

"The conviction has completely changed me. For the longest time,

Rapist Darrell Boyd.
Courtesy of Charlotte Police Department.

I felt a sense of powerlessness, frustration, and anger. These emotions took hold at the core of me, and they affected everything I said and did. I now feel empowered. I feel like I can make an impact. I feel heard.

"I no longer see my daughter as a vulnerable person with no impact on her world. Closing my rape case has changed my perspective on my daughter's life and future.

"Just identifying the rapist started the healing process. And if I had known they were actively looking for him, I would have felt better much sooner.

"Now I want to do what I can to see other cold cases closed. I work with databases in my profession, and I try to keep updated on what's happening with DNA databases. I'm looking for ways I can be involved in working with DNA databases. I know the databases are only as effective as the evidence that is entered into them. Until we get a criminal's DNA in national databases, he can continue to harm others.

"My view of law enforcement has completely changed because of Troy Armstrong. After years of trying to get someone interested in my case, I had decided that police officers see crime all the time and it doesn't impact them. But Troy was so human, so caring. I mattered to him. I could have been his sister. Being in partnership with a man in prosecuting this case was very healing for me. Troy was sensitive and understanding. He 'got it.'

"During the trial, he and his wife invited my family and the other victim and her family to a barbecue at their home. Then, when we heard the verdict, we decided to all take an impromptu trip to Florida to celebrate and heal. So our three families went to Florida the day after the trial, and this year my family and Troy's family went to Florida together again. (The other woman's family could not make it.)

"I've come a long way since the trial, but I'll never be the same person I was before the rape. I'll never be able to live without dogs. Currently, we have five dogs, including two Dobermans and a pit bull. One dog will never be enough for me. I look at that as a kind of disability that's a result of what I've been through.

"I travel in my work, and I find it very difficult to sleep when I'm out of town alone.

"I talk freely about my rape because I want people to understand that it can happen to anyone and rape victims have nothing to be ashamed of. One of the most difficult responses I've had to deal with is when people say, 'He would have had to kill me.' The implication that I should have fought harder is awful. They don't have a concept of what happens during a rape. Your life is no longer your own. Someone can take it from you arbitrarily. At any moment, the rapist could have snapped my neck and killed me. Until you've experienced that type of helplessness, you don't know how you'd react.

"Troy's caring attitude has done a great deal to help me finally start to heal. I hope other cold case detectives will realize what a tremendous effect they have on victims and their families. If I could say just one thing to cold case detectives, it would be this: Know that the enthusiasm that your living victims have when you solve a case is also reflective of the victims who didn't make it. A lot of people can't be there to advocate like I did. They're depending on you to speak for them."

Index